Information Technology Law in Slovenia

Information Technology Law in Slovenia

Aleš Završnik

Pika Šarf

Karmen Lutman

Primož Gorkič

This book was originally published as a monograph in the International Encyclopaedia of Laws/Privacy and Technology Law.

Founding Editor: Roger Blanpain
General Editor: Frank Hendrickx
Volume Editors: Jos Dumortier, Pieter Gryffroy, Ruben Roex & Yung Shin Van Der Sype

Wolters Kluwer

Published by:
Kluwer Law International B.V.
PO Box 316
2400 AH Alphen aan den Rijn
The Netherlands
E-mail: lrs-sales@wolterskluwer.com
Website: www.wolterskluwer.com/en/solutions/kluwerlawinternational

Sold and distributed by:
Wolters Kluwer Legal & Regulatory U.S.
7201 McKinney Circle
Frederick, MD 21704
United States of America
E-mail: customer.service@wolterskluwer.com

ISBN 978-94-035-2266-1

e-Book: ISBN 978-94-035-2476-4
web-PDF: ISBN 978-94-035-2486-3

The Authors

Dr Aleš Završnik is a Senior Research Fellow at the Institute of Criminology at the Faculty of Law, Ljubljana and a Professor at the Faculty of Law at the University of Ljubljana, Slovenia.

Dr Karmen Lutman is an Assistant Professor at the Faculty of Law at the University of Ljubljana, Slovenia.

The Authors

Dr Primož Gorkič is a judge at the Supreme Court of the Republic of Slovenia and an Associate Professor at the Faculty of Law at the University of Ljubljana, Slovenia.

Dr Pika Šarf is a Researcher at the Institute of Criminology at the Faculty of Law, Ljubljana.

The research leading to this monograph has received funding from the Slovenian Research Agency, research programme 'Social Surveillance, Criminal Justice, Prevention of Violence and Victimisation in the Context of High Technology Society' (No. P-0221).

Table of Contents

Table of Contents

List of Abbreviations

ADR	Alternative Domain Name Dispute Resolution
ADR Rules	Alternative Domain Name Dispute Resolution Procedure for .si Top-Level Domains
AKOS	*Agencija za komunikacijska omrežja in storitve* (Agency for Communication Networks and Services of the Republic of Slovenia)
Arnes	*Akademska in raziskovalna mreža Slovenije* (Academic and Research Network of Slovenia)
AVK	*Javna agencija Republike Slovenije za varstvo konkurence* (Slovenian Competition Protection Agency)
CRPP	*Centralni register podatkov o pacientu* (Central Registry of Patient Data)
CSIRT	Computer Security Incident Response Team
CJEU	Court of Justice of the European Law
CIA	Confidentiality, Integrity and Availability
ECHR	European Court on Human Rights
EU	European Union
EUR	European Currency
FURS	*Finančna Uprava Republike Slovenije* (Financial Administration of the Republic of Slovenia)
GDP	Gross Domestic Product
GDPR	General Data Protection Regulation
ICT	Information and Communication Technology
ISDN	Integrated Services Digital Network
ISP	Internet Service Providers
KZ	*Kazenski zakonik* (Criminal Code from 1994)
KZ-1	*Kazenski zakonik* KZ-1 (Criminal Code from 2008)
MMS	Multimedia Messaging Service
MJU	*Ministrstvo za javno upravo* (Ministry of Public Administration)
NATO	North Atlantic Treaty Organization

List of Abbreviations

NIJZ	*Nacionalni inštitut za javno zdravje* (National institute of Public Health)
NUTS	Nomenclature of Territorial Units for Statistics
OECD	Organisation of Economic Co-operation and Development
OSCE	Organization for Security and Co-operation in Europe
OZ	*Obligacijski zakonik* (Obligations code)
PM	Prime Minister
PSTN	Public Switched Telephone Network
SDS	Slovenian Democratic Party
SFRJ	Socialist Federative Republic of Yugoslavia
SMS	Short Message Service
TARIC	Tarif Intégré de la Communauté
UN	United Nations
UNICITRAL	United Nations' Commission of International Trade Law
URS	Ustava Republike Slovenije (Constitution of the Republic of Slovenia)
URST	*Uprava Republike Slovenije za telekomunikacije* (Telecommunications Administration of the Republic of Slovenia)
VoIP	Voice Over Internet Protocol
WTO	World Trade Organizations
ZASP	*Zakon o avtorski in sorodnih pravicah* (Copyright and Neighbouring Rights Act)
ZDR-1	*Zakon delovnih razmerjih* (Employment Relationships Act)
ZEISZ	*Zakon o elektronski identifikaciji in storitvah zaupanja* (Electronic Identification and Trust Services Act)
ZEKom-1	*Zakon o elektronskih komunikacijah* (Electronic Communications Act)
ZEPEP	*Zakon o elektronskem poslovanju in elektronskem podpisu* (Electronic Commerce and Electronic Signature Act)
ZEPT	*Zakon o elektronskem poslovanju na trgu* (Electronic Commerce Market Act)
ZGD-1	Zakon o gospodarskih družbah (Companies Act)
ZIL-1	*Zakon o industrijski lastnini* (Industrial Property Act)
ZIN	*Zakon o inšpekcijskem nadzoru* (Inspection Act)
ZInfP	*Zakon o informacijskem pooblaščencu* (Information Commissioner Act)
ZInfV	*Zakon o informacijski varnosti* (Information Security Act)
ZKP	*Zakon o kazenskem postopku* (Criminal Procedure Act)

ZKUASP	*Zakon o kolektivnem upravljanju avtorske in sorodnih pravic* (Collective Management of Copyright and Neighbouring Rights Act)
ZMed	*Zakon o medijih* (Mass Media Act)
ZOIzk-1	*Zakon o osebni izkaznici* (Identity Card Act)
ZOPOKD	*Zakon o odgovornosti pravnih oseb za kazniva dejanja* (Liability of Legal Persons for Criminal Offences Act)
ZP-1	*Zakon o prekrških* (Minor Offences Act)
ZpacP	*Zakon o pacientovih pravicah* (Patients' Rights Act)
ZPOmK	*Zakon o preprečevanju omejevanja konkurence* (Prevention of Restriction of Competition Act from 1993)
ZPOmK-1	*Zakon o preprečevanju omejevanja konkurence* (Prevention of the Restriction of Competition Act from 2008)
ZPotK-2	*Zakon o potrošniških kreditih* (Consumer Credit Act)
ZPS	*Zveza potrošnikov Slovenije*
ZSOVA	*Slovenski obveščevalno-varnostni agenciji* (Slovene Intelligence and Security Agency Act)
ZUP	*Zakon o splošnem upravnem postopku* (General Administrative Procedure Act)
ZVK	*Zakon o varstvu konkurence* (Protection of Competition Act)
ZVOP-1	*Zakon o varstvu osebnih podatkov* (Personal Data Protection Act)
ZVOP-2	*Zakon o varstvu osebnih podatkov* (Personal Data Protection Act)
ZVOPOKD	*Zakon o varstvu osebnih podatkov na področju obravnavanja kaznivih dejanj* (Act on the Protection of Personal Data in the Area of Treatment of Criminal Offences)
ZVPot	*Zakon o varstvu potrošnikov* (Consumer Protection Act)
ZZPPZ	*Zakon o zbirkah podatkov s področja zdravstvenega varstva* (Healthcare Databases Act)

List of Abbreviations

General Introduction

Chapter 1. General Background of the Country

§1. Historical, Geographical, and Demographic Features

I. Historical Landmarks

1. The predecessors of the Slovenians settled in the region that is nowadays the territory of the Republic of Slovenia in the sixth century CE.[1] With the weakening of Avar rule over the Slavs in the Eastern Alps and Pannonia, a relatively independent Slavic landscape (*marca Vinedorum*) with its own prince developed in southern Carinthia at the beginning of the seventh century. Between 623 and 658, the Alpine Slavs were united under King Sam in the so-called Sam's Tribal Union, which collapsed after Sam's death, but independence was retained by a tribal principality in the area of present-day Austrian Carinthia, called *Carantania*. The Slavic ancestry of the Slovenes is also documented in 670 in the vicinity of Chedad. In the eighth century, this territory was incorporated into the Frankish empire of Charlemagne, and in the tenth century, it came under Franks (Germanic peoples) as part of the medieval empire (later the Holy Roman Empire). Except for the period from 1809 to 1814, when Napoleon ruled the area, most of the lands belonged to the Austro-Hungarian Empire until the formation of the State of Slovenes, Croats, and Serbs in 1918 (which subsequently transformed into the Kingdom of Serbs, Croats, and Slovenes the same year).

2. Slovenia was incorporated into the Kingdom of Serbs, Croats, and Slovenes (called Yugoslavia at the beginning of 1929 in order to fight nationalism and stress loyalty to Yugoslav ('South Slav') patriotism) after World War I. During World War II, Slovenia was trisected, with two parts being annexed by Nazi Germany and Fascist Italy and the Prekmurje region in the east being annexed by Hungary. In south-central Slovenia, annexed by Fascist Italy and renamed the Province of Ljubljana, the Slovenian National Liberation Front was organized in April 1941. Led by the Communist Party, it formed the Slovenian Partisan units as part of the Yugoslav Partisans led by the Communist leader Josip Broz Tito.[2]

---

1. Britannica, Slovenia summary, available at: www.britannica.com/summary/Slovenia, accessed 14 Jul. 2022.
2. Wikipedia, Slovenia, available at: https://en.wikipedia.org/wiki/Slovenia, accessed 14 Jul. 2022.

3. During the re-establishment of Yugoslavia in World War II, the first Slovenian republic, the Federal Republic of Slovenia, was created as part of the Federal Republic of Yugoslavia. It was a socialist state, but due to the Tito–Stalin split in 1948, its economic and personal freedoms were broader than in Eastern Bloc countries.[3]

4. In 1987 a group of intellectuals demanded Slovenian independence in the 57th edition of the magazine *Nova Revija.* Ideas as regards democratization and greater Slovenian autonomy were sparked. A mass democratic movement, coordinated by the Committee for the Defence of Human Rights, pushed the ruling communist party in the direction of democratic reforms. In September 1989, numerous constitutional amendments were passed in order to introduce parliamentary democracy to Slovenia. On 7 March 1990, the Slovenian Assembly changed the official name of the state to the 'Republic of Slovenia'. In April 1990, the first democratic elections in Slovenia took place, and the DEMOS movement – united in opposition to the communist ruling structure – emerged victorious.

5. In 1992, Slovenia became a member of the United Nations (UN). It is also a member of the Council of Europe, the World Trade Organization (WTO), the Organization for Security and Co-operation in Europe (OSCE), North Atlantic Treaty Organization (NATO), and several other international organizations. In 2004, Slovenia joined the European Union and in 2007 it became a member of the Monetary Union and adopted the single European currency, the euro, and it further became a member of the Schengen Area, the European border control-free travel area. It became a member of the Organisation of Economic Co-operation and Development (OECD) in 2010.

II. Geographical Features

6. Slovenia is located at the junction of central and southeast Europe, bordering (from west to east) Italy, Austria, Hungary, and Croatia. Geographically, it is a diverse country, made up of portions of four major European geographic landscapes: (1) the European Alps, (2) the karstic Dinaric Alps, (3) the Pannonian and Danubian lowlands and hills, and (4) the Mediterranean coast. More than half of Slovenian territory is forested, amounting to 11,823 km^2, ranking third in Europe according to the percentage of area forested, right after Finland and Sweden. The climate is influenced by the variety of relief and the influence of the Alps and the Adriatic Sea. In the northeast, continental climate type, with the greatest difference between winter and summer temperatures, prevails. The coastal region has a sub-Mediterranean climate, while a severe Alpine climate is present in the high mountain regions. There is a strong interaction between these three climatic systems across most of the country. Regarding geographical diversity, Slovenia signed the

---

3. Wikipedia, Slovenia, available at: https://en.wikipedia.org/wiki/Slovenia, accessed 14 Jul. 2022.

Rio Convention on Biological Diversity on 13 June 1992. The biological diversity of the country is high, with 1% of the world's organisms on 0.004% of the Earth's surface area.

III. Demographic Characteristics

7. Ethnically, 90% of Slovenia's population are Slovenian, a South Slavic people with a unique South Slavic language (e.g., in addition to the singular and plural, Slovenian also has the dual form). Historians agree that most Slovenians are descendants of settlers who arrived in the sixth century CE, Slavs that migrated westward from the vast Russian Plain, probably from an area in between the Black Sea and the Carpathian Mountains.[4]

8. Italians and Hungarians constitute Slovenia's two official as well as the main ethnic minority groups. Italians live primarily in Primorska (southwestern Istria) and Hungarians in the north-eastern Prekmurje region. In those two regions, the Italian and Hungarian languages, alongside the Slovenian language, enjoy the status of official languages. Communities of Roma are also autochthonous in Slovenia and are found mostly in north-eastern Slovenia or scattered throughout southern Slovenia near the border with Croatia.

9. In terms of demographic trends, Slovenia has an ageing population; its birth rate is among the lowest in Europe. Life expectancy compares favourably with former communist countries in eastern and central Europe, standing at approximately 78 years (2019) for men and 84 for women (2019). The largest concentrations of Slovenians outside Slovenia now reside in the Italian region of Friuli-Venezia Giulia, in the Austrian states of Kärnten and Steiermark, and in the Hungarian counties of Vas and Zala.

§2. Social, Cultural, and Economic Features

10. The transition from a socialist to a pluralistic and market-oriented model was probably the most far-reaching and difficult of all transitions for the country in the twentieth century.[5] The positive sides of the previous socialist system, especially the job security it provided, along with public social and medical care and relatively higher gender equality, came under great strain after independence in 1991, when the positive effects of the open market regime were not clearly evident and felt by the majority of the population. The demands for political freedoms, a more efficient economy, and a high standard of living have not been completely met. Relatively

4. Britannica, Climate of Slovenia, available at: https://www.britannica.com/place/Slovenia/Climate, accessed 14 Jul. 2022.
5. A. Šelih (ed.), A. Završnik (ed.) (2012). Crime and transition in Central and Eastern Europe. New York [etc.]: Springer, p. 3.

high social protection costs, i.e., a 40.4% tax burden on labour costs,[6] are not met with the corresponding efficiency of welfare services, with healthcare services being the most striking example of such inconsistency. The parallel healthcare system services, i.e., a hardly accessible public system for the masses and a private system attuned to patients' rights for those that can afford it; strong right-wing populism that has put greater strain on gender equality and the reproductive rights of women; threats to an independent media; political pressure on supervisory bodies, such as the Court of Audit, the Information Commissioner, and the Ombudsman, are some of the serious concerns in the past few years.

11. At-risk-of-poverty rates were between 11% and 15% in the period between 2005 and 2021, e.g., in 2021, the poverty line threshold was EUR 771 per month, and 11.7% of the population of Slovenia lived below this line. Social transfers, including pensions, continued to reduce poverty in 2021 and remain an important factor in reducing poverty in Slovenia. If social transfers (family and social benefits) were not counted as income, the risk of poverty would be 21.2%. If pensions were subtracted from income, the risk of poverty would rise to 40.3%.[7]

12. The risk of social exclusion was 13.2%, and the inequality of income distribution (Gini coefficient) was 23% (2021),[8] i.e., approximately 275,000 inhabitants were at risk of social exclusion.[9]

13. The labour market situation after the COVID-19 pandemic in 2021 was favourable, with the highest number of people in employment (900,262) since 1991. The unemployment rate was 4.7%, the lowest since such survey began.[10]

14. The labour market in Slovenia is changing, including an increasing share of foreigners in the labour force. In 2010, it accounted for 7% of the total labour force and 12% in 2021.[11] In all years, men have dominated among foreigners in employment in Slovenia, and the largest share of employed EU citizens worked in manufacturing (30%), while the largest share of those from other countries worked in construction (30%).

---

6. Statistical Office of the Republic of Slovenia (*Statistični urad RS* – SURS), Work Incentives Indicators, 2021, available at: https://www.stat.si/StatWeb/News/Index/10333, accessed 14 Jul. 2022.
7. Statistical Office of the Republic of Slovenia (*Statistični urad RS* – SURS), Income, poverty and social exclusion indicators, 2021, 16 Jun. 2022. Available at: https://www.stat.si/StatWeb/News/Index/10400, accessed 14 Jul. 2022.
8. Statistical Office of the Republic of Slovenia (*Statistični urad RS* – SURS), Income, poverty and social exclusion indicators, 2021, 16 Jun. 2022. Available at: https://www.stat.si/StatWeb/News/Index/10400, accessed 14 Jul. 2022.
9. Statistical Office of the Republic of Slovenia (*Statistični urad RS* – SURS), Quality of life, 2021, 16 Jun. 2022. Available at: https://www.stat.si/StatWeb/Field/Index/10, accessed 14 Jul. 2022.
10. Statistical Office of the Republic of Slovenia (*Statistični urad RS* – SURS), Slovenia from 1991 to the present, 20 Jun. 2022. Available at: https://www.stat.si/StatWeb/News/Index/10349, accessed 14 Jul. 2022.
11. Statistical Office of the Republic of Slovenia (*Statistični urad RS* – SURS), Slovenia from 1991 to the present, 20 Jun. 2022. Available at: https://www.stat.si/StatWeb/News/Index/10349, accessed 14 Jul. 2022.

15. Gross domestic product (GDP)[12] per capita was EUR 24,678 in 2021, almost five times the EUR 5,131 at the time of Slovenia's independence in 1991. Since the first years after independence, GDP fell the most in real terms at the start of the Great Depression in 2009 (–7.5%) and in 2020, when Slovenia was hit by the COVID-19 pandemic (–4.2%).[13]

16. Inflation[14] was the highest in Slovenia's history in 1991, at the time of gaining independence, reaching 247.1%. It also had deflation for two years (2015: –0.5% and 2020: –1.1%). At the monthly level, inflation has been on the rise since March 2021 to June 2022. In April 2022, inflation was 6.9% compared to April 2021. Transport has risen the most, by 15.1%. The most significant impact on inflation has been the rise in the price of diesel (by 29.7%) after the Russian invasion of Ukraine, while the rise in communication services amounted to 2.7%, and within this group internet access became the cheapest service.

17. General government gross debt was estimated at EUR 38.9 billion, or 74.7% of GDP, at the end of 2021. This amounts to EUR 43,163 of debt for every person under employment. At the average gross monthly wage of EUR 1,970, every employee would have to work one year and ten months to pay off the corresponding share of the public debt.

18. The value of imports is higher than exports, with the largest share of imports coming from Germany (14.9% of the total value of imports), followed by Italy (11.4%) and Switzerland (10.2%).[15] With regard to energy, Slovenia met 53% of its energy needs with domestic energy sources and imported the rest (2021). The supply of petroleum products was entirely imported. In all years, the energy supply structure was dominated by petroleum products (31%), with natural gas accounting for the smallest share (12%). Nuclear energy provided 23.2% of total energy needs (2021).

§3. The Use of ICT[16]

19. In 2021, already 93% of households had internet access, while 89% of 16–74-year-olds regularly used the internet. Of households with internet access,

---

12. Statistical Office of the Republic of Slovenia (*Statistični urad RS* – SURS), Slovenia from 1991 to the present, 20 Jun. 2022. Available at: https://www.stat.si/StatWeb/News/Index/10349, accessed 14 Jul. 2022.
13. Statistical Office of the Republic of Slovenia (*Statistični urad RS* – SURS), Economy of Slovenia. Available at: https://www.britannica.com/place/Slovenia/Economy, accessed 14 Jul. 2022.
14. Statistical Office of the Republic of Slovenia (*Statistični urad RS* – SURS), Slovenia from 1991 to the present, 20 Jun. 2022. Available at: https://www.stat.si/StatWeb/News/Index/10349, accessed 14 Jul. 2022.
15. Statistical Office of the Republic of Slovenia (*Statistični urad RS* – SURS), Slovenia from 1991 to the present, 20 Jun. 2022. Available at: https://www.stat.si/StatWeb/News/Index/10349, accessed 14 Jul. 2022.
16. Statistical Office of the Republic of Slovenia (*Statistični urad RS* – SURS). Internet usage in households and individuals, Slovenia, 7 Oct. 2021. Available at: https://www.stat.si/StatWeb/News/Index/9704, accessed 14 Jul. 2022.

83% accessed the internet via a fixed internet connection, while the most common way for regular internet users to access the internet was by smartphone (95%). More than two-thirds of 16–74-year-olds carried out health-related activities online, 81% used e-mail, 75% searched for goods and services information, and 68% used internet to search for news. More than half of users aged 16–74 (58%) have seen untrue or dubious information or content on news websites or social media; 37% of these have checked the veracity of such content, and 39% already knew that the source was unreliable. Almost a third of households with fixed broadband access faced problems with frequent disconnections or reduced connection speeds, and almost a quarter of households faced connection speeds lower than contractually guaranteed.

20. Mobile network users made more calls and wrote more messages (Q1 2022).[17] The number of mobile network users in Slovenia exceeded 2,613,000 at the end of Q1 2022, which is a 2% increase at the annual level. In total, almost 475 million outgoing calls were detected from Slovenian mobile networks (2022). Domestic outgoing calls were up 1% and have increased on all networks (Q1 2022). International outgoing calls increased by 12% (Q1 2022). However, the number of hours has decreased: in total, there were approximately 23 million hours of outgoing traffic from Slovenian mobile networks in Q1 2022, which was 6% less than in the same period a year earlier. Some 577 million Short Message Service (SMS) (7% more than in Q1 2021) and almost 29 million Multimedia Messaging Service (MMS) messages were sent in Q1 2022. Data traffic via mobile broadband continues to grow significantly (data from 2022), e.g., almost 71 million gigabytes of data were downloaded via mobile broadband, which was 27% more compared to the same period in 2021. Half of all internet users accessed the internet via fibre-optic access (Q1 2022).[18]

21. Among companies in Slovenia with at least ten employees and the self-employed,[19] 83% have a website, and 24% of such companies generated revenue from online sales (2020).[20] The percentage of people aged 16–74 who ordered or bought goods or services on the internet in the past twelve months amounted to 71% in 2021.

22. The older population's (aged 65–74) use of Information and Communication Technology (ICT) was still under the EU-27 average in 2022. The digital divide was relatively sharp, e.g., 31% of the older population had never used the internet,

17. Statistical Office of the Republic of Slovenia (*Statistični urad RS* – SURS), Electronic communications services, Q1 2022, 20 Jun. 2022. Available at: https://www.stat.si/StatWeb/News/Index/10385, accessed 14 Jul. 2022.
18. All data from the Statistical Office of the Republic of Slovenia (*Statistični urad RS* – SURS), Electronic communications services, Q1 2022, 20 Jun. 2022. Available at: https://www.stat.si/StatWeb/News/Index/10385, accessed 14 Jul. 2022.
19. Statistical Office of the Republic of Slovenia (*Statistični urad RS* – SURS), Development and technology. Available at: https://www.stat.si/StatWeb/Field/Index/25, accessed 14 Jul. 2022.
20. Statistical Office of the Republic of Slovenia (*Statistični urad RS* – SURS), Online sales, Slovenia, 2020, 4 Nov. 2021. Available at: https://www.stat.si/StatWeb/News/Index/9890, accessed 14 Jul. 2022.

and 45% had no digital skills (2021). The share of this group in the overall population is slightly more than 20%. However, 96% of them use mobile phones and 58% use smartphones (2022).[21] Of those that use the internet, 48% carry out health-related activities online.[22]

§4. Political, Constitutional, and Legal Features[23]

I. Political System[24]

23. Slovenia is a parliamentary democratic republic with a proportional electoral system. All power in the country comes from the people and belongs to the people. All citizens of the Republic of Slovenia of legal age (at least 18 years of age) have the right to vote for representatives of the people in general, multiparty, and free elections. Power is divided into legislative, executive, and judicial branches. The *legislative* branch of power is vested in the bicameral parliament, *executive* power is vested in the Government, and the *judiciary* is separate from both the legislature and the executive. The mechanisms of checks-and-balances between the mentioned three powers are in place.

24. The head of state is the President of the Republic of Slovenia, who is elected for a term of five years. The Government of the Republic of Slovenia is made up of ministers and is headed by the Prime Minister (PM). The PM is nominated by the President and confirmed by a vote of the National Assembly of the Republic of Slovenia.

25. Slovenia's incomplete bicameral parliament is made up of the National Assembly and the National Council. The National Assembly has ninety seats, with one seat each for the Italian and Hungarian minorities. The National Council has forty seats and is made up of social, economic, professional, and local interest groups. The National Council does not have the function of a second (upper) chamber of parliament, as the Constitution does not grant it these powers. Regular parliamentary elections are held every four years, and elections to the National Council every five years.

---

21. Statistical Office of the Republic of Slovenia (*Statistični urad RS* – SURS), World Telecommunication and Information Society Day, 12 May 2022. Available at: https://www.stat.si/StatWeb/News/Index/10317, accessed 14 Jul. 2022.
22. Statistical Office of the Republic of Slovenia (*Statistični urad RS* – SURS), World Telecommunication and Information Society Day, 12 May 2022. Available at: https://www.stat.si/StatWeb/News/Index/10317, accessed 14 Jul. 2022.
23. Wikipedia, Politics of Slovenia, available at: https://en.wikipedia.org/wiki/Politics_of_Slovenia, accessed 14 Jul. 2022.
24. Wikipedia, Slovenia, available at: https://sl.wikipedia.org/wiki/Slovenija, accessed 14 Jul. 2022.

II. The Constitutional Principles

26. The Constitution of the Republic of Slovenia was adopted on 23 December 1991[25] and stipulates that Slovenia is a democratic republic (Article 1) and a social state governed by the rule of law (Article 2). The Constitution introduces the principle of the separation of the legislative, executive, and judicial powers (Article 3). The Constitutional Court of the Republic of Slovenia is the highest body of the judicial power for the protection of constitutionality, legality, human rights, and fundamental freedoms.

27. The Constitution provides human rights and political freedoms (Chapter 2), on the one hand, and social and economic rights (Chapter 3), on the other. It establishes the organization of the state with the following pillars (Chapter IV): (a) the National Assembly, (b) the National Council, (c) President of the Republic, (d) The Government, (e) the State Administration, (f) National Defence, (g) the Judiciary, (h) the State Prosecutor's Office, and (i) the Attorneyship and Notariat.

28. The subject matter of constitutional regulation includes self-government, public finance, constitutionality and legality, the Constitutional Court, and the procedure for amending the Constitution.

III. The Judicial System[26]

29. The judicial system is unified and consists of general and specialized courts. The specialized courts operate only in the field of (a) labour and social law (reflected in four first instance labour courts and one Higher Labour and Social Court) and (b) administrative law (one Administrative Court), while the general courts are local (44), district (11), higher (4), and supreme (1) courts. The general courts hence operate at four levels of subject matter jurisdiction, and territorial jurisdiction is also determined by the system of the territorial distribution of the courts. The Supreme Court is the highest authority among state judicial authorities, adjudicating at the third instance on regular legal remedies against the decisions of second instance courts and, as a rule, on extraordinary legal remedies against the final decisions of courts.

IV. Administrative Division[27]

30. Slovenia does not have a regional level of division, although the Constitution provides for such. The only form of local self-government is the municipality,

---

25. In order to honour the adoption and implementation of the Constitution, as the fundamental legal basis for the deciding of the judges of the Constitutional Court, every year on 23 December Constitutionality Day is celebrated.
26. More about Slovenian court system can be found at: https://www.gov.si/en/state-authorities/courts/, accessed 14 Jul. 2022.
27. More on the administrative division of the Republic of Slovenia is available at: https://sl.wikipedia.org/wiki/Upravna_delitev_Slovenije, accessed 14 Jul. 2022.

with relatively broad public powers, whose main roles are the provision of early childhood education and primary healthcare, the provision of essential public services (including public transport and library services), and spatial planning. Slovenia is administratively divided into 212 municipalities, 11 of which have the status of city municipality. By international comparisons, local self-government is highly fragmented, which has only become more pronounced in the years since independence; e.g., more than half of the Slovenian municipalities in 2022 had fewer than 5,000 inhabitants.

31. In addition to municipalities and the various informal divisions into provinces, there are 12 statistical regions according to the standard scheme for the classification of territorial units for statistics in the European Union, Nomenclature of Territorial Units for Statistics (NUTS-3). The statistical regions, which are grouped into two cohesion regions – West and East Slovenia (NUTS-2), have no administrative function. The cohesion regions also exist for the sole purpose of implementing European regional policy.

V. Political Parties

32. Slovenia uses a proportional system to elect its ninety members to the National Assembly. An exception is made for members of the Italian and Hungarian national minorities, who are elected under a majority voting system in the areas where the minorities live. Under the proportional system, seats are distributed in proportion to the support given by each group to individual candidates and lists in elections.[28]

33. Slovenia has a 4% electoral threshold for entry into the National Assembly (four seats), which means that only lists that win at least 4% of the total number of votes in the whole country are taken into account in the distribution of seats.

34. A political party can be founded in Slovenia by at least two-hundred adult citizens who sign a declaration of establishment. A political party is an association of citizens pursuing their political objectives, as set out in the party's programme, by democratically shaping the political will of citizens and nominating candidates in elections to the National Assembly, the Presidency of the Republic, and local authorities. A political party shall act publicly. The public nature of a political party's activities shall, as a rule, be ensured by informing the public of its activities. The financial and material operations of a political party shall be public. No political party may operate in the Republic of Slovenia that is not registered in accordance with the law or that has its seat abroad. A political party may not operate or

28. More about the Slovenian electoral process is available on the State Electoral Commission website: https://www.dvk-rs.si/en/election-education/, accessed 14 Jul. 2022. Books in Slovenian: (1) Brezovšek, M., Haček, M., Zver, M. (2008). Organizacij oblasti v Sloveniji. Ljubljana: Fakulteta za družbene vede. Available at: https://www.zrss.si/projektiess/gradiva/add/Organizacija_oblasti_v_Sloveniji_knjiga_Brezovšek_Haček_Zver.pdf, accessed 14 Jul. 2022; (2) Lukšič, I. (2001). Politični sistem Republike Slovenije: Očrt. Ljubljana. Sophia.

establish its organizational forms in companies, institutions, and other organizations, or in state bodies. A political party may not function as a military or armed association and may not be established for that purpose.

35. At the beginning of the democratic transition, the electorate was predominantly in favour of left and centre-left parties. By 1996, however, there was a shift on the left-right continuum from a predominantly centre-left orientation to a centre orientation (about half of the electorate was in the ideological centre). The party LDS, which followed this shift of voters towards the centre, gained a large number of votes, although it also lost some of its distinctiveness. After the October 2004 elections, however, there was a major shift on the left-right continuum, as voters showed strong confidence in right-wing parties. The reverse was true in the 2008 national elections, where voters showed strong trust in centre-left parties.

36. The Slovenian political space has been dominated by conflicts of a symbolic or ideological nature (cultural struggles, attitudes towards recent – Yugoslavian – history), which perpetuate elements of political or social polarization.

37. The parliamentary elections held in 2011 were the first early elections in Slovenian history. The election was surprisingly won by the centre-left Positive Slovenia party, led by businessman Zoran Janković. However, he failed to be elected as the new Prime Minister in the National Assembly, and the new Government was instead formed by a right-leaning coalition of five parties led by the Slovenian Democratic Party (SDS).

38. Parliamentary elections were held in Slovenia in 2014 following the resignation of Alenka Bratušek's Government. The Party of Miro Cerar (SMC), a new party led by lawyer and professor Miro Cerar, won the election with over 34% of the vote. Three political parties left the National Assembly, including Zoran Janković's Positive Slovenia, the winner of the 2011 election. A leftist United Left party entered the National Assembly for the first time, winning six seats.

39. However, in 2018, all parties called for snap elections after the early resignation of Prime Minister Miro Cerar. These were the third consecutive snap elections after 2011 and 2014. The nationalist SDS came out ahead in the snap elections, and Janez Janša was elected the Prime Minister–designate on 3 March 2020 to form the 14th Government of Slovenia from 2020 to 2022.

40. In the 2022 elections, a newly founded political party, the Freedom Movement, won a landslide victory, winning 34.45% of the vote and 41 seats, the most in the history of the Republic of Slovenia. The reasons for its victory can be attributed to the authoritarian rule of the right-wing Government of the nationalist Janez Janša, with its strong anti-migrant right-wing populism and attacks on the judiciary, supervisory bodies, and the media.

Chapter 2. Telecommunications Infrastructure

§1. Overview

41. An overview of the telecommunications infrastructure shows that this sector in Slovenia is stable and on the rise. The overall positive trends are demonstrated by the steady rise in the number of employees and self-employed in the sector in the 2010–2020 decade (12.6%). The number of operators (fixed and mobile network) and internet service providers remained stable. A downward trend is noticeable in the field of cable and satellite communication service providers (Table 1).

Table 1 Operators, Infrastructure, and Employment in Electronic Communications[29]

Year	*2010*	*2011*	*2012*	*2013*	*2014*	*2015*	*2016*	*2017*	*2018*	*2019*	*2020*
Fixed network operators	12	11	13	15	16	16	14	14	12	13	13
International operators	15	16	17	19	20	20	16	19	17	18	18
Mobile network operators	6	6	7	7	7	7	6	8	7	7	7
Cable and satellite service providers	67	61	60	58	57	56	52	50	47	48	53
Internet service providers	57	58	64	63	62	65	62	61	61	60	55
Employees and self-employed	5,497	5,404	5,537	5,782	5,709	5,643	5,453	5,442	5,344	5,845	6,187

§2. Main Telephone Lines

42. The stability of the rise in the telecommunications infrastructure is first reflected in the number of household connections via main telephone lines (fixed location). Even though the 2010–2020 period shows a slight decrease in the overall number of connections (–2.5%), the rise in Voice Over Internet Protocol (VoIP) household connections is significant (approx. 73%) and compensates for the phase-out of Public Switched Telephone Network (PSTN) and Integrated Services Digital Network (ISDN connections (–84%) (Table 2).

29. *Source*: https://pxweb.stat.si, accessed 14 Jul. 2022.

Table 2 Fixed-Location Connections (Main Telephone Lines): Households[30]

Year	*2010*	*2011*	*2012*	*2013*	*2014*	*2015*	*2016*	*2017*	*2018*	*2019*	*2020*
Total number of connections	571,604	564,863	556,597	556,127	555,349	556,678	545,612	561,785	557,490	551,538	557,523
PSTN	240,988	209,473	181,854	154,526	129,506	110,300	92,033	70,319	59,362	48,357	38,871
PSTN Centrex	–	–	–	–	–	–	–	–	–	–	–
ISDN BA	31,139	23,763	18,116	13,202	9,017	6,392	4,406	3,100	2,401	1,822	1,357
ISDN PA	–	–	–	–	–	–	–	–	–	–	–
ISDN Centrex	–	–	–	–	–	–	–	–	–	–	–
VoIP	299,477	331,627	356,627	388,399	416,826	439,986	449,173	488,366	495,727	501,359	517,295

30. *Source*: https://pxweb.stat.si, accessed 14 Jul. 2022.

43. Business users, however, show a strong trend as regards phasing out main telephone lines altogether, with the total number of connections decreasing from 2010 to 2020 by 46%, in spite of the 182% increase in VoIP connections (Table 3).

Table 3 Fixed-Location Connections (Main Telephone Lines): Business Users[31]

Year	*2010*	*2011*	*2012*	*2013*	*2014*	*2015*	*2016*	*2017*	*2018*	*2019*	*2020*
Total number of connections	248,857	233,352	210,711	190,653	174,871	164,869	158,009	156,221	147,074	139,930	134,135
PSTN	36,328	33,256	30,179	26,449	22,933	19,634	17,339	15,462	13,827	12,406	10,874
PSTN Centrex	80,532	71,917	62,763	52,630	44,800	39,591	35,046	31,695	27,308	23,401	20,367
ISDN BA	42,445	37,149	31,037	25,019	18,633	13,995	11,139	9,156	7,741	6,699	5,680
ISDN PA	649	574	462	372	322	300	279	270	251	224	210
ISDN Centrex	57,549	48,176	37,893	30,596	24,569	19,926	16,220	13,601	11,231	9,797	8,447
VoIP	31,354	42,280	48,377	55,587	63,614	71,423	77,986	86,037	86,716	87,403	88,557

§3. MOBILE NETWORKS

44. In the recent decade, the number of mobile network users has been steadily increasing in both the private and business sectors. Overall, the number of private users has increased by 12%, whereas the number of users in the business sector has increased by more than 50% (Table 4). The increase can mainly be attributed to the increase in subscribers, with a noticeable decrease in pre-paid access to mobile networks in the private sector (more than 25%). It appears that the strong rise in business mobile users is compensating for the phasing out of fixed-location phone connections (Table 5).

31. *Source*: https://pxweb.stat.si, accessed 14 Jul. 2022.

Table 4 Mobile Network Users – Private Users[32]

Year	*2010*	*2011*	*2012*	*2013*	*2014*	*2015*	*2016*	*2017*	*2018*	*2019*	*2020*
Total number of mobile network users	1,713,815	1,746,261	1,805,308	1,833,356	1,863,045	1,866,860	1,887,419	1,907,681	1,907,050	1,924,711	1,935,833
Pre-paid	635,313	627,241	636,192	619,886	613,555	578,666	550,552	534,097	498,713	491,502	475,390
Subscribed	1,078,502	1,119,020	1,169,116	1,213,470	1,249,490	1,288,194	1,336,867	1,373,584	1,408,337	1,433,209	1,460,443

Table 5 Mobile Network Users: Business Users[33]

Year	*2010*	*2011*	*2012*	*2013*	*2014*	*2015*	*2016*	*2017*	*2018*	*2019*	*2020*
Total number of mobile network users	408,135	422,287	435,852	450,217	463,341	487,066	498,338	535,491	558,807	587,268	615,062
Prepaid	277	231	209	171	149	125	–	–	–	–	–
Subscribed	407,858	422,056	435,643	450,046	463,192	486,941	498,338	535,491	558,807	587,268	615,062

32. *Source*: https://pxweb.stat.si, accessed 14 Jul. 2022.
33. *Source*: https://pxweb.stat.si, accessed 14 Jul. 2022.

§4. Internet Access

45. Similarly, the number of broadband internet connections is steadily rising, resulting in an approximately 38% increase over the past decade in both household and business internet access (Tables 6 and 7).

Table 6 Internet Access: Households[34]

Year	*2010*	*2011*	*2012*	*2013*	*2014*	*2015*	*2016*	*2017*	*2018*	*2019*	*2020*
Total number of broadband connections	407,294	422,630	437,037	453,185	479,555	491,065	506,147	517,618	527,203	540,974	562,246
xDSL	226,683	212,488	205,541	199,102	195,320	191,480	182,167	168,698	157,883	148,150	133,066
Cable modem	118,356	129,929	140,799	147,870	164,610	164,065	164,121	164,815	162,799	161,414	168,267
Optical fibre access connections	57,118	70,617	78,957	93,811	106,782	122,427	147,824	171,457	194,336	219,580	250,907
Other	5,137	9,596	11,740	12,402	12,843	13,093	12,035	12,648	12,185	11,830	10,006
Dial-up access connections	9,926	4,211	1,918	876	459	246	61	30	4	–	–

34. *Source*: https://pxweb.stat.si, accessed 14 Jul. 2022.

Table 7 Internet Access: Business Users[35]

Year	*2010*	*2011*	*2012*	*2013*	*2014*	*2015*	*2016*	*2017*	*2018*	*2019*	*2020*
Total number of broadband connections	64,927	74,403	75,900	75,640	76,283	77,961	83,171	84,202	85,542	86,965	89,358
xDSL	51,820	58,746	57,554	54,632	52,401	51,858	48,988	45,052	42,318	39,782	35,904
Cable modem	5,286	6,026	6,873	7,295	8,029	7,740	12,258	12,965	13,004	13,027	14,558
Optical fibre access connections	6,997	8,694	10,437	12,560	14,588	16,915	20,379	24,298	28,169	31,868	36,625
Other	824	937	1,036	1,153	1,265	1,448	1,546	1,887	2,051	2,288	2,271
Dial-up access connections	423	200	309	171	145	125	–	–	–	–	–

35. *Source*: https://pxweb.stat.si, accessed 14 Jul. 2022.

46. Trends in internet access are reflected in the internet access penetration levels, nearing a 20% increase in households enjoying access over the last decade and a 60% increase in mobile broadband access penetration (Tables 8 and 9).

Table 8 Broadband Access Penetration: Households[36]

Year (%)	*SURS (EU-SILC) (%)*	*SURS (2015)*
2012	68.96	
2013	70.61	
2014	73.11	
2015	73.64	72.15
2016		76.39
2017		80.24
2018		81.45
2019		83.24
2020		84.84
2021		86.72

Table 9 Mobile Broadband Internet Access Penetration: Population[37]

Year	*SURS (%)*
2012	33.14
2013	37.89
2014	44.27
2015	47.82
2016	62.16
2017	70.5
2018	77.72
2019	83.45
2020	86.46
2021	91.24

36. *Source*: https://eanalitik.akos-rs.si/, accessed 14 Jul. 2022.
37. *Source*: https://eanalitik.akos-rs.si/, accessed 14 Jul. 2022.

§5. ADMINISTRATIVE BODIES

47. Currently, the overall oversight of the telecommunication infrastructure falls within the competence of an independent public agency, Agencija za komunikacijska omrežja in storitve (Agency for Communication Networks and Services of the Republic of Slovenia)(AKOS).[38] The first forerunner of AKOS was established in 2001 by the Slovenian Government[39] after the enactment of the Telecommunications Act (no longer in force).[40]

48. The scope of the tasks of AKOS is at this time regulated by the Government's decision on its establishment,[41] pursuant to the provisions of Zakon o elektronskih komunikacijah (ZEKom-1).[42] The main goals of the Agency are to encourage competition in the field of providing electronic communications networks and services (Article 195 ZEKom-1), to promote the development of the internal market (Article 196 ZEKom-1), and to support the interests of citizens (Article 197 ZEKom-1), e.g., access to universal services and ensuring consumer protection.

49. AKOS cooperates closely with other public and state bodies in the field, such as competition protection bodies, the Information Commissioner, and bodies responsible for network security and integrity. Under Zakon o informacijski varnosti (ZInfV),[43] the two central bodies responsible for network security and integrity are SI-CERT[44] and the Government Information Security Office.[45]

50. SI-CERT acts as the national Computer Security Incident Response Team (CSIRT) and is tasked with, *inter alia*, providing methodological support, assistance, and cooperation in the event of an incident and with receiving information on risks and vulnerabilities in the field of information security, forwarding such to the administrators of the affected systems, and with publishing warnings (Article 28 ZInfV).

51. The Information Security Office's primary tasks are to coordinate the operation of the national information security system, to develop cyber defence capabilities, to provide professional support in the field of information security, and to provide analyses, methodological support, and preventive actions in the area of information security (Article 27 ZInfV).

---

38. General website available at https://www.akos-rs.si/en, accessed 25 Jun. 2022.
39. Ruling on the establishment of the Telecommunications and Broadcasting Agency, Official Gazette of the Republic of Slovenia, No. 60/01, with subsequent amendments.
40. Official Gazette of the Republic of Slovenia, No. 30/01, as amended.
41. Decision on the establishment of the Agency for Communication Networks and Services of the Republic of Slovenia, Official Gazette of the Republic of Slovenia, No. 41/13, as amended.
42. Official Gazette of the Republic of Slovenia, No. 109/12, as amended.
43. Official Gazette of the Republic of Slovenia, Nos. 30/18 and 95/21.
44. *See*: https://www.cert.si/, accessed 25 Jun. 2022.
45. General information available at https://www.gov.si/en/state-authorities/government-offices/government-information-security-office/, accessed 25 Jun. 2022.

52. The CSIRT for state administration bodies (Article 29 ZInfV) is organized as a part of the Ministry of Public Administration (*Ministrstvo za javno upravo* – MJU), Sector for Information Security (*Sektor za informacijsko varnost*).[46]

46. For general information, *see*: https://www.gov.si/drzavni-organi/ministrstva/ministrstvo-za-javno-upravo/o-ministrstvu/direktorat-za-informatiko/sektor-za-informacijsko-varnost/, accessed 25 Jun. 2022.

Chapter 3. The Information and Communication Technology Market

§1. Overview

53. In the Socialist Federative Republic of Yugoslavia (SFRJ), all telecommunication services were regulated at the federal level. They were monitored by an organization established in accordance with the eastern European practice of post, telegraph, and telephone companies – PTT, and named the Community of Yugoslav Post, Telegraph, and Telephone Companies (*Skupnost jugoslovanskih post, telegrafov in telefonov* – JPPT). Since Slovenia became an independent state, the Slovenian ICT market has been subject to several significant changes, all aimed at the denationalization and liberalization of the market.

54. The first significant change was introduced in 1993, when the Administration of the Republic of Slovenia for Telecommunications (*Uprava Republike Slovenije za telekomunikacije* (URST)) was established, which assumed some of the tasks handled by the Community of the Slovenian PPT. The Slovenian PPT was still responsible for post and telecommunications until the next important milestone in the history of the Slovenian ICT market – the year 1995, when the PTT was divided into two entities, formally separating postal and telecommunication services (following the pattern of several other European states that had used the PTT model). The first entity was *Pošta Slovenije d.o.o.*, which took over postal activities.[47] The second one was Telekom Slovenije p.o., which assumed the monopoly over the provision of public service of telegraph and telephone services.[48]

55. In 2001, the Telecommunications Act was adopted, which was aimed at liberalizing and ensuring competition in the market.[49]

56. The Slovenian National Programme for the Development of Telecommunications, adopted in 2000, already foresaw that the Slovenian ICT market, at the time consisting of several telecommunications networks for different telecommunications services, historically developed in isolation or lose integration with one another, would in the following years be characterized by diversity and competition between the different specialized services offered by different networks.[50] This has indeed been the case in the past two decades, despite the consolidation process,[51] as the Slovenian ICT market remains quite saturated.

---

47. Regulation on the Establishment of Pošte Slovenije d.o.o.; Official Gazette of the Republic of Slovenia, No. 64/94.
48. Decree on the Reorganization of PTT Slovenije p.o. into Telekom Slovenije p.o.; Official Gazette of the Republic of Slovenia, No. 76/94
49. *See* the amended Art. 2(1) of the Telecommunications Act, Official Gazette of the Republic of Slovenia, No. 30/01.
50. Official Gazette of the Republic of Slovenia, No. 23/00.
51. *See*: The Slovenian Press Agency (STA), Slovenian telecoms market in an intensive phase of consolidation, 8 Jun. 2015, available at: https://www.sta.si/2144005/slovenski-telekomunikacijski-trg-v-intenzivni-fazi-konsolidacije, accessed 27 Jun. 2022.

57. At the end of 2020, 13 fixed network operators and seven mobile network operators were active on the market, 53 cable and satellite providers, and 55 internet service providers.[52] The competition between operators is therefore strong. For this reason, operators are trying to retain users and attract new ones with tempting offers, which include specific discounts, faster internet access speed, and often a mandatory twelve or twenty-four-month tethering period and a bundled package of services. The Slovenian Consumers Association (*Zveza potrošnikov Slovenije* (ZPS)) reports a lack of consumer awareness in this area and notes that the methods used by the operators do not enable consumers to choose specific services and instead force them into bundled contracts.[53]

58. An important actor in the ICT market is the ICT Association of Slovenia (*Združenje za informatiko in telekomunikacije* – ZIT), which is a part of the Slovenian Chamber of Commerce and Industry (*Gospodarksa zbornica Slovenije* – GZS), that is aimed at representing the Slovenian ICT industry within the country and abroad.[54]

§2. Operators and Their Market Shares

59. Currently, 147 operators are registered in the register of operators (the Register) established and monitored by the Agency for Communication Networks and Services of the Republic of Slovenia (*Agencija za komunikacijska omrežja in storitve Republike Slovenije* – AKOS).[55]

60. The Slovenian ICT market is, however, to a large extent divided between the four companies with the most significant market shares. These are: A1 Slovenija, T-2, Telekom Slovenije, and Telemach.

61. The highest market share in the mobile broadband internet access field belongs to Telekom Slovenije, in the field of fixed broadband internet access to Telemach, and in the field of mobile telephony users again to Telekom Slovenije (*see* Figures 1–3).

52. *See*: https://www.stat.si/StatWeb/News/Index/9846, accessed 27 Jun. 2022.
53. *See*: https://www.zps.si/trg-in-cene-topmenu-306/cene/9108-pregled-trga-storitev-elektronskih-komunikacij-6-2018, accessed 26 Jun. 2022.
54. *See*: https://www.gzs.si/en_zit, accessed 27 Jun. 2022.
55. *See*: https://www.akos-rs.si/registri/seznam-registrov/operaterji, accessed 27 Jun. 2022.

Figure 1 The Mobile Broadband Internet Access Market Shares of the Four Largest Operators[56]

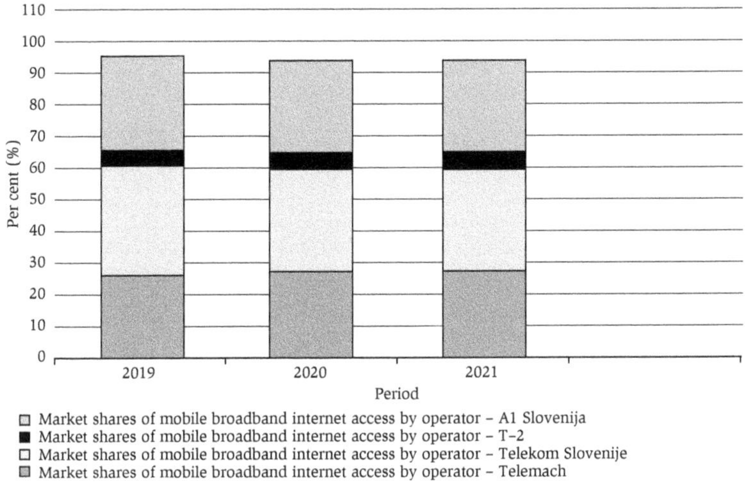

Figure 2 The Fixed Broadband Internet Access Market Shares of the Four Largest Operators[57]

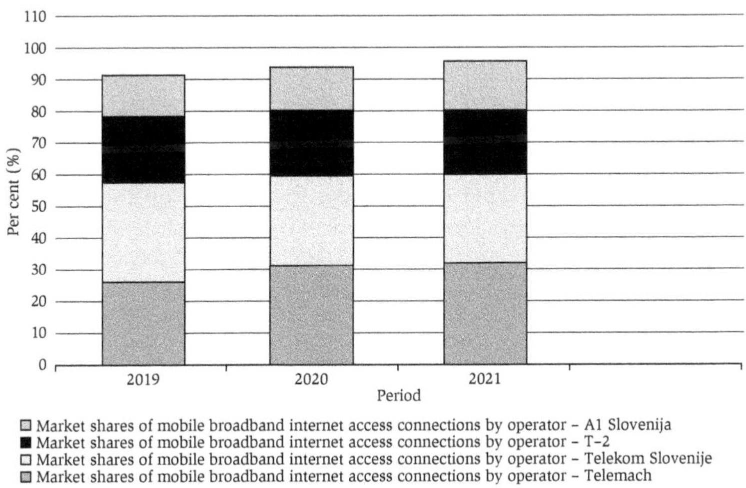

56. The Agency for Communication Networks and Services of the Republic of Slovenia, available at: https://eanalitik.akos-rs.si/en/?tx_agindicator_filter%5Baction%5D=advanced&tx_agindicator_filter%5Bcontroller%5D=Filter&cHash=9aace9ee40eeb4c97d74d05ab2a9f8ec, accessed 14 Jul. 2022.
57. Agency for Communication Networks and Services of the Republic of Slovenia, available at: https://eanalitik.akos-rs.si/en/?tx_agindicator_filter%5Baction%5D=advanced&tx_agindicator_filter%5Bcontroller%5D=Filter&cHash=9aace9ee40eeb4c97d74d05ab2a9f8ec, accessed 14 Jul. 2022.

Figure 3 The Market Shares of the Four Largest Operators Regarding Active Mobile Telephony Users[58]

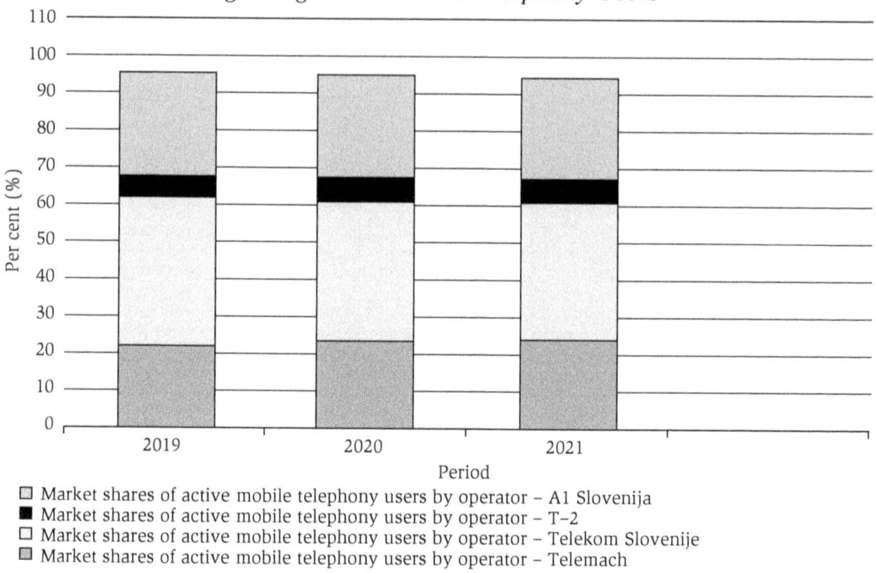

§3. Trends on the ICT Market

62. In Slovenia, the range of providers of both fixed and mobile services is very wide, but there are no significant differences between their offers, which can lead to uninformed consumer choice. This is compounded by the fact that, despite the bundled package of services, switching between service providers is still relatively easy. It can be observed from the data collected by AKOS in its quarterly reports that the market remains divided between the four largest operators, and with the number of users or subscribers growing, there is much switching between them. The operators are therefore quite aggressive with their offers to attract new subscribers while retaining existing ones, whom other operators target with favourable offers. A constant trend deriving from these characteristics is the increased flexibility of the ICT market.

63. AKOS analysed products and services in the retail broadband access market, gathering data from operators providing electronic communications broadband access services in December 2020 and registering them as active operators in the

58. The Agency for Communication Networks and Services of the Republic of Slovenia, available at: https://eanalitik.akos-rs.si/en/?tx_agindicator_filter%5Baction%5D=advanced&tx_agindicator_filter%5Bcontroller%5D=Filter&cHash=9aace9ee40eeb4c97d74d05ab2a9f8ec, accessed 14 Jul. 2022.

Register.[59] The analysis showed, *inter alia*, that the quadruple package (INT+TV+TEL+MOB) was the most frequently chosen combination of end-user services during the period under review, followed by the triple package (INT+TV+TEL+TEL).[60] During the period under review, 89% of broadband connections included a TV service.[61] For connections with a TV service, the average number of TV channels included in the basic service package was 178.[62] This data confirms the trend regarding an increase in bundled packages of service offers, which are the most frequently chosen option and continue to be on the rise.

64. Another trend is the increase in the number of mobile broadband internet users, which in the first quarter of 2020 was experienced by all mobile broadband internet access providers, except Telekom Slovenije, d.d. and A1 Slovenija, d.d.[63]

65. The predictions for the future are that the ICT market will continue towards greater consolidation.

§4. Turnover and Investments in the ICT Market

66. Turnover and investments in the ICT sector in the past few years were relatively stable. The COVID-19 pandemic, however, had a substantial impact on the ICT market. On the one hand, certain services offering remote connectivity and secure communications witnessed significant growth, while on the other, some long-term planned projects on the market were put on hold indefinitely (Table 10).[64]

---

59. The Agency for Communication Networks and Services of the Republic of Slovenia (*Agencija za komunikacijska omrežja in storitve Republike Slovenije* – AKOS). Analysis of products and services in the retail broadband access market, 7 Dec. 2021. Available at: https://www.akos-rs.si/telekomunikacije/raziscite/porocila-raziskave-in-analize/telekomunikacije/novica/analiza-produktov-in-storitev-na-maloprodajnem-trgu-sirokopasovnega-dostopa-5, accessed 28 Jun. 2022.
60. The Agency for Communication Networks and Services of the Republic of Slovenia (*Agencija za komunikacijska omrežja in storitve Republike Slovenije* – AKOS). Analysis of products and services in the retail broadband access market, 7 Dec. 2021. Available at: https://www.akos-rs.si/telekomunikacije/raziscite/porocila-raziskave-in-analize/telekomunikacije/novica/analiza-produktov-in-storitev-na-maloprodajnem-trgu-sirokopasovnega-dostopa-5, accessed 28 Jun. 2022.
61. The Agency for Communication Networks and Services of the Republic of Slovenia (*Agencija za komunikacijska omrežja in storitve Republike Slovenije* – AKOS). Analysis of products and services in the retail broadband access market, 7 Dec. 2021. Available at: https://www.akos-rs.si/telekomunikacije/raziscite/porocila-raziskave-in-analize/telekomunikacije/novica/analiza-produktov-in-storitev-na-maloprodajnem-trgu-sirokopasovnega-dostopa-5, accessed 28 Jun. 2022.
62. The Agency for Communication Networks and Services of the Republic of Slovenia (*Agencija za komunikacijska omrežja in storitve Republike Slovenije* – AKOS). Analysis of products and services in the retail broadband access market, 7 Dec. 2021. Available at: https://www.akos-rs.si/telekomunikacije/raziscite/porocila-raziskave-in-analize/telekomunikacije/novica/analiza-produktov-in-storitev-na-maloprodajnem-trgu-sirokopasovnega-dostopa-5, accessed 28 Jun. 2022.
63. The Agency for Communication Networks and Services of the Republic of Slovenia (*Agencija za komunikacijska omrežja in storitve Republike Slovenije* – AKOS). Electronic communications market development report for the first quarter of 2020, July 2020. Available at: https://www.akos-rs.si/fileadmin/user_upload/Cetrtletno_porocilo_Q1_2020_za_objavo.pdf, accessed 28 Jun. 2022.
64. *See*: https://www.trade.gov/country-commercial-guides/slovenia-information-and-communications-technology, accessed 27 Jun. 2022.

Table 10 Turnover and Investments in the Field of Electronic Communications in Slovenia[65]

	2019	2020	2020/2019
	EUR	*EUR*	*Index*
Turnover from electronic communications services – total	1,085,649	1,066,433	98.2
Turnover from the public telephone network at a fixed location	471,205	482,630	102.4
Turnover from publicly available mobile telephone services	353,015	338,603	95.9
Turnover from interconnection services	135,483	120,358	88.8
Other revenues	125,946	124,842	99.1
Investments	231,953	284,349	122.6

67. Total turnover from electronic communications services in 2020 amounted to EUR 1,066 million. Turnover from the public telephone network at a fixed location represented 45% of the total turnover, which is approximately EUR 483 million. Turnover from publicly available mobile telephone services represented 32% or approximately EUR 339 million. Turnover from interconnection services was 11%, i.e., EUR 120 million. Other revenues represented 12% of the total turnover, which amounted to EUR 125 million. Total turnover from electronic communications services was 2% lower in 2020 compared to 2019, with lower turnover from interconnection services and publicly available mobile telephony services, the former by EUR 15 million or 11%, and the latter by EUR 14 million or 4%. By contrast, turnover from public fixed telephony services was higher, by EUR 11 million or 2%.

68. The value of investment in electronic communications services in 2020 was EUR 284 million, which is EUR 52 million or 23% more compared to 2019.

69. Overall, the 98.2 index of total turnover from electronic communications services and the 122.6 index of the investments show that the ICT market maintained growth.[66]

65. *Source*: https://www.stat.si/StatWeb/News/Index/9846, accessed 27 Jun. 2022. To compare, for example, the turnover from 2017 and 2018, *see*: https://www.stat.si/StatWeb/news/Index/8345, accessed 27 Jun. 2022.

66. ICT sector maintains robust growth, The Slovenia Times, 18 Sep. 2021. Available at: https://sloveniatimes.com/ict-sector-maintains-robust-growth/, accessed 27 Jun. 2022.

Chapter 4. e-Commerce: Facts and Figures

70. In 2021, Slovenia was the 77th largest market (worldwide) for e-commerce, with an income of approximately EUR 600 million.[67] With an increase of 16%, the Slovenian e-commerce market contributed to the worldwide growth rate of 29%.[68] According to the current trend, incomes from e-commerce will continue to increase.

71. The leading platform in the Slovenian e-commerce market is mimovrste-.com. The store had an income of EUR 56 million in 2021, followed by merkur.si with EUR 29 million in income, and mercator.si with almost EUR 23 million. Altogether, the top three stores account for 20% of online income in Slovenia.[69] These rankings are based on every store that generates income in Slovenia, while the stores may be focused on either domestic sales or operate on a global level. For the above-mentioned evaluation, only revenue created in Slovenia was considered.

72. With 30% of Slovenian e-commerce income, fashion is the most important segment in the Slovenian e-commerce market. The toys, hobby, and 'do it yourself' sector is – at 26% – in second place. The electronics and media sector is in third place (23%) followed by furniture and home appliances (11%), and food and personal care (10%).[70]

73. e-commerce is governed by Zakon o varstvu potrošnikov (ZVPot),[71] in which a number of European directives on consumer protection and e-commerce have been transposed. If a business is conducting e-commerce and pursues its commercial or professional activities in Slovenia or targets consumers in Slovenia (the concept of targeted activity as introduced by EU international private law), its activity must comply with Slovenian consumer legislation. If a business conducting e-commerce is registered in Slovenia, it must provide website information to Slovenian consumers in the Slovenian language.[72]

74. e-commerce businesses in general fall under the authority of the Market Inspectorate, which is responsible, e.g., for administrative inspections and minor offence procedures concerning consumer protection, unfair commercial practices, the general safety of products, and the use of the Slovenian language. The Information Commissioner, on the other hand, is the competent authority for breaches of data protection rules. The competent body in the field of competition law is Javna agencija Republike Slovenije za varstvo konkurence (AVK) (as further explained in Part I below).

---

67. eCommerceDB, The eCommerce market in Slovenia, available at: https://ecommercedb.com/en/markets/si/all, accessed 17 Jun. 2022.
68. *Ibid.*
69. *Ibid.*
70. Edwards, K. European Ecommerce Overview: Slovenia, eCommerce Germany, https://ecommercegermany.com/blog/european-ecommerce-overview-slovenia, accessed 17 Jun. 2022.
71. Official Gazette of the Republic of Slovenia, No. 98/04 with further amendments.
72. *See*: Art. 32(1) b) of the Public Use of the Slovenian Language Act (*Zakon o javni rabi slovenščine* – ZJRS), Official Gazette of the Republic of Slovenia, No. 86/04 with further amendments.

Chapter 5. e-Government Initiatives

§1. Introduction

75. The development of e-Government in Slovenia started later than in other European countries in the 1990s. In 1993, the Government Informatics Centre (*Center Vlade Republike Slovenije za informatiko*) was established; however, the first important step in the direction of the informatization of the public administration was only made in 2000, when the Electronic Business and Electronic Signature Act (*Zakon o elektronskem poslovanju in elektronskem podpisu* (ZEPEP))[73] was enacted. Based on the provisions of the ZEPEP, the electronic form of documents gained the same legal value as documents in physical (paper) format, provided that the information contained therein is accessible and can be used for subsequent reference.[74]

76. In 2001 (a) he Strategy for E-business in the Public Administration of the Republic of Slovenia for the Period 2001–2004 (*Strategija e-poslovanja v javni upravi RS za obdobje od leta 2001 do leta 2004*) was adopted, which was implemented by means of the Action Plan adopted in 2002; (b) the first generation of e-Government portal (*eUprava*) was established; (c) the Trust Service Authority of Slovenia (SI-TRUST) was established to issue digital certificates to natural persons, legal entities, and public authorities.

77. Building on the priorities set in the strategic documents relating to the use of information and communication technology in the public sector, in the following years, public administration authorities started to exploit the possibilities offered by the development of ICT. New governmental portals and online platforms were established, and the existing e-services were reformed with the aim of enabling direct access to public registers (e.g., the Land Registry, the Central Register of the Population), the electronic submission of various documents and forms, and access to relevant information in order to facilitate the exercise of the rights of individuals, businesses, and other legal entities.

78. The development of public administration and electronic commerce between 2009 and 2015 was guided by the Strategy on IT and Electronic Services Development and the Connection of Official Records (*Strategija razvoja elektronskega poslovanja ter izmenjave podatkov iz uradnih evidenc* – SREP)[75] and the Action Plan for E-government Development 2010–2015 (*Akcijski načrt elektronskega poslovanja javne uprave od 2010 do 2015* – AN SREP).[76] With the purpose of ensuring that all users – individuals, legal entities, and governmental institutions –

73. Official Gazette of the Republic of Slovenia, No. 98/04 – official consolidated text, last amendment No. 121/21 – ZEISZ.
74. *See*: Art. 13 ZEPEP.
75. *See*: https://nio.gov.si/nio/cms/download/document/893dcfa487eda5b432e7634ceac12b9a8db4a71d-1498051266322, accessed 22 Jun. 2022.
76. *See*: http://nio.gov.si/nio/cms/download/document/e5ba92cd6fa02565d6d77e4ada2567284306da11-1376404012316, accessed 22 Jun. 2022.

benefit from e-Government solutions, they were focused on four strategic goals: (1) to ensure efficient and effective public administration by making use of electronic commerce; (2) to increase the take-up of electronic public administration services; (3) to develop interoperability solutions and the products of the public sector; (4) to support the establishment of the European common market and cross-border services not just in the EU, but also globally.

79. The Public Administration Development Strategy 2015–2020 (*Strategija razvoja javne uprave 2015–2020*)[77] and the Information Society Development Strategy 2020 – Digital Slovenia 2020 (*Strategija razvoja informacijske družbe do leta 2020 – Digitalna Slovenija 2020*),[78] adopted in 2015 and 2016, respectively, evaluated the progress made in the field of electronic commerce and the digitalization of the public administration. While recognizing the importance of the goals and objectives set in older strategic documents, the Public Administration Development Strategy 2015–2020 highlighted the need to adapt the priorities of the development of public administration to international standards and guidelines, taking into account the recent evolution of ICT (e.g., cloud computing). With the aim of achieving the efficient use of information technology, increasing the take-up of e-services, and ensuring the interoperability of information systems, it envisaged various technical and organizational measures, focusing, on the one hand, on users (better and more accessible services), and on the other, on public authorities and services (more efficient performance and resource exploitation).

§2. e-Government Services in Slovenia

80. e-Government services in Slovenia can be divided into four categories depending on their end users:

(i) e-Government services for **individuals**: *eAdministration*, *eTax*, *eHealth*, initiatives for the promotion of e-Participation;
(ii) e-Government services for **legal entities**: The Slovenia Business Portal, Electronic Public Procurement, *eTax*;
(iii) e-Government services for **public authorities**: the Slovenian State Cloud, the National Interoperability Framework Portal, the Open Data Portal Slovenia (OPSI), the KRPAN Information System;
(iv) **Other** e-Government initiatives: the GOV.SI Portal, Statist, Erar, the Single Contact Centre.

77. *See*: https://www.gov.si/assets/ministrstva/MJU/Kakovost-in-inovativnost-v-javni-upravi/Strategija/Strategija-razvoja-javne-uprave-2015-2020.pdf, accessed 22 Jun. 2022.
78. *See*: https://www.gov.si/assets/ministrstva/MJU/DID/Strategija-razvoja-informacijske-druzbe-2020.pdf, accessed 22 Jun. 2022.

I. e-Government Services for Individuals

A. *The e-Government Portal (Portal e-Uprava)*

81. The e-Government portal[79] is a central focal point for citizens. It offers various electronic public administration services and connects a number of public databases. The portal is managed by the MJU. First established in 2001, it has undergone a major transformation since then in order to make it more user-friendly, provide additional electronic services, and enable access to (personal) data.

82. The portal and the electronic services it offers are divided into subgroups on the basis of so-called *life events*, e.g., family, children, and marriage, labour and retirement, travel, personal documents and residence, real estate, and the environment, which are further divided into subsections in which citizens can easily and efficiently find relevant information, download various forms, or submit them electronically. Applications may only be submitted electronically by using certain qualified digital certificates, which are also necessary to sign in into the My e-Government module (Moja eUprava), by means of which citizens can gain insight into the current status of their applications and their personal data stored in public administration databases and registers (e.g., the access your own personal data service (*Vpogled v lastne osebne podatke*)).

B. *The eTax (eDavki)*

83. The eTax portal[80] is one of the electronic services offered by the Financial Administration of the Republic of Slovenia (*Finančna uprava Republike Slovenije* (FURS)), which enables natural and legal persons to easily and securely submit and verify various tax forms. Any taxable person may use eTax. Electronically submitted documents are equivalent to documents in paper form and can be managed anytime, anywhere, and free of charge. The eTax platform is integrated with user support tools that help taxable persons to independently and correctly complete and file relevant tax forms.

C. *eHealth (eZdravje)*

84. eHealth (*eZdravje*) is an information system aimed at the digitalization of the Slovenian healthcare system by enabling the processing of healthcare and other data and the implementation of the electronic health services.[81] From 2008 to 2015

---

79. *See*: https://e-uprava.gov.si, accessed 22 Jun. 2022.
80. *See*: https://edavki.durs.si/EdavkiPortal/OpenPortal/CommonPages/Opdynp/PageA.aspx, accessed 22 Jun. 2022.
81. *See*: Art. 14 of the Healthcare Databases Act (*Zakon o zbirkah podatkov s področja zdravstvenega varstva* – ZZPPZ), Official Gazette of the Republic of Slovenia, No. 65/00, last amended 206/21 – ZDUPŠOP.

it was managed by the Ministry of Health and co-financed by the European Social Fund. Since the management of the project was taken over by the National Institute of Public Health (*Nacionalni inštitut za javno zdravje* (NIJZ)) in 2015, more than 20 eHealth solutions have been successfully implemented into the healthcare environment, e.g., the *eHealth* website, the *zVem* portal, ePrescription (*eRecept*), eAppointment (*eNaročanje*), eReferral (*eNapotnica*), the Central Registry of Patient Data, and the Electronic Registry of Vaccinated Persons and Adverse Reactions after Vaccination.

85. The core of the Slovenian eHealth system is the Central Registry of Patient Data *Centralni Register Podatkov o Pacientu* (CRPP), which is a database on patients with permanent or temporary residence in the Republic of Slovenia and on other patients receiving healthcare in the Republic of Slovenia.[82] The CRPP enables access to and the exchange of healthcare data, e.g., information on health insurance, patients' medical records, as well as written declarations about a patient's wishes under the law governing patients' rights (e.g., persons entitled to make decisions about his or her healthcare). The Healthcare Databases Act (*Zakon o zbirkah podatkov s področja zdravstvenega varstva* (ZZPPZ)) stipulates the purposes for which data may be processed, the categories of personal data contained therein, and their data retention periods.[83]

86. ePrescription enables the electronic prescription and dispensing of medications. It was fully implemented in 2016 and has almost entirely replaced physical prescriptions: in 2019 more than 90% of medications were prescribed electronically.[84]

D. Initiatives for the Promotion of e-Participation

87. One of the priorities of the e-Government Strategy of the Republic of Slovenia for the period 2006–2010 (*Strategija e-uprave Republike Slovenije za obdobje 2006 do 2010* – SEP-2010) was to include a variety of actors – citizens, NGOs, business entities – in the decision-making process in order to gain their insight into relevant societal questions with the aim of improving public policies and legislation.[85] Three initiatives to enhance the dialogue between civil society and the state have been operationalized by the establishment of the following platforms: eDemocracy (*eDemokracija*),[86] I propose to the Government (*Predlagam vladi*),[87] and STOP the bureaucracy (*STOP birokraciji*).[88] They all provide an online platform to

82. *See*: Art. 14b ZZPPZ.
83. *See*: Articles 14a–14d ZZPPZ.
84. Ž. Rant, D. Stanimirović, *Analiza uporabe rešitev eZdravja v Sloveniji: izzivi in prihodnje usmeritve*, 39th International Conference on Organizational Science Development. Organizations at Innovation and Digital Transformation Roundabout (2020).
85. e-Government Strategy of the Republic of Slovenia, p. 15.
86. *See*: https://e-uprava.gov.si/drzava-in-druzba/e-demokracija.html, accessed 16 Jun. 2022.
87. *See*: https://predlagam.vladi.si, accessed 16 Jun. 2022.
88. *See*: https://www.stopbirokraciji.gov.si/domov, accessed 16 Jun. 2022.

propose new ideas, comment on and discuss existing proposals, and express support or opposition thereto; however, the method of and procedure for participation varies between them. Views, comments, and suggestions on pending legislation may be submitted via the eDemocracy portal. *I propose to the Government* presents a communication channel between citizens, the state, and other citizens: citizens may propose their own ideas, and if their suggestion attracts enough support from other users of the portal, the proposal is sent to the competent Ministry for treatment in a further procedure. STOP the bureaucracy is a similar mechanism, which is focused solely on the de-bureaucratization and simplification of the (administrative) procedures of the public administration. Although three different portals have been established in order to foster the participation of civic society, the level of participatory political culture in Slovenia remains low as citizens are rarely involved in policy formulation.[89]

II. e-Government Services for Legal Entities

A. *The SPOT Portal (Portal SPOT)*

88. The SPOT Portal is the national business portal operating as a part of the Slovenian business point (*Slovenska poslovna točka*), which is a government-operated system that offers business entities various advisory, support, and similar services. The SPOT Portal enables businesses, companies, and entrepreneurs to conduct business with the state easily, quickly, and securely.[90] It provides existing and future business entities information about conducting business in Slovenia and enables them to file various forms and initiate procedures electronically.

B. *The Electronic Public Procurement Information System*

89. The Electronic Public Procurement Information System (*Elektronsko javno naročanje Republike Slovenije*) enables the electronic execution of public procurement procedures. It provides a platform for the exchange of various electronic documents, which simplifies and rationalizes public procurement procedures, increases transparency, and reduces costs and administrative barriers.

III. e-Government Services for Public Authorities

A. *The Open Data of Slovenia Portal* (Odprti podatki Slovenije (OPSI))

90. The Open Data of Slovenia Portal is a national open-data portal that provides users with open data on the public sector. It was set up on the basis of Directive (EU) 2019/1024 of the European Parliament and of the Council of 20 June 2019

89. Public Administration Development Strategy 2015-2020, p. 88.
90. *See*: https://spot.gov.si/sl/portal-in-tocke-spot/predstavitev-sistema-spot/, accessed 16 Jun. 2022.

on open data and the reuse of public sector information and national legislation regulating access to public information by the Slovenian MJU. The main objective of the portal is to enhance cooperation with all stakeholders in order to maximize the use of open data for the creation of applications that will provide high-quality and efficient services to citizens and businesses.[91]

91. All datasets published on OPSI are made available under the Attribution 4.0 International License (CC BY 4.0) and therefore can be further reused under the condition that reference is made to the source material.

B. *The Slovenian State Cloud* (Državni računalniški oblak (DRO))

92. The Slovenian State Cloud[92] is a computing infrastructure owned and operated by the Slovenian MJU. It provides cloud storage service for governmental institutions, organs, and other public administration bodies, including the safe storage of highly sensitive data that cannot be stored on third-party storage capacities.

C. *The National Interoperability Framework* (Nacionalni interoperabilnostni okvir (NIO))

93. The National Interoperability Framework is a website that enables (1) the publishing of interoperability solutions and products from the public sector; (2) connecting the catalogue of interoperability solutions with best practices for reusing its content. It is a cornerstone of the Slovenian interoperability initiatives aimed at aligning the interoperability policy and strategy with the European Interoperability Framework.

IV. Other e-Government Initiatives

A. *GOV.SI Portal*

94. The GOV.SI Portal is a website that provides information about the State Administration of the Republic of Slovenia. It is a result of the project 'The Renewal and Optimisation of the State Administration Websites', which was completed in 2021 with the transfer of all presentation websites of the state administration bodies to the single GOV.SI website. It provides users with an overview of the functioning and organization of the Government, including the function and competences of the prime minister, ministries, constituent bodies, government departments, and administrative units.

---

91. *See*: https://podatki.gov.si/o-portalu, accessed 16 Jun. 2022.
92. *See*: https://nio.gov.si/nio/asset/drzavni+racunalniski+oblak+dro?lang=en, accessed 16 Jun. 2022.

Part I. The Regulation of the ICT Market

Chapter 1. The Regulatory Framework of the Telecommunications Sector

§1. Slovenian Legislation

95. On the statutory level, the telecommunications sector in Slovenia is mainly regulated by ZEKom-1. It implements European Union directives in this field, such as Directive No. 2002/19/EC, Directive No. 2002/20/EC, Directive No. 2002/21/EC, Directive No. 2002/22/EC, Directive No. 2002/58/EC, Directive No. 2002/77/EC, and Directive No. 2014/61/EU.

96. ZEKom-1 – as the main legal source in the field – lays down the conditions for the provision of electronic communications networks and electronic communication services. According to its wording, any natural or legal person may provide electronic communications networks or electronic communications services if the statutory requirements are met and provided it does not endanger public order, life and human health, public security, and national defence.[93] ZEKom-1 also establishes sector-related competition rules. It furthermore contains legal rules on the management of the radio frequency spectrum, the efficient construction and installation of electronic communications networks, and the sharing of the existing physical infrastructure. ZEKom-1 also determines the sector-related rights of users (including the right to privacy), regulates the security of networks and services and their operation in exceptional situations and dispute resolution in the field.

§2. The Slovenian Telecommunications Authority

97. AKOS is the competent body for the regulation and supervision of the electronic communications market. It also performs tasks related to radio and television and regulates and supervises postal services and railway traffic. It is an independent body – a public authority – established by ZEKom-1 and is regulated in detail by the Statutes of the Agency for Communication Networks and Services of the Republic of Slovenia.[94] It was founded in 2001.

93. Article 4 of the Electronic Communications Act.
94. Statute of the Agency for Communication Networks and Services of the Republic of Slovenia

98. AKOS aims to ensure the effective development of communications networks and services and the equitable operation of the operators in the field, protects user rights, and regulates the content of radio and television programming and audiovisual media services.[95]

99. AKOS manages a number of web portals that primarily serve consumers:

'e-Analitik' (intended for the presentation of data on the electronic communications market in Slovenia);
'Primerjaj operaterje' (which provides access to the offers of operators (both fixed and mobile) and gives consumers a comparison of offers according to their needs);
'Geoportal AKOS' (the central web portal for access to and the review of spatial data, including data on electronic communications infrastructure, network connection points, coverage with fixed and mobile networks, and data on planned public infrastructure constructions); and
'Akos test net' (a system that gives consumers an overview of the speed and quality of broadband connections on fixed and wireless networks).

100. One of the important tasks of AKOS is also the out-of-court resolution of consumer disputes in the field. Furthermore, it is responsible for the promotion of competition in the telecommunications sector. However, it is up to AVK to control illegal actions in this regard.

(*Statut Agencije za komunikacijska omrežja in storitve Republike Slovenije*, Official Gazette of the Republic of Slovenia, No. 43/18).

95. For more on the Agency for Communication Networks and Services of the Republic of Slovenia, *see*: https://www.akos-rs.si/en/about-akos#:~:text=The%20Agency%20for%20Communication%20Networks,and%20railway%20traffic%20in%20Slovenia, accessed 16 Jun. 2022.

Chapter 2. The Regulation of Competition in the ICT Market

§1. Slovenian Legislation

101. In 1993, i.e., two years after the transition to a market economy, the Slovenian legislature passed the first legislation on the protection of competition. Zakon o varstvu konkurence (ZVK) of 1993[96] contained rules on the prohibition of: (i) restrictive agreements; (ii) the abuse of a dominant position; and (iii) unfair competition. Within the EU accession process, several changes followed in order to align the national legislation with the European Union *acquis*. In 1999, Zakon o preprečevanju omejevanja konkurence (ZPOmK)[97] was enacted, which introduced rules on the concentration of undertakings. With this amendment the antitrust rules and rules on unfair competition were separated into two different acts. The antitrust rules were covered by the newly introduced ZPOmK, whereas the rules on unfair competition remained in the ZVK. In one of the later amendments this changed again and as of 2015 antitrust and unfair competition are both contained in the umbrella competition act (ZPOmK-1).[98]

102. Besides these general rules on the protection of competition, there are also sector-specific rules enhancing and safeguarding competition in certain segments of the ICT market. The field of telecommunications is regulated by specific rules contained in ZEKom-1. Imperfect telecommunications markets (upstream and downstream) are mostly regulated through asymmetric rules that apply to incumbent operators – on prices and on access to the network infrastructure. The interplay of *ex ante* sector-specific regulation and the *ex post* application of general competition protection rules in the telecommunications market opens several highly interesting legal and economic questions that have been, as in other Member States, the subject of discussions among scholars and proven important also in practice.

§2. The Slovenian Competition Authority

103. The central national guardian of competition is AVK. It is an independent administrative authority responsible for the public enforcement of antitrust and merger control rules in Slovenia. In cases of restrictive agreements, concerted practices, and the abuse of a dominant position, the proceedings consist of two phases. First, in ex officio administrative proceedings, AVK establishes whether there were breaches of the relevant provisions of the ZPOmK-1. If the findings are affirmative, AVK initiates the second phase – minor offence proceedings against the offender. With newer amendments of the ZPOmk-1, AVK obtained broader powers in the investigation phase, making its work and proceedings more effective.

96. Official Gazette of the Republic of Slovenia, No. 18/93.
97. Official Gazette of the Republic of Slovenia, No. 64/07.
98. Official Gazette of the Republic of Slovenia, No. 36/08 with further amendments, last amendment No. 23/17.

104. AVK may issue interim measures, and the investigated companies may, in line with the EU legislation, offer commitments that are intended to address the competition concerns identified by AVK.

105. The available legal remedies against the AVK's decisions are administrative lawsuits and requests for judicial protection. The administrative court decides on lawsuits against the AVK's administrative judgments and a minor offence court decides on legal remedies against the AVK's decisions in minor offence proceedings.

106. Besides public enforcement, the law also provides for private enforcement. Thus far, private enforcement has rarely been used in practice and consequently the case law is very scarce. One of the very few private enforcement cases was the lawsuit of a market entrant telecommunications operator against the incumbent operator regarding the damage allegedly caused by several instances of abuse of its dominant position. The case, however, was settled by the parties by means of a court settlement that is not publicly available.

107. As stated above, the telecommunications sector is also subject to *ex ante* sector-specific regulation governed by the ZEKom-1. The relevant authority responsible for the enforcement of the ZEKom-1 provisions is the AKOS. It carries out regular market research and adopts measures to enhance competition in the electronic communications market.

§3. Slovenian Antitrust Law

108. In line with EU legislation, Slovenian antitrust law consists of the following three pillars: (i) the prohibition of restrictive agreements (including concerted practices); (ii) the prohibition of the abuse of a dominant position; and (iii) merger control rules. The majority of the AVK's proceedings and decisions are in the field of merger clearance (approximately 30 per year), whereas cases involving restrictive agreements and the abuse of a dominant position are rarer (few per year). AVK publishes its decisions on its website.[99]

109. There are no particular country-specific antitrust rules that would deviate from the EU legislation.

99. AVK (*Javna agencija Republike Slovenije za varstvo konkurence*), Decisions on restrictive practices. Available at: http://www.varstvo-konkurence.si/en/antitrust/decisions/, accessed 28 Jun. 2022.

Chapter 3. The Regulation of Cryptography and Other Dual Use Goods

§1. The Regulation of Cryptography

110. Cryptography is one of the central aspects of information security, as it prevents unauthorized access to information, thus maintaining and ensuring the information's confidentiality and integrity. The strength of a cryptographic algorithm is measured by the length of the security key it uses. Access to cryptographic algorithms exceeding a certain key length has been regulated and restricted, while intelligence and law enforcement agencies have worked to break or circumvent encryption in order to access data.

111. Regulation on cryptography in Slovenia is scarce. Article 43 of the Act Amending the Electronic Business and Electronic Signature Act (*Zakon o spremembah in dopolnitvah Zakona o elektronskem poslovanju in elektronskem podpisu* – ZEPEP-B) stipulates in the chapter Electronic Signature (the sub-section Qualified Certificates and Certification Service Providers) that a certification service provider must use reliable systems and equipment that are tamper-proof and which ensure the technical and cryptographic security of the processes in which they are used. Moreover, the General Data Protection Regulation (GDPR) repeatedly highlights encryption and pseudonymization as 'appropriate technical and organizational measures' of personal data security.

112. Generally, systems, equipment, and components designed or modified to perform or use cryptanalytic functions are considered dual-use goods that are subject to export and import restrictions.

§2. The Regulation of Dual-Use Goods

113. Dual-use goods are civilian goods, software, and technology and are normally intended for civilian use but may also be used for military purposes because of their characteristics or technical characteristics. This also includes all goods that can be used for non-explosive uses as well as for any use in the production of nuclear weapons or other nuclear explosive devices.

I. Software as a Dual-Use Good

114. The feature of a software product that may cause it to be classified as a dual-use product is a cryptographic function, i.e., encryption, even if it is not the main purpose or application of the software. Producers of software that has encryption functions and that is exported from Slovenia or imported into Slovenia need to consider whether their product uses an encryption protocol with a symmetric key length exceeding 56 bits or equivalent (many commonly used protocols exceed this key length). If so, the software may constitute a dual-use product, unless it falls under the exclusions specified in Regulation (EU) 2021/821.[100] Certain software products, sold universally and easy to use (typically COTS – commercial off-the-shelf or commercially available off-the-shelf products) may be excluded if they meet the following criteria: a wide range of buyers, universal availability in retail outlets, the possibility of self-installation, and a cryptographic function that cannot be modified.

II. The EU Export Control System

115. The establishment of a common European regulatory framework was necessary to ensure compliance with the commitments and responsibilities of the Member States and of the European Union. It was also considered a prerequisite for promoting the free movement of dual-use items inside the Community. With the control of the export, transit, brokering, and technical assistance of dual-use items, the EU contributes to international peace and security and the prevention of the proliferation of Weapons of Mass Destruction (WMD). The export controls take into account the EU and its Member States' international obligations, including: (1) UN Security Council Resolution 1540; (2) the Nuclear Non-Proliferation Treaty; (3) the Chemical Weapons Convention; and (4) the Biological Weapons Convention. Trade in dual-use goods accounts for a significant part of the EU's external trade as the latest figures confirm that the volume of exports of controlled dual-use items from the EU has already reached EUR 85 billion.[101]

116. Dual-use items may in principle be traded freely within the EU, except for some particularly sensitive items, whose transfer within the EU remains subject to prior authorization (*see* Annex IV of Regulation (EU) 2021/821). The EU clearly defines what falls under such control and what does not. However, there is no uniformity of export regulations among the EU Member States. While countries are united in their dedication to liberal encryption regulation and export control laws are subject to European law, the implementation of these laws can be subject to the interpretation of the Member States. In some cases, they may interpret the regulation differently or have additional national laws.

117. The EU established a common regulatory framework that subjects dual-use goods to effective control when exported from the Community, which evolved in the following way:

– Council Regulation (EC) No 3381/94 of 19 December 1994 Setting up a Community regime for the control of exports of dual-use goods.

100. Regulation (EU) 2021/821 of the European Parliament and of the Council of 20 May 2021 setting up a Union regime for the control of exports, brokering, technical assistance, transit and transfer of dual-use items (recast).

101. For more on the European regulation of dual-use goods exports, *see*: https://policy.trade.ec.europa.eu/help-exporters-and-importers/exporting-dual-use-goods_en, accessed 14 Jul. 2022.

- Repealed by Council Regulation No 1334/2000 of 22 June 2000 (in effect from 28 September 2000 until 26 August 2009).
- Repealed by Council Regulation (EC) No 428/2009 of 5 May 2009 setting up a Community regime for the control of exports, transfer, brokering and transit of dual-use items (Recast). This established a general framework for export controls on dual-use items listed on a regularly updated annex which includes a range of items from uranium to certain types of sealants.
- Repealed by Regulation (EU) 2021/821 of 20 May 2021, which is now the key legal act applicable to dual-use products in the EU setting up a Community regime for the control of exports, brokering, technical assistance, transit and transfer of dual-use items.

118. The new Export Control Regulation upgrades and strengthens the EU's export control toolbox to respond effectively to evolving security risks and emerging technologies and allows the EU to effectively protect its interests and values. Regulation 2021/821 set up a network of competent authorities supporting the exchange of information and the consistent implementation and enforcement of controls throughout the EU. In certain cases, EU Member States may introduce additional controls on non-listed dual-use items due to public security or human rights considerations. The regulation is directly applicable throughout the EU, but Member States need to take national measures to implement some of their provisions, e.g., enforcement and penalties. The Commission regularly holds public consultations and has a constant dialogue with industry, academia, and civil society, in an effort to strike the right balance between security and trade.

119. There are four types of export authorizations in place in the EU export control regime:

(1) EU General Export Authorisations (EUGEAs) allow the export of dual-use items to certain destinations under certain conditions (*see* Annex II of the Regulation). Regulation (EU) 2021/821 provides for the following EUGEAs:
   (a) exports to Australia, Canada, Iceland, Japan, New Zealand, Norway, Switzerland, Liechtenstein, the United Kingdom, and the United States of America;
   (b) the export of certain dual-use items to certain destinations;
   (c) export after repair/replacement;
   (d) temporary export for exhibitions or fairs;
   (e) telecommunications;
   (f) chemicals;
   (g) intra-group technology transfers, and;
   (h) encryption.
(2) National General Export Authorisations (NGEAs) may be issued by EU Member States if they are consistent with existing EUGEAs and do not refer to items listed in Annex IIg of the Regulation.

(3) Global licences can be granted by competent authorities to one exporter and may cover exports of multiple items to multiple countries of destination or end users.
(4) Individual licences can be granted by competent authorities to one exporter and cover exports of one or more dual-use items to one end user or consignee in a third country.

III. The Slovenian Export Control System

120. The Financial Administration of the Republic of Slovenia (*Finančna uprava RS* – FURS), more specifically, the customs authorities within FURS, controls the export, transfer within the customs territory of the European Union, brokering, and transit of dual-use goods, as well as the provision of technical assistance.

121. The Ministry of Economic Development and Technology is responsible for issuing licences and provides all the necessary information for applicants, such as on the legislation establishing the dual-use export control regime, the list of dual-use items, and information on the procedure for obtaining an export licence.[102] The applications that can be lodged with the Ministry are:

(a) an application for an export licence for dual-use items;[103]
(b) an application for an international import certificate for dual-use items;[104]
(c) an application for a certificate of the delivery of dual-use items.[105]

122. Natural or legal persons must obtain prior authorization if they wish to *export* the dual-use item listed in Annex I or to *transfer* the dual-use items listed in Annex IV to Regulation (EU) 2021/821. A person must also obtain prior authorization for the *brokering* of the dual-use items listed in Annex I between two third countries and for the provision of technical assistance where certain conditions are met. A licence is also required for the *export* of non-Annex I dual-use items if certain conditions are met (the so-called *Catch-all Clause*),[106] in accordance with Article 4 of the Regulation.

102. More information is available at: https://www.gov.si/teme/nadzor-strateske-trgovine/, accessed 14 Jul. 2022.
103. More information is available at: https://www.gov.si/zbirke/storitve/zahtevek-za-izdajo-izvoznega-dovoljenja-za-blago-z-dvojno-rabo/, accessed 14 Jul. 2022.
104. More information is available at: https://www.gov.si/zbirke/storitve/izdaja-mednarodnega-uvoznega-potrdila/, accessed 14 Jul. 2022.
105. More information is available at: https://www.gov.si/zbirke/storitve/izdaja-potrdila-o-dostavi-blaga-z-dvojno-rabo/accessed 14 Jul. 2022.
106. The catch-all clause' in the EU Dual-use Regulation empowers national authorities to prohibit the export of non-listed dual-use items where they believe those items might be for illicit use.

123. In Slovenia, dual-use is regulated by the Act Regulating the Control of the Exports of Dual-Use Items[107] (*Zakon o nadzoru izvoza blaga z dvojno rabo* – ZNIBDR) and the Decree on Procedures for Issuing Authorizations and Certificates and on the Competence of the Commission for the Control of Exports of Dual-Use Items (*Uredba o načinu izdaje dovoljenj in potrdil ter vlogi Komisije za nadzor izvoza blaga z dvojno rabo*, hereinafter: the Decree).[108] The ZNIBDR regulates measures for the control of dual-use items to the extent that European Union rules in this area do not or to the extent that EU rules empower the Member States to further regulate this area in national legislation. The ZNIBDR establishes the competent authority for licensing and supervision, as well as criminal provisions. The ZNIBDR regulates the control of the provision of technical assistance in accordance with Council Joint Action 2000/401/CFSP of 22 June 2000 on the control of technical assistance related to certain military applications (OJ L 159, 30 June 2000, p. 216).

124. The ZNIBDR also stipulates the role, powers, and obligations of the Ministries and other bodies of the state administration in the exercise of control dual-use items. These authorities have the right to inspect and access data regardless of the provisions on the confidentiality of information and the right and duty to provide each other with all information on exporters and exported dual-use goods that they need for the purpose of exercising controls under the ZNIBDR. An exporter, bank, other financial organization, or anyone else who has the information necessary for the control of the export of dual-use items is, upon request, obliged to provide the Ministry, customs, and law enforcement authorities its books, correspondence, and any other information necessary for the exercise of control.

125. It is the exporter's responsibility to verify whether the goods it intends to export are dual-use goods, in accordance with the applicable EU and national legislation. Using the TARIC Consultation application,[109] the exporter is informed if the tariff code of the goods it is exporting may be linked to a dual-use code. The tool also provides information on which dual-use code(s) the exporter needs to check in the list of dual-use items. Based on this guidance, the exporter has to check in the dual-use list whether its goods meet the technical parameters indicated in the list under the codes offered by TARIC and are classified therein. If the exporter finds that its goods are included in the dual-use list, it must be authorized to export them to any third country. If the exporter finds that the goods it intends to export are classified as dual-use items and the goods cannot be exported under an EU General Export Authorisation, it must initiate a licensing procedure and submit an application to the Ministry of Economic Development and Technology (the Strategic Trade Controls website of the Ministry; the contact point is the DNT – Trade Policy Department).

---

107. Official Gazette of the Republic of Slovenia, Nos. 37/04, 8/10.
108. Official Gazette of the Republic of Slovenia, Nos. 34/10, 42/12.
109. The TARIC application is available at: https://ec.europa.eu/taxation_customs/dds2/taric/taric_consultation.jsp?Lang=sl, accessed 14 Jul. 2022.

126. The ZNIBDR also provides for fines: (a) a legal person may be fined from EUR 1,200 to EUR 125,000 for an offence it has committed, and (b) the person responsible for the offence is liable for a fine from EUR 120 to EUR 4,100.

Chapter 4. Legal Status of Standardization

§1. Regulatory Framework

127. The regulatory framework of standardization is provided in two acts: ZEKom-1 and ZInfV. While ZEKom-1 allows for a softer approach, ZInfV requires the mandatory application of international security standards.

128. Under ZEKom-1, AKOS and other competent state authorities are required to encourage the use of standards applicable to the 'provision of services, technical interfaces and network functions and where urgently required to ensure the interoperability of services and improve freedom of choice for users' (paragraph 1 of Article 202 ZEKom-1). Until the publication of the non-obligatory standards compiled by the European Commission, the use of standards adopted by European standards organizations (e.g., the European Committee for Standardization, the European Committee for Electrotechnical Standardization, the European Telecommunications Standards Institute) should be encouraged (paragraph 2 of Article 202 ZEKom-1).

129. AKOS is also the competent agency setting the minimal requirements applicable to providers of electronic communications, for example:

- the Act on Internet Access Services and the Related Rights of End Users;[110]
- the Act on the Radio Frequency Usage Plan (NURF-4);[111]
- the Act on Number Portability;[112]
- the Act on Data Transfer Rates Suitable for Functional Internet Access;[113]
- the Act on the Minimum Requirements for the Planning and Operation of Access and Distribution Points;[114]
- the Act on the Quality of Universal Service;[115]
- the Act on Transparency Regarding Planned Construction Works and the Joint Construction of Public Utility Infrastructure;[116]
- the Act on Network and Service Security.[117]

110. Official Gazette of the Republic of Slovenia, No. 54/19.
111. Official Gazette of the Republic of Slovenia, No. 10/18, as amended.
112. Official Gazette of the Republic of Slovenia, No. 62/13.
113. Official Gazette of the Republic of Slovenia, No. 27/18.
114. Official Gazette of the Republic of Slovenia, No. 39/18.
115. Official Gazette of the Republic of Slovenia, No. 27/18.
116. Official Gazette of the Republic of Slovenia, No. 9/18.
117. Official Gazette of the Republic of Slovenia, Nos. 75/13 and 64/15.

130. The mandatory requirement of observing applicable security standards in ICT is regulated by ZInfV. ZInfV requires providers of essential services[118] to follow the prescribed methodology in order to ensure the security and maintenance of their information systems (Articles 11–12 ZInfV).[119] This includes:

(1) a risk management analysis with an assessment of the acceptable level of risk;
(2) a business continuity policy with a management plan;
(3) a list of its key, control, and monitoring information systems and the parts of the network and associated data which are essential for the operation of essential services;
(4) the plan for the restoration and re-establishment of the operation of the information systems referred to in the previous indent;
(5) an incident response plan with a national CSIRT notification protocol; and
(6) a security measures plan to ensure the integrity, confidentiality, and availability of network and information systems that take into account sectoral specificities.

131. As for (other) digital service providers, Article 14 ZInfV requires that they 'identify and adopt appropriate and proportionate technical and organizational measures to manage the risks to the security of the networks and information systems they use to provide services in the EU'. In doing so, they need to take into account, *inter alia*, that the measures taken comply with international standards.

§2. Conformity Assessment

132. Insofar as the application of standards or minimum requirements is a legal obligation, conformity assessments are entrusted to AKOS and the information security inspectorate.

133. Under Article 221 ZEKom-1, AKOS is competent to monitor the implementation of the provisions of the Act as well as the regulations and general acts issued pursuant to the Act (with the exception of the provisions on personal data protection). AKOS also supervises the implementation of all individual acts and measures adopted pursuant to this Act and pursuant to regulations and general acts issued on its basis.

134. The information security inspectorate forms a part of the Government Information Security Office. Under Article 31 ZInfV, the Inspectorate is competent

118. This includes providers in the fields of energy, digital infrastructure, drinking water supply and distribution, health care, traffic, banking, financial market infrastructure, food supply and environmental protection. *See*: the Decree determining essential services and the detailed methodology for determining essential service operators (Official Gazette of the Republic of Slovenia, No. 39/19).
119. Further elaborated in the Rules on Security Documentation and Security Measures of Operators of Essential Services (Official Gazette of the Republic of Slovenia, No. 32/19, as amended).

to supervise both providers of essential services and other digital service providers. In doing so, the inspectorate may require service providers to provide information and evidence necessary to assess the security of their network and information systems, including documented security rules (paragraph 2 of Article 32 and paragraph 4 of Article 33 ZInfV).

Chapter 5. The Legal Status of Out-of-Court Dispute Settlements in the ICT Sector

§1. General Statement

135. In Slovenia, two general out-of-court dispute settlement mechanisms are available, namely, arbitration and mediation.[120] They are generally applicable to a variety of disputes, including disputes in the ICT sector. However, regarding disputes in the ICT sector, the Agency for Communication Networks and Services of the Republic of Slovenia (*Agencija za komunikacijska omrežja in storitve Republike Slovenije* – AKOS) plays a significant role, as described in the following section.

§2. The Agency for Communication Networks and Services of the Republic of Slovenia

136. The Agency for Communication Networks and Services of the Republic of Slovenia resolves disputes between entities on the Slovenian ICT market (Article 217(1) ZEKom-1). The ZEKom-1 distinguishes between two kinds of disputes that fall under the jurisdiction of AKOS, namely:

(1) inter-operator disputes: disputes between natural and legal persons providing electronic communications networks or services, if the dispute relates to rights and existing obligations under the ZEKom-1, regulations issued pursuant thereto, general and individual acts, as well as disputes between natural and legal persons providing electronic communications networks or services and other natural and legal persons benefiting from an access or interconnection obligation imposed or agreed on in accordance with the ZEKom-1 or a general or individual act of AKOS;[121] and
(2) end-user disputes: disputes between natural and legal persons providing electronic communications networks and services and end users, insofar as the dispute relates to rights and obligations under the ZEKom-1, regulations issued pursuant thereto, and rights and obligations under contracts for the provision of electronic communications networks or services.[122]

137. Besides these two categories, AKOS may further resolve disputes arising from a reduction in the cost of electronic communications networks.[123]

---

120. *See* the Arbitration Act (*Zakon o arbitraži* – ZArbit), Official Gazette of the Republic of Slovenia, No. 45/08; the Mediation in Civil and Commercial Matters Act (*Zakon o mediaciji v civilnih in gospodarskih zadevah* – ZMCGZ), Official Gazette of the Republic of Slovenia, No. 56/08; and the Act on Alternative Dispute Resolution in Judicial Matters (*Zakon o alternativnem reševanju sodnih sporov* – ZARSS, Official Gazette of the Republic of Slovenia, Nos. 97/09 and 40/12.
121. Article 217(1,2) ZEKom-1.
122. Article 217(1) ZEKom-1.
123. Article 220a(1) ZEKom-1.

138. In carrying out the dispute settlement tasks assigned to it by the ZEKom-1, AKOS must act independently and must not seek or receive instructions from other public authorities.[124] The exception to this rule is the possibility of AKOS consulting the competition authority or the consumer protection authority, when deemed appropriate.[125] A dispute settlement procedure is conducted in accordance with the rules on administrative procedure.[126]

139. Dispute settlement as regulated by the ZEKom-1 does not interfere with judicial jurisdiction.[127] In the event, any of the parties to a dispute initiates litigation before a court of competent jurisdiction on the same matter or withdraws a request for dispute settlement, the dispute settlement procedure before AKOS shall be terminated.[128] This means that the out-of-court dispute settlement procedure specifically provided for the ICT sector does not take precedence over litigation and is therefore secondary in nature.

I. Inter-operator Disputes

140. The Agency is obliged to make public decisions relating to inter-operator disputes.[129] They must be published in a manner that respects the prohibition on the publication of business secrets of the parties to a particular dispute settlement procedure, such that individual parts of the text are adequately protected, unless the parties propose the publication of their business secrets.[130]

II. Disputes Involving Consumers or Other End Users

141. According to Article 142(1) of the ZEKom-1, every end user has the right to object to a decision or the conduct of an operator in relation to the rights and obligations determined by the ZEKom-1 and the regulations issued pursuant thereto, and by contracts for the provision of electronic communications networks or services, to the appropriate authority or body established by the operator.

142. If the operator does not comply with the objection within fifteen days of the objection being lodged, or if the operator fails to issue a decision regarding the objection within fifteen days, or, finally, if the operator accepts the end user's objection but then fails to fulfil its obligations within fifteen days of the service of the decision, the end user may file a dispute with AKOS.[131]

124. Article 217(4) ZEKom-1.
125. Article 217(4) ZEKom-1.
126. Article 218(3) ZEKom-1.
127. Article 217(3) ZEKom-1.
128. Article 218(4) ZEKom-1.
129. Article 218(8) ZEKom-1.
130. Article 218(8) ZEKom-1.
131. Article 142(8,9,10) ZEKom-1.

143. According to the most recent quarterly report from 2022 on the resolution of end-user disputes in the field of electronic communications and postal services, AKOS received 123 proposals for dispute resolution in the field of electronic communications.[132] Compared to the last quarter of the previous year – 2021 (141 dispute settlement proposals received in the field of electronic communications and 7 in the field of postal services), the number of disputes received in the field of electronic communications decreased slightly by 12.8%.[133]

144. Content-wise, disputes regarding broadband services dominated, as they represented 43% of all disputes, followed by disputes relating to mobile telephony services, representing 32%.[134]

145. From the point of the parties to the dispute, AKOS received the highest number of disputes concerning mobile services against T-2 d.o.o., in terms of both criteria available, i.e., the criterion of the number of end users per operator and the criterion of the number of connections per operator.[135]

146. Besides the AKOS mechanism for resolving consumer disputes, there are several other options for consumers to seek an out-of-court dispute settlement.[136] There is a list of providers of out-of-court dispute settlement services which may be contacted directly or – for disputes arising from online services, through the platform for online out-of-court dispute settlement in Slovenia.[137] This platform provides a list of online dispute settlement providers, including the Slovenian Association of Mediators.[138] A consumer may choose primarily one of such out-of-court dispute settlement mechanisms; however, if such proceedings do not result in a binding decision in accordance with the law governing the out-of-court settlement of consumer disputes, the consumer may refer the dispute to AKOS.[139]

---

132. *See*: https://www.akos-rs.si/uporabniki-storitev/raziscite/porocila-raziskave-in-analize/uporabniki-storitev/novica/prvo-cetrtletje-2022-porocilo-agencije-o-resevanju-uporabniskih-sporov-s-podrocja-elektronskih-komunikacij-in-postnih-storitev-1, accessed 29 Jun. 2022.
133. *See*: https://www.akos-rs.si/uporabniki-storitev/raziscite/porocila-raziskave-in-analize/uporabniki-storitev/novica/prvo-cetrtletje-2022-porocilo-agencije-o-resevanju-uporabniskih-sporov-s-podrocja-elektronskih-komunikacij-in-postnih-storitev-1, accessed 29 Jun. 2022.
134. *See*: https://www.akos-rs.si/uporabniki-storitev/raziscite/porocila-raziskave-in-analize/uporabniki-storitev/novica/prvo-cetrtletje-2022-porocilo-agencije-o-resevanju-uporabniskih-sporov-s-podrocja-elektronskih-komunikacij-in-postnih-storitev-1, accessed 29 Jun. 2022.
135. *See*: https://www.akos-rs.si/uporabniki-storitev/raziscite/porocila-raziskave-in-analize/uporabniki-storitev/novica/prvo-cetrtletje-2022-porocilo-agencije-o-resevanju-uporabniskih-sporov-s-podrocja-elektronskih-komunikacij-in-postnih-storitev-1, accessed 29 Jun. 2022.
136. *See*: https://www.gov.si/teme/resevanje-potrosniskih-sporov/, accessed 29 Jun. 2022. *See also* the Out-of-Court Settlement of Consumer Disputes Act (*Zakon o izvensodnem reševanju potrošniških sporov* – ZIsRPS, Official Gazette of the Republic of Slovenia, No. 81/15).
137. *See*: https://www.gov.si/teme/resevanje-potrosniskih-sporov/, accessed 29 Jun. 2022.
138. *See* the full list of online out-of-court dispute settlement options at: https://ec.europa.eu/consumers/odr/main/?event=main.adr.show2&lng=SL, accessed on 29 Jun. 2022.
139. Article 142(11) ZEKom-1.

Part II. Protection of Intellectual Property in the ICT Sector

Chapter 1. The Application of Copyright in the Area of ICT

§1. NORMATIVE FRAMEWORK

147. Since the turn of the twenty-first century, the use of information technology has spread to all areas of life. New software, platforms, and communication systems have changed everyday life and are transforming the law as well. Although technology is changing faster than the law can keep up with, there have been some important improvements in Slovenian intellectual property law in the area of ICT in the past decades, with copyright being no exception.

148. Copyright in Slovenia stems from the Constitution of the Republic of Slovenia (*Ustava Republike Slovenije* (URS)),[140] more precisely from Article 60, which guarantees copyright protection. Most of the rules on copyright are laid down in Zakon o avtorski in sorodnih pravicah (ZASP).[141] Since its adoption in 1995, the Act has been subject to several amendments, mostly as a consequence of the implementation of numerous EU directives on copyright law, such as:

- Directives 91/250/EEC and 2009/24/EC on the legal protection of computer programs.
- Directives 92/100/EEC and 2006/115/EC on rental right and lending right and on certain rights related to copyright in the field of intellectual property.
- Directive 93/83/EEC on the coordination of certain rules concerning copyright and rights related to copyright applicable to satellite broadcasting and cable retransmission.
- Directive 2011/77/EU amending Directive 2006/116/EC on the term of protection of copyright and certain related rights, Directive 96/9/EC on the legal protection of databases.
- Directive 2001/29/EC on the harmonisation of certain aspects of copyright and related rights in the information society.
- Directive 2001/84/EC on the resale right for the benefit of the author of an original work of art;

140. Official Gazette of the Republic of Slovenia, No. 33/91-I, last amendment No. 92/21 – UZ62a.
141. Official Gazette of the Republic of Slovenia, No. 16/07, last amendment No. 59/19.

– Directive 2004/48/EC on the enforcement of intellectual property rights.
– Directive 2012/28/EU on certain permitted uses of orphan works.
– Directive 2017/1564/EU on certain permitted uses of certain works and other subject matter protected by copyright and related rights for the benefit of persons who are blind, visually impaired or otherwise print-disabled.

149. As part of Slovenian copyright law, Zakon o kolektivnem upravljanju avtorske in sorodnih pravic (ZKUASP)[142] should also be mentioned, which implements Directive 93/83/EEC on the coordination of certain rules concerning copyright and rights related to copyright applicable to satellite broadcasting and cable retransmission, and Directive 2006/116/EC on the term of protection of copyright and certain related rights.

150. It should be noted that Slovenian copyright law in the area of ICT is very much 'international', since it is strongly influenced by international treaties and European legislation. While the copyright protection in the ICT sector garners attention among scholars, case law on this matter is rather scarce.

§2. General Features of Slovenian Copyright Law

I. Works Protected

151. When defining the object of copyright, ZASP combines two methods – the method of general definition and the method of enumeration by way of example. According to the general clause, copyright works are 'individual intellectual creations in the domain of literature, science and art which are expressed in any mode, unless otherwise provided by ZASP'.[143] Ideas, principles, discoveries, official legislative, administrative, and judicial texts, and folk literary and artistic creations are exempt from copyright protection.[144]

152. There are five fundamental requirements of copyrightable subject matter:

(1) the work must be expressed in any form, tangible or intangible, which is humanly perceivable;[145]
(2) it must be a product of human activity;
(3) it must be a work of art, science, or literature;
(4) it must be 'a work of the mind', which means that it has a spiritual content and is an expression of the author's thoughts, feelings, etc.;

142. Official Gazette of the Republic of Slovenia, No. 63/16.
143. Article 5(1) ZASP.
144. Article 9(1) ZASP. *See*: M. Trampuž, 29 (M. Trampuž et al. eds., GV Založba 1997).
145. The idea as such is not protected. However, the Slovenian law does not require 'fixing' copyrighted works in a tangible form. *See*: M. Trampuž, 30 (M. Trampuž et al. eds., GV Založba 1997).

(5) the work must be individual, which means that it is a product of the author's personal and individual effort.[146]

153. In the interest of clarity, ZASP lays down a list of examples of copyright works. The list should not be deemed a limitative catalogue. According to it, works of authorship include, in particular, the following categories:[147]

(1) spoken works such as speeches, sermons, and lectures;
(2) written works such as belletristic works, articles, manuals, studies, and computer programs;
(3) musical works with or without words;
(4) theatrical or theatrico-musical works and works of puppetry;
(5) choreographic works and works of pantomime;
(6) photographic works and works produced by a process similar to photography;
(7) audiovisual works;
(8) works of fine art such as paintings, graphic works, and sculptures;
(9) works of architecture such as sketches, plans, and built structures in the field of architecture, urban planning, and landscape architecture;
(10) works of applied art and industrial design;
(11) cartographic works;
(12) presentations of a scientific, educational, or technical character (technical drawings, plans, sketches, tables, expert opinions, three-dimensional representations, and other works of a similar nature).

II. The Content and Duration of Copyright

154. Copyright in a work gives the author moral, economic (pecuniary), and some other rights, such as the right of access and of delivery, the resale right, the public lending right, and the right to remuneration.

155. The substantive content of such moral rights is a bundle of specific prerogatives, such as: (i) the right to disclose the work to the public, (ii) the right to the recognition of authorship (the paternity right), (iii) the right to the integrity of the work, and (iv) the right to retract.[148] They cannot be transferred and remain with the author, if pecuniary rights are assigned.

156. The pecuniary rights protect the author with respect to his or her economic interests by giving him an exclusive right to authorize or prohibit the use of his or her work or copies thereof. The pecuniary rights listed in ZASP are in particular: (i) the right of reproduction, (ii) the right of distribution, (iii) the rental right, (iv) the right of public performance, (v) the right of public transmission, (vi) the right of

---

146. M. Trampuž, 30-32 (M. Trampuž et al. eds., GV Založba 1997).
147. Article 5(2) ZASP.
148. *See*: Articles 16–20 ZASP.

public communication by means of phonograms or videograms, (vii) the right of public presentation, (viii) the right of broadcasting, (ix) the right of making the work available, and (x) the right of transformation.[149] However, it should be noted that the list of pecuniary rights laid down in ZASP is a non-exhaustive list.[150]

157. In Slovenian law, copyright runs for the life of the author and for seventy years after his or her death, unless otherwise provided by ZASP.[151] Due to the monistic concept of copyright adopted in Slovenian law, the expiry of such protection refers to the copyright as a whole, including moral and pecuniary rights.[152]

§3. Copyright Protection of Computer Programs

158. When implementing Directives 91/250/EEC and 2009/24/EC on the legal protection of computer programs into the Slovenian legal order, computer programs were explicitly included in ZASP as works enjoying copyright protection. For copyright purposes, they are treated as 'written works', among belletristic works, articles, manuals, and studies. They are deemed to be a work of science.[153]

159. Like all other works laid down in the list, computer programs should fulfil the five above-mentioned fundamental requirements of copyrightable subject matter.[154] However, it is explicitly stipulated in ZASP that a computer program shall be protected if it is original in the sense that it is the author's own intellectual creation.[155]

160. Similar to the Software Directive (2009/24/EC), ZASP does not define the notion of computer programs.[156] However, it says that computer programs are programs expressed in any form, including preparatory design materials for their creation.[157] Only the expression of a computer program is protected and such protection cannot be extended to the ideas and principles underlying any program component, including those that underlie its interfaces. All expressions of computer programs that are (directly or indirectly) humanly perceivable, including expression in the form of an object code or a source code, are protected.[158]

---

149. Articles 22–33 ZASP.
150. B. Oman, 90 (M. Trampuž et al. eds., GV Založba 1997).
151. Article 59 ZASP.
152. M. Trampuž, 174 (M. Trampuž et al. eds., GV Založba 1997).
153. *Ibid.*, p. 264.
154. *Ibid.*, p. 268.
155. Article 111(3) ZASP.
156. The lack of a definition results from the express choice of the legislature to avoid the Directive 'becoming outdated'. *See*: Explanatory Memorandum 1989, para. 1.1.
157. Article 111(1) ZASP.
158. M. Damjan, *Problemi pravnega varstva računalniških programov*, Podjetje in delo 3-4/2008/XXXIV, 471, 479 (2008); M. Damjan, *Pravni temelj prostega programja*, Pravnik 4-6/2004/59, 280, 281 (2004); M. Trampuž, 265 (M. Trampuž et al. eds., GV Založba 1997).

161. Since it is a general principle of copyright law that it does not protect mathematical formulas, general rules or scientific theories and algorithms[159] do not enjoy protection under Slovenian copyright legislation,[160] unless they go beyond the abstract description of the solution or basic instructions. Their copyright protection depends on the level of abstractness and generality.

162. ZASP contains a separate set of rules on computer programs,[161] which is considered to be a *lex specialis* in relation to other rules laid down in the Act.[162] It addresses the issue of works created by employees within their scope of employment, defines the author's rights and their limitations, and addresses the notion of decompilation and special measures of protection.

163. Copyright vests initially in the author of a computer program – the natural person who created the work[163] ('the creator doctrine'). In Slovenian law, legal persons cannot be the original copyright holder of a computer program. If a work created through the collaboration of two or more persons constitutes an inseparable whole, all co-authors of such work shall have a joint copyright.[164]

164. If a program was created by employees within their scope of employment or by an author under a contract for a work made for hire, it is deemed that the economic rights and other rights of the author to such program are assigned to the employer or person ordering the work, exclusively and without limitations, unless otherwise provided by a contract. Therefore, employers are entitled to exercise the economic rights to computer programs created by their employees, while a document confirming the transfer of rights is not required. However, moral rights are not transferred to the employer.[165] This provision was transposed into the Slovenian legal order from the Software Directive. It has been noted that computer programs constitute the only subject matter in relation to which European law has been able to impose this so-called work-for-hire rule.[166] However, the attribution of economic

---

159. An algorithm is 'a procedure for solving a mathematical problem in a finite number of steps that frequently involves the repetition of an operation and whereby these steps are usually described on a rather high level of abstraction.' *See*: M. C. Janssens, *The Software Directive*, 99, para. 5.27 (I. Stamatoudi, P. Torremans eds. Edward Elgar Publishing Limited 2014).
160. M. Trampuž, *Predmet avtorskopravnega varstva pri računalniških programih*, Podjetje in delo 5-6/1996, 1018 (1996).
161. Articles 111–117 ZASP.
162. M. Damjan, *Problemi pravnega varstva računalniških programov*, Podjetje in delo 3-4/2008/XXXIV, 471, 479 (2008); M. Damjan, *Prodajna ali licenčna pogodba za računalniško programje*, Pravnik, 1-3/2002/60, 143, 145 (2002); M. Trampuž, 264 (M. Trampuž et al. eds., GV Založba 1997).
163. Article 10 ZASP.
164. Article 12 (1) ZASP.
165. M. Trampuž, 270 (M. Trampuž et al. eds., GV Založba 1997).
166. M. C. Janssens, *The Software Directive*, 108, para. 5.47 (I. Stamatoudi, P. Torremans eds. Edward Elgar Publishing Limited 2014).

rights applies only in relation to computer programs that were created 'in the execution of the employee's duties or following the instructions given by the employer'.[167]

165. Copyright belongs to the author by the mere fact of the creation of a work. When implementing the Software Directive, ZASP adopted a set of author's exclusive rights, which are adapted to the technical-industrial nature of computer programs. Thus, Article 113 ZASP defines more precisely the author's economic rights to a computer program (the right of reproduction, the right of alteration, and the right of distribution). According to the wording of this provision, the author has an exclusive right, in particular: (i) to make permanent or temporary reproductions of a computer program by any means and in any form, in part or in whole;[168] (ii) to make translations, adaptations, arrangements, and any other alterations of a computer program and the reproduction of the results thereof, without prejudice to the rights of a person who alters the program; and (iii) to distribute the original of the computer program or copies thereof in any form, including its rental.

166. The author may assign the above-mentioned rights to a third person with a licence agreement. The theory stresses the difference between a licence agreement and a copyright transfer agreement.[169] While in the case of a copyright transfer agreement the recipient is a singular legal successor and becomes the holder of all his or her economic rights, the licence agreement entitles him or her to only certain aspects of exploitation, since it is the author who retains the economic rights that have not been transferred to the recipient by the licence agreement.[170]

167. Since the licence agreement, as a rule, does not entitle the licensee to the source code, the theory stresses the need to conclude an escrow agreement, which aims to regulate the deposit of the source code of the software with a third party (an escrow agent).[171] Escrow is typically requested by the licensee to ensure the maintenance of the software instead of its abandonment or orphaning. The source code is released to the licensee if the licensor files for bankruptcy or otherwise fails to maintain and update the software as promised in the software licence agreement.[172] In practice, some notaries in Slovenia offer source code escrow services.

---

167. Article 112 ZASP. *See, e.g.*, Judgment of the Higher Court of Ljubljana No. II Cp 4750/2008 of 6 May 2009 (concluding that the plaintiff's involvement in post-graduate studies at a centre owned by the applicant cannot be regarded as a relationship between an employer and employee).
168. Insofar as the loading, displaying, running, transmission, or storage of a computer programme necessitates its reproduction, the author's permission shall be necessary for such acts.
169. M. Damjan, *Pravni temelj prostega programja*, Pravnik 4-6/2004/59, 280, 284 (2004).
170. *Ibid.*
171. G. Peljhan, *Naročanje in izdelave programske opreme*, Pravna praksa No. 2, 12 (1996).
172. *Ibid.*

168. Limitations of the author's rights set out in Article 113 can be found in Articles 114 and 115 ZASP.[173] This is in line with the Software Directive determining that these exceptions must be given a restrictive interpretation. However, publicly available case law on this issue is scarce.

169. Article 114 ZASP enumerates certain forms of use of computer programs that do not infringe the author's exclusive rights. According to this article, reproductions, translations, adaptations, etc. (including error corrections) may be done by the lawful acquirer of the program without the authorization of the author if they are necessary for using the computer program in accordance with its intended purpose.[174] A person having the right to use a computer program may, without the authorization of the author, make a maximum of two back-up copies of it, if that is necessary for its use.[175] A person having the right to use a copy of a computer program shall be entitled, without the authorization of the author, to observe, study, or test the functioning of the program in order to determine the ideas and principles that underlie any element of the program, if he or she does so while performing any of the acts of loading, displaying, running, transmitting, or storing the program that he or she is entitled to perform.[176]

170. Article 115 ZASP regulates the issue of the decompilation (reverse engineering) of computer programs. Decompilation is 'the act whereby a programmer disassembles software to translate the object code, a machine-readable language which is indecipherable to the user, into intelligible source code, or more precisely into a form of source code ('pseudo source code')'.[177] These acts are only allowed for the purpose of achieving the interoperability of programs.[178]

171. Article 115 determines: '(1) The reproduction of the code and the translation of its form, within the meaning of items 1 and 2 of Article 113 of this Act, shall not require the authorization of the author, where such reproduction or translation is indispensable to obtain the information necessary to achieve the interoperability of an independently created computer programme with other programmes, or with hardware, provided that the following conditions are met: 1. these acts are performed by the licensee or by another authorized user, or on their behalf, by a person authorized to do so; 2. the information necessary to achieve interoperability has not been previously readily available to the persons referred to in the foregoing item; and 3. these acts are confined only to those parts of the pre-existing programme which are necessary to achieve interoperability. (2) The information obtained through the application of the foregoing paragraph may not be: 1. used for goals other than to achieve the interoperability of an independently created computer programme; 2. given to others, except when necessary for the interoperability of an

173. *See also*: Judgment of the Higher Court of Ljubljana No. V Cpg 697/2017 of 12 Oct. 2017.
174. Article 114 (1) ZASP.
175. Article 114 (2) ZASP.
176. Article 114 (3) ZASP.
177. M. C. Janssens, *The Software Directive*, 133, para. 5.111 (I. Stamatoudi, P. Torremans eds. Edward Elgar Publishing Limited 2014).
178. *Ibid.*

independently created computer programme; 3. used for the development, production, or marketing of another computer programme substantially similar in its expression, or for any other act that infringes copyright. (3) The provisions of this Article may not be interpreted in such a way so as to allow its application to be used in a manner that unreasonably prejudices the legitimate interests of the author or conflicts with the normal use of the computer programme. (4) Contractual stipulations contrary to the provision of this Article shall be null and void.'

172. It follows from Recital 15 and Article 6 of the Software Directive that decompilation is a very narrow right and should be allowed only in specific circumstances.[179] In order to prevent the author from abuses of his or her copyright, Slovenian theory also stresses the importance of a narrow interpretation of the provision on decompilation.[180]

§4. Copyright Protection of Databases

173. When implementing the Database Directive[181] into the Slovenian legal order in 2001, some new provisions on the protection of databases[182] were included in ZASP. It follows from the Database Directive that the protection of databases is twofold.[183] On the one hand, databases enjoy copyright protection,[184] while on the other hand, they are protected by sui generis rights.[185] The same applies to databases under Slovenian law.[186] While the section on the protection of databases (Articles 141a–141g ZASP) applies to the sui generis database right, which is considered a neighbouring right in Slovenian law, provisions on the copyright protection of databases are spread throughout the Act.[187]

174. Databases are protected by copyright due to the fact that they constitute the author's own intellectual creation by reason of the selection or arrangement of their content.[188] In Slovenian law, databases are considered to be collections, similar to

179. M. C. Janssens, *The Software Directive*, 133, para. 5.112 (I. Stamatoudi, P. Torremans eds. Edward Elgar Publishing Limited 2014).
180. M. Trampuž, 277 (M. Trampuž et al. eds., GV Založba 1997).
181. Directive 96/9/EC of the European Parliament and of the Council of 11 Mar. 1996 on the legal protection of databases.
182. Articles 141a–141g ZASP.
183. *See also*: J. Levovnik, *Pravno varstvo podatkovnih baz – izbrani pravni vidiki*, 116 (M. Damjan ed., GV Založba 2014).
184. Articles 3–6 of the Database Directive.
185. Articles 7–11 of the Database Directive.
186. J. Levovnik, *Pravno varstvo podatkovnih baz – izbrani pravni vidiki*, 116 (M. Damjan ed., GV Založba 2014).
187. E.g., Articles 8, 53(a), 102.
188. Article 3 (1) of the Database Directive. *See also* Decision of the Higher Court of Ljubljana, No. I Cpg 1150/2007 of 10 Jan. 2008.

encyclopaedias, anthologies, collections of documents, etc. More precisely, a database is defined as a 'collection of independent works, data, or other materials in any form, arranged in a systematic or methodical way and individually accessible by electronic or other means'.[189]

175. The author of a database is the natural person or group of natural persons who created the database. In Slovenian law, legal persons cannot be the original copyright holder of a database.

176. The author of a database enjoys the copyright according to the general rules of ZASP. He or she is the holder of the moral rights, economic rights, and some other rights (e.g., the right of access and of delivery, the resale right, the public lending right, the right to remuneration). However, there are certain limitations to his or her copyright. Namely, ZASP ensures that a lawful user can access and use the database's contents normally. According to Article 53(a) ZASP, a lawful user of a disclosed database or of a copy thereof may freely reproduce or alter that database if this is necessary for the purposes of access to its contents and the normal use of such contents. Where the user is authorized to access only a part of the database, this rule applies only to that part. Any contractual provision contrary to this rule is null and void.

177. Similar as in the case of computer programs, ZASP contains a provision concerning databases authored by employees.[190] Since the Database Directive does not have a rule on this matter, this situation is regulated entirely by national law.[191] It is a general rule of ZASP that when a copyright work is created by an employee in the execution of his or her duties or following instructions given by his or her employer, it shall be deemed that the economic rights and other rights of the author to such work are exclusively assigned to the employer for a period of ten years from the completion of the work, unless otherwise provided by a contract.[192] However, Article 102 ZASP stipulates that it shall be deemed that the economic rights and other rights of the author to a database and to a collective work are assigned exclusively and without limitations to the employer, unless otherwise provided by a contract.

189. Article 8 (3) ZASP.
190. Article 102 ZASP.
191. E. Derclaye, *The Database Directive*, 311, para. 9.19 (I. Stamatoudi, P. Torremans eds. Edward Elgar Publishing Limited 2014). However, Recital 29 of the Directive says that nothing prevents Member States from stipulating in their legislation that where a database is created by an employee in the execution of his or her duties or following the instructions given by his or her employer, the employer shall exclusively be entitled to exercise all economic rights in the database so created, unless otherwise provided by contract.
192. Article 101 (1) ZASP.

Chapter 2. Legal Protection of Software

§1. Introduction

178. The legal protection of computer software is governed by different areas of law, mostly by copyright law. In general, computer software includes computer programs (including interfaces, which provide for interconnection and interaction to permit all elements of the software and hardware to work with other software and hardware and with users[193]) and software documentation (preparatory design materials, user documentation, technical documentation, etc.).[194] Computer programs are protected under copyright law or by a sui generis right. Since interfaces are regarded as parts of the computer programs, they are also copyright protected.[195] However, under certain circumstances, it is permitted to be acquainted with the information contained in interfaces by observing the operation of a program[196] and decompilation.[197,198] User interfaces are in practice also protected by the law on unfair competition.[199] According to an explicit provision of ZASP, the preparatory design materials for the creation of computer programs are considered to be a computer program[200] and therefore enjoy the same protection. User documentation, on the other hand, is not covered by the term 'computer program'. Therefore, general rules of copyright law apply, including the right to withdrawal, the public lending right, and the right of private internal reproduction.[201]

179. The name of the software may be protected as a trademark according to the provisions of ZIL-1.[202] Article 42(1) ZIL determines that a 'sign, or any combination of signs, capable of distinguishing the goods or services of one undertaking from those of another undertaking, and capable of being graphically represented, in particular words, including personal names, letters, numerals, figurative elements, three dimensional images, including the shape of goods or of their packaging, combinations of colours, as well as any combination of such signs, shall be eligible for registration as trademarks'. A trademark confers on its owner the exclusive right to

193. The preamble to Directive 91/250/EEC.
194. *See also*: M. Trampuž, *Predmet avtorskopravnega varstva pri računalniških programih*, Podjetje in delo 5-6/1996, 1018 (1996).
195. *Ibid.*
196. Article 114 (3) ZASP.
197. Article 115 ZASP.
198. M. Trampuž, *Predmet avtorskopravnega varstva pri računalniških programih*, Podjetje in delo 5-6/1996, 1018 (1996)
199. According to Art. 63a ZPomK-1; *see*: M. Trampuž, *Predmet avtorskopravnega varstva pri računalniških programih*, Podjetje in delo 5-6/1996, 1018 (1996).
200. Article 111 (1) ZASP.
201. M. Trampuž, *Predmet avtorskopravnega varstva pri računalniških programih*, Podjetje in delo 5-6/1996, 1018 (1996).
202. Official gazette of the Republic of Slovenia No 51/06 with further amendments.

use the trademark and to prevent all third parties from using any sign that is identical or similar to the trademark, taking into account also the identity or similarity of the goods or services covered by the trademark and the sign and the likelihood of confusion on the part of the public.[203]

§2. Legal Protection of Computer Programs

180. Legal protection of computer programs in Slovenia is multifold. Although computer programs are considered to be copyrighted works, the source code could at the same time be protected as a trade secret and the algorithms may under certain conditions enjoy patent protection.[204] Therefore it might occur that the same actions will come into conflict with different fields of protection.[205]

181. As already noted, computer programs enjoy copyright protection according to ZASP. However, computer programs may also enjoy patent protection under ZIL-1,[206] although copyright is considered to be a more suitable means for the protection of computer programs. Following the trends of the European Patent Office and the TRIPS Agreement, the Slovenian legislature decided to amend ZASP in 2001, so as to change the provision according to which computer programs were not patentable. Thereafter, a patent could also be granted for a computer program. In practice, this provision is interpreted in line with the European Patent Convention, according to which a patent should not be granted for a computer program 'as such'. The reason behind this is that computer programs are abstract (non-technical), whereas a patentable invention must relate to a technical field and have a technical character. Although a computer program 'as such' is not patentable, it is to be examined whether it can be defined as a 'computer-implemented invention'.[207] As the practice of the European Patent Office and the Slovenian patent office indicates, computer-implemented inventions are patentable provided that such an invention has a technical character that involves what is called a 'technical contribution to the prior art' or the 'solution of a technical problem'.

---

203. Article 47 ZASP.
204. M. Damjan, *Problemi pravnega varstva računalniških programov*, Podjetje in delo 3-4/2008/XXXIV, 471, 475 (2008).
205. *Ibid.*
206. Official Gazette of the Republic of Slovenia, No. 51/06, last amendment No. 100/13.
207. http://www.innovaccess.eu/sites/default/files/es_patentabilitycomputer_0000006548_00.xml.pdf accessed on December 2019.

Chapter 3. Legal Protection of Databases

§1. Introduction

182. As already noted, the legal protection of databases is twofold. On the one hand, databases enjoy copyright protection, while on the other they are protected by a sui generis right. While the copyright protects only the database's structure[208] (what is protected is the database as such if it meets the requirements of an individual and intellectual creation), the sui generis right protects its contents and the investment in making the database.[209]

183. However, a sui generis right only comes into existence if the creation of the database has resulted from a *substantial* investment that went into gathering, verifying, or otherwise presenting the contents. The investment can be financial, material, or human.[210] A sui generis right on a database prohibits third parties from taking actions that could unreasonably prejudice the database maker's legitimate interests related to such investment.[211] According to Slovenian case law, the sui generis right has also been recognized to a person who had received a database gratuitously from its maker. The Court of Appeal in Ljubljana held that 'in order to assess the value of an investment, the legal basis on which the beneficiary came to the database is not important, but the value of the investment itself'.[212] Due to the fact that the database maker invested 1,500 hours of work and EUR 5,000 to establish the database, the court held that the creation of the database resulted from a substantial investment and therefore the beneficiary is entitled to the sui generis right.[213]

184. In Slovenia, the sui generis right has been classified as a neighbouring right. By implementing the Database Directive into ZASP, the Slovenian legislature included it among other neighbouring rights in a new section on the protection of databases ('the rights of makers of databases').[214] Although almost twenty years have passed since then, publicly available case law on this matter is scarce.[215] The sui generis right lasts for fifteen years after the completion of the making of the database and can be licensed and transferred.[216]

---

208. The structure of a database results from the arrangement and/or selection of its contents.
209. J. Levovnik, *Pravno varstvo podatkovnih baz – izbrani pravni vidiki*, 116 (M. Damjan ed., GV Založba 2014).
210. E. Derclaye, *The Database Directive*, 321, para. 9.33 (I. Stamatoudi, P. Torremans eds. Edward Elgar Publishing Limited 2014).
211. J. Levovnik, *Pravno varstvo podatkovnih baz – izbrani pravni vidiki*, 116 (M. Damjan ed., GV Založba 2014).
212. Decision of the Higher Court of Ljubljana, No. I Cpg 159/2013 of 20 Nov. 2014.
213. *Ibid.*
214. Articles 141a–141g ZASP.
215. *See, e.g.*, Judgment of the Supreme Court of Slovenia No. III Ips 26/2017 of 25 Sep. 2018 (a ruling on the obligation to pay compensation for unjustified use of a database); decision of the Higher Court of Ljubljana, No. I Cpg 159/2013 of 20 Nov. 2014 (the reproduction of a database).
216. E. Derclaye, *The Database Directive*, 320, para. 9.31 (I. Stamatoudi, P. Torremans eds. Edward Elgar Publishing Limited 2014).

§2. The Definition of a Database

185. In ZASP, a database is defined as 'a collection of independent works, data or other materials in any form, arranged in a systematic or methodical way and individually accessible by electronic or other means, whereby either the obtaining, verification, or presentation of its contents demands a qualitatively or quantitatively substantial investment'.[217] This definition is relatively broad and corresponds to the definition in the Database Directive.

§3. Object of Protection

186. Sui generis protection of a database applies to:

(1) the whole contents of a database;
(2) every qualitatively or quantitatively substantial part of its contents;
(3) qualitatively or quantitatively insubstantial parts of its contents, when they are used repeatedly and systematically, which conflicts with the normal exploitation of that database or which unreasonably prejudice the legitimate interests of the maker of the database.[218]

187. However, the protection of databases does not apply to computer programs used in the making or operation of electronic databases. This is in line with the Database Directive, according to which computer programs used in the making or operation of databases or any collection included in such computer programs which could qualify as a database cannot be protected as a database by copyright or the sui generis right.[219] However, a computer program or a part thereof which is not used in the making or operation of electronic databases can benefit from the sui generis right if it can be classified as a database.[220]

§4. The Content of the Right

188. Article 141c ZASP lays down the rights of the maker of databases. These are entitlements arising from his or her sui generis database right. It says that the maker of a database has the exclusive right:

(1) to reproduce the database;
(2) to distribute copies of the database;
(3) to rent copies of the database;

217. Article 141a (1) ZASP.
218. Article 141b (1) ZASP.
219. E. Derclaye, *The Database Directive*, 303, para. 9.07 (I. Stamatoudi & P. Torremans eds, Edward Elgar Publishing Limited 2014).
220. *Ibid.*

(4) to make available to the public the database;
(5) to other forms of communication with the public regarding the database.

189. The protection of a database or its contents by a sui generis right applies irrespective of their protection by copyright or by other rights. The inclusion of material into a database and its use is without prejudice to rights existing in respect of that material. The aim of such rules is to avoid conflicts between norms of different laws on intellectual property.

§5. Rights and Obligations of Lawful Users

190. Neither ZASP nor the Database Directive provides a definition of 'lawful user'. According to the Explanatory Memorandum of a Database Directive, which is used for the interpretation of the Slovenian Act as well, a lawful user is 'a person having acquired the right to use a database'.[221] However, this definition does not say how a user acquires the right to use a database.[222] It is considered that the definition of a lawful user should be interpreted broadly so as to cover any user who lawfully acquires a database.[223]

191. A lawful user of a disclosed database or a copy thereof is free to use qualitatively or quantitatively insubstantial parts of its contents for any purposes whatsoever. However, a lawful user may not perform acts which are in conflict with the normal exploitation of that database or which unreasonably prejudice the legitimate interests of the maker of the database. A lawful user may also not cause prejudice to the copyright or neighbouring rights in respect of the works or subject matter contained in that database. According to ZASP, any contractual provision contrary to these rules is void.[224]

§6. Limitations of the Right of a Database Maker

192. ZASP provides for three exceptions to the sui generis right of a database maker – the teaching exception, the private use exception, and the public security exception. A lawful user of a published database is free to use a substantial part of its contents for the purposes of teaching and for private or other internal use of the contents of a non-electronic database (if the conditions of the teaching and private use exception to the copyright are met).[225] The use of the database is also free for

221. Paragraph 52 of the Explanatory Memorandum.
222. *See*: E. Derclaye, *The Database Directive*, 333, para. 9.56 (I. Stamatoudi & P. Torremans eds, Edward Elgar Publishing Limited 2014).
223. *Ibid.*
224. Article 141d (4) ZASP.
225. Article 141g (1) ZASP.

the performance of tasks relating to public security or the performance of any official proceedings such as proceedings in the National Assembly or National Council of the Republic of Slovenia, or judicial, administrative or arbitrary proceedings, if this is deemed necessary in the particular case.[226]

226. Article 141g (2) ZASP.

Chapter 4. Legal Protection of Computer Chips

193. Not applicable in this jurisdiction (in Slovenia there is no specific legislation/theory/case law on this issue).

Chapter 5. Other Intellectual Property Rights in the ICT Sector

194. Not applicable in this jurisdiction (all important aspects of the protection of intellectual property rights in the ICT sector have already been addressed in other chapters and subchapters).

Chapter 6. Internet Domain Name Registration

§1. The Slovenian Registry and General Rules for the Registration of Domain Names under the .SI Top-level Level Domain

195. The internet country code top-level domain for Slovenia is'.si'.[227] In June 2022, the number of Slovenian domains reached 148,270. The Slovenian Registry ('Register.si') is the registry for the '.si' top-level domain and operates within the Academic and Research Network of Slovenia *Akademska in raziskovalna mreža Slovenije* (Arnes). It was established in 1992 and since then has been responsible for the registration of domain names under .si and for the management of the top-level domain name system server for .si. Arnes is a public institution and was established by the Ordnance Establishing the Academic and Research Network of Slovenia Public Institution[228] and replaced by the Resolution Establishing the Academic and Research Network of Slovenia Public Institution.[229]

196. Arnes had been the only competent body for the registration of domain names under the .si top-level domain until 2005. However, in April 2005, the rules on registration changed and since then applicants may file a request for the registration of a .si top-level domain with every domain name registrar that has a contractual relationship with Arnes. In June 2022 there were 97 registrars offering the registration of .si domains.[230] Only applicants that use the Arnes network may file an application for registration directly with Arnes.[231]

197. In order to become a registrar of .si top-level domains, a foreign or domestic company must fulfil the following requirements:[232]

– it is registered to carry out the business activity of registration with the corresponding company registry or relevant authority;
– it is located in the European Union;
– it is ICANN accredited, if it is not located in the European Union;
– it has its own domain name registered under .si and an active website;
– it carries out the Operational Test & Evaluation (OT&E);
– it performs annual quota as stated in the registrar agreement.

198. In 2016, Arnes adopted new General Terms and Conditions for the registration of domain names under the .si top level domain. These general terms regulate the contractual relations between Arnes as the registry and registrars and domain name holders associated with the registration of the domain names. They

227. According to ISO 3166.
228. Official Gazette of the Republic of Slovenia, No. 23/92.
229. Official Gazette of the Republic of Slovenia, No. 24/2014.
230. https://www.register.si/choosing-a-domain-name-registrar/, accessed 28 Jun. 2022.
231. M. Bogataj Jančič et al., *Pravni vodnik po internetu*, 112.
232. https://www.register.si/registrars/be-a-registrar/?lang=en_US, accessed 28 Jun. 2022.

also contain some rules pertaining to technical procedures for registration. By submitting an application to register a domain name via a registrar, the domain name holder agrees to be bound by these General Terms and Conditions. A contractual legal relation between Arnes and a domain name holder arises at the moment the domain name is registered.

According to the General Terms and Conditions, a domain name may be registered if it meets the following conditions:

- The minimum length of a domain name is two characters. For an IDN, the minimum length relates to the IDN (č.si is not allowed, even though the ACE string is xn--bea.si).
- The maximum length of a domain name is 63 characters, whereas the maximum length of an IDN relates to the ACE string.
- Neither the first nor the last character of a domain name may be a hyphen.
- A domain name may not contain consecutive hyphens as the third and fourth characters, unless it is an ACE string of an allowed IDN.
- 113.si is reserved for the police, 112.si is reserved for the needs of the Administration of the Republic of Slovenia for Civil Protection and Disaster Relief, and si.si and rs.si are reserved for the needs of the Slovenian government.

199. The period of a domain name registration and the renewal of a domain name is one, two, three, four, or five years. The period commences on the date of the registration of the domain name and ends on the same day in the month as the domain name was registered.[233] A domain name may be renewed for a period of at least one and at most five years[234] on the basis of a timely application and payment.

200. Domain names are granted on a first-come, first-served basis.[235] An application is deemed to have been received when it is accepted from the registrar by the registry's server for the registration of domain names in the prescribed manner.[236] If an application for the renewal of a domain name is not filed before its expiration, the domain is allocated pending quarantine status on the date of its expiry. A pending quarantine status means that the registrar has deactivated the domain name by removing the pointers from the .si top-level domain DNS server. A status is set for a period of thirty days. Afterwards the domain name is deleted and is again available for registration. According to the General Terms and Conditions for the registration of domain names, registrars are responsible for the timely notification of domain name holders of the expiry of domain periods.

201. If a domain name is subject to alternative domain name dispute resolution or to court proceedings, the domain name is blocked. A blocked domain name cannot be transferred to other users or deleted. However, the domain name holder can

233. Article 5.1 of the General Terms and Conditions for the registration of domain names under the .si top-level domain (available at: https://www.register.si/domains/general-information/policies-and-forms/?lang=en_US, accessed 28 Jun. 2022).
234. Which starts to run on the same day in the month as the domain name was registered.
235. M. Bogataj Jančič et al., *Pravni vodnik po internetu*, 117.
236. *See*: Art. 5.2 of the General Terms and Conditions for the registration of domain names.

continue to use it in accordance with the contractual rights and duties arising from the relationship between the holder and the registrar. The registry may also lock a domain name upon a registrar's request in order to provide a greater degree of protection against unintentional changes, transfers, and deletions.[237]

202. A registry is furthermore entitled to deactivate a domain name for a certain period of time if the domain name holder has violated its duties arising from the contractual relationship with the registrar or due to a court decision.

203. During the period for which a domain name is registered, the domain name holder is entitled to change the registrar or to transfer the domain to a third party. However, none of these actions should alter the period of registration.

204. It follows from the principles of consumer protection that a domain name holder who is considered to be a consumer according to ZVPot has the right to withdraw from a contract within fourteen days of concluding a domain name registration agreement remotely (the 'cooling-off period'), without being obliged to state the reason for doing so. In such a case, the consumer is also entitled to be reimbursed for the money paid for the registration, unless he or she has already started to consume the service. In the particular case of domain name registration, this means that a refund is not possible if the domain name has been activated before the consumer decides to withdraw from the purchase. In practice, the registry considers a domain name to be activated as soon as the name server records have been submitted to its domain name activation systems.[238]

§2. Domain Name Disputes

205. In general, domain name disputes are of two kinds. First, a dispute might arise from the fact that a domain name holder made a registration in bad faith in order to gain profit from such registration (e.g.,, cybersquatting). Second, it might occur that two (or more) legitimate owners of similar trademarks (trademarks that have been registered for the same sign but for different goods or services) claim to have priority for the registration of the domain name. A trademark owner should either file a complaint in a competent court against the domain name holder (or where appropriate, an in rem action concerning the domain name) or, in cases of abusive registration, submit a complaint to an approved dispute-resolution service provider. A trademark owner might also claim to have priority by referring to the right to use its own name, copyright, company name, etc.[239]

---

237. *See*: Art. 5.6. of the General Terms and Conditions for the registration of domain names.
238. https://www.register.si/domains/domain-registration-and-management/withdrawing-from-contract/?lang=en_US accessed 25 Mar. 2019.
239. M. Bogataj Jančič, *Alternativno reševanje domenskih sporov v Sloveniji*, Zbornik znanstvenih razprav LXIV/2004, 77, 87 (2004).

206. In Slovenian law, the registration of a domain name does not confer intellectual property rights or other rights with *erga omnes* effect.[240] However, domain names may come into conflict with intellectual property rights, especially trademarks[241] and company names.[242]

207. In contrast to the system of trademarks, which is territorially oriented, domain names are global. Therefore, one of the most common disputes is when the registration of a domain name comes into collision with a previously registered trademark that the domain name is identical or similar to. The collision might occur not only as a consequence of a bad-faith registration but also due to the fact that trademarks are (in contrast to domain names) based on the principles of territoriality and specialty. According to the latter, a trademark can only be asserted with regard to those goods and services in respect of which it is protected. Therefore, it might occur that owners of identical trademarks that have been registered for different goods or services would attempt to register the same domain name (this cannot be the case when it comes to well-known trademarks).[243] Since domain name registration with the same top-level and second-level domain is not possible, a domain name is registered according to the first-come, first-served rule.

208. A domain name might also collide with a company name, which is considered to be an industrial property right in Slovenian law.[244] In practice, there have been cases of a bad-faith registration where the applicants registered domain names that were identical or similar to company names. However, the company name might also be registered as a sign and in such cases is protected by a trademark.

209. As mentioned above, domain name disputes are resolved in court or by means of alternative dispute resolution methods. It also follows from the Uniform Domain-Name Dispute-Resolution Policy of ICANN, which must be followed by national registrars, that most types of trademark-based domain name disputes must be resolved by agreement, court action, or arbitration before a registrar cancels, suspends, or transfers the domain name.[245]

---

240. M. Bogataj Jančič et al., *Pravni vodnik po internetu*, 119; *see also*: M. Bogataj Jančič, *Alternativno reševanje domenskih sporov v Sloveniji*, Zbornik znanstvenih razprav LXIV/2004, 77, 80–83 (2004).
241. The following could be registered as a trademark: 'any sign, or any combination of signs, capable of distinguishing the goods or services of one undertaking from those of another undertaking, which are also capable of being graphically represented'. *See*: Art. 42 ZIL-1.
242. A corporate name is the name under which a company operates. According to the provisions of the Companies Act (*Zakon o gospodarskih družbah* – ZGD-1, Official Gazette of the Republic of Slovenia, No. 65/09 with further amendments), it shall not include words or signs that are contrary to the law or public morality, include the trademarks or service marks of other entities, or include or imitate official marks. Further rules on corporate names can be found in Articles 12–28 ZGD-1.
243. M. Bogataj Jančič et al., *Pravni vodnik po internetu*, 120.
244. M. Bogataj Jančič, *Alternativno reševanje domenskih sporov v Sloveniji*, Zbornik znanstvenih razprav LXIV/2004, 77, 81 (2004).
245. https://www.icann.org/resources/pages/help/dndr/udrp-en, accessed 28 Mar. 2019.

§3. Alternative Dispute Resolution Methods

210. Slovenian law provides alternatives to court proceedings, which is in line with the Uniform Domain-Name Dispute-Resolution Policy of ICANN. Disputes alleged to arise from abusive registrations of domain names (i.e., cybersquatting) are addressed in expedited administrative proceedings that the holder of trademark rights initiates by filing a complaint with the Registry 'Register.si', which is an approved dispute-resolution service provider in Slovenia.

211. When registering a domain name under the top-level domain'.si' and by accepting Arnes's General Terms and Conditions for the registration of domain names under this domain, domain name holders consent to be subjected to expedited administrative proceedings in instances of the abusive registration of domain names. In Slovenia, this procedure is known as alternative domain name dispute resolution (hereinafter referred to as ADR and was established by the Registry.[246] These proceedings are subject to the Rules on the Alternative Domain Name Dispute Resolution Procedure for .si Top-Level Domains Alternative Domain Name Dispute Resolution Procedure for .si Top-Level Domains (ADR Rules).[247]
In order to initiate the ADR procedure, three conditions must be met:[248]

(1) the domain name of the holder is identical to or interchangeable with its trademark valid in the territory of the Republic of Slovenia, or its company name, as taken from the court register in the Republic of Slovenia, or it violates its copyright under Slovenian law or a registered geographic designation to which it is entitled, or encroaches on its rights to its personal name or upon other rights recognized by Slovenian legislation;
(2) the domain name holder has no legally recognized interest with regard to the registered domain name; and
(3) the domain name was registered or is being used in bad faith.

212. The ADR is considered to be a time and cost-efficient[249] mechanism to resolve internet domain name disputes. However, it does not exclude the possibility of using other legal remedies, such as court litigation.

213. Disputes are resolved by an arbiter or panel of three arbiters[250] appointed from the list of arbiters established by the registrar. Arbiters are appointed to the list of arbiters for a period of three years and may be reappointed after the expiry of such term.

---

246. Article 18.1 of the General Terms and Conditions for the registration of domain names.
247. Available at: https://www.register.si/wp-content/uploads/2017/01/ARDS_eng.pdf, accessed 29 Mar. 2019.
248. Article 18.2 of the General Terms and Conditions for the registration of domain names.
249. In case there are 1-5 disputed domain names, the fee for the ADR is EUR 700, and for 6-10 disputed domain names it is EUR 1,200. If the number of disputed domain names is more than 10, the fee is determined by the administrator (the Registry).
250. The complaint is decided by a panel at the request of a complainant or a holder and upon the payment of the supplement for the panel.

214. After filing a complaint with the Registry, the competent person of the Registry examines whether the complaint meets the formal requirements.[251] If it is complete and the fee for the proceedings has been paid, the Registry should block the disputed domain name. This prevents the domain name from being deleted or transferred to a third party until the procedure is finished. The domain name holder has the right to respond to the complaint within twenty-one days of the day the domain name was blocked. The Registry should also inform the registrar that registered the disputed domain name of the filed complaint and that the domain name has been blocked. The domain name holder may respond to a complaint within twenty-one days of the day the domain name was blocked.

215. If the parties reach a settlement before an arbiter or panel of arbiters, the Registry suspends the ADR procedure. However, if the parties do not settle the case, the arbiter adopts a decision on the basis of the statements made by the parties and the proof submitted in accordance with the ADR Rules. In its decision, the arbiter or panel may reject a complaint as unfounded or uphold it partly or fully. It follows from the ADR Rules that if a complaint is partly or fully upheld, the decision shall order the deletion of the domain name or its transfer to the complainant in line with the content of the complaint. If the complainant has requested in its complaint that a specific domain name be transferred to it and the arbiter or panel finds that there is no basis for doing so, at the same time finding that there is a basis for deleting the domain name, the decision shall order the domain name to be deleted.[252] The arbiter or panel are bound by judicial and arbitration decisions.

216. It follows from the ADR Rules that there is no appeal against a decision issued in an ADR procedure.[253]

251. The preliminary examination should be completed within five days of receiving the complaint and the payment of the fee (Art. 11.1 of the ADR Rules).
252. Article 17.3 of the ADR Rules.
253. Article 17.7 of the ADR Rules.

Part III. ICT Contracts

Chapter 1. Introduction

217. Since information and communication technology contracts are of relatively recent origin, the Slovenian literature on this topic is very limited. In Slovenian law, these modern, innominate types of contacts are still in a rather nascent stage of development. They combine elements of different contracts laid down in the Obligations Code (*Obligacijski zakonik* (OZ))[254] – purchase contracts, service contracts, licensing contracts, etc. However, foreign literature and contract templates from abroad are usually of great help to practising lawyers when drafting or revising such contracts.

254. Official Gazette of the Republic of Slovenia, No. 97/07 with further amendments.

Chapter 2. Hardware Contracts

218. Hardware is usually supplied by a purchase,[255] rental, or leasing contract.[256] There is no special piece of legislation dedicated specifically to the supply of hardware, which entails that the general rules of contract law apply in such cases.

219. Hardware purchase agreements are governed by the general rules on purchase agreements as contained in the Obligations Code (for B2B and C2C relationships) or in the Consumer Protection Act (for B2C relationships). The subject of a purchase agreement can be the entire device or individual hardware components. For this reason, it is of great importance to define the subject of a purchase agreement carefully. While the seller should provide the buyer with the operating instructions, installation is not as a rule included in the seller's performance. The latter usually depends on the price and complexity of the hardware.[257] With regard to liability for defects, the general rules of contract law apply, which differentiate between liability in B2B and C2C relationships and liability in B2C relationships.

220. If hardware is supplied for a limited period of time and in return for payment, the relationship between the contracting parties is governed by the rules of rental contracts. Since the price of hardware may in certain cases be very high, this type of contract can be very useful in practice. Due to the rapid development of technology, it may be in the interest of a renter to change its hardware over time. For this reason, a contract may impose a duty on the hardware provider to subsequently replace the device with an updated one.

221. Hardware may also be supplied by a leasing agreement. Different from a rental contract, a lessee as a party to a leasing agreement bears the risk of the subsequent deterioration or destruction of the hardware.[258] However, the leasing of IT does not differentiate it from other leasing agreements. In Slovenian law, a leasing contract is not a part of statutory law but is considered to have elements of rental, loan, and purchase agreements.[259] If a lessor wants to include the general terms and conditions of the supplier in the leasing agreement, this should be done in an explicit, unambiguous, and clear manner.[260]

---

255. If the transfer is made on a permanent basis.
256. If it is transferred for a limited period of time.
257. A. von dem Bussche et al., *IT Vertragsgestaltung*, para. 367 (A. Leupold et al. eds., Münchener Anwaltshandbuch IT-Recht, C.H. Beck 3rd ed. 2013).
258. Judgment of the Higher Court of Ljubljana, No. I Cp 123/2014 of 9 Jul. 2014. *See also*: A. von dem Bussche et al., *IT Vertragsgestaltung*, para. 379 (A. Leupold et al. eds., Münchener Anwaltshandbuch IT-Recht, C.H. Beck 3rd ed. 2013).
259. For more on leasing agreements in Slovenian law and their legal nature, *see*: P. Grilc, *Pravna narava pogodbe o leasingu*, Zbornik znanstvenih razprav, Vol. LIII, 67–90 (1993); A. Berden, *Pogodba o leasing* (1978); V. Kranjc, *Gospodarske pogodbe* (GV Založba 2020), 413–436.
260. Von dem Bussche, Schelinski: IT: Vertragsgestaltung, in: Münchener Anwaltshandbuch IT-Recht, 3. Edition, 2013, para. 381.

Chapter 3. Software Contracts

222. Similar to hardware, there is no legislation that comprehensively deals with the supply of software. Such is governed by the rules of purchase contracts, contracts for services, and licensing agreements. Standard software, i.e., software that does not need to be adapted to the individual needs or requirements of its users (e.g., mobile apps), is usually supplied on the grounds of a purchase agreement.[261] However, software can also be supplied by a licensing agreement, which is quite common in practice, or by a combination of both – a purchase and a licensing agreement.[262] The position is usually as follows: a contract between a user and a seller is a purchase agreement, while a contract between a producer and a user is considered to be a licensing agreement.[263] The regulative framework of licensing agreements is laid down in the Obligations Code.[264] A licensing agreement is a written contract in which the software owner permits another party to use the software under a specific set of conditions and in return for the payment of a licence fee.[265] A licensing agreement causes the formation of a continuing contractual relationship for a definite or indefinite period of time. Since it is usually prepared in advance by the software owner, it is to be interpreted in a user-friendly manner.[266]

223. If software is developed upon the request of a contracting party or is adapted to its individual needs, the relationship between the contracting parties should be based on a contract for services unless the adaptation plays only a minor role.[267] Furthermore, such a contract should also contain elements of licensing and copyright agreements. According to the Copyright and Related Rights Act, moral rights and other author's rights on the program developed on the basis of a copyright agreement are transferred to the principal unless otherwise agreed by the parties.[268] The principal is usually entitled to the source code, which enables him or her to subsequently change or modify the program.[269] If the copyright does not pass to the principal, he or she acquires a licence that enables him or her to use the

261. A. von dem Bussche et al., *IT Vertragsgestaltung*, para. 142 (A. Leupold et al. eds., Münchener Anwaltshandbuch IT-Recht, C.H. Beck 3rd ed. 2013). *See also*: Judgment of the Higher Court of Ljubljana, No. I Cpg 349/2015 of 10 Jun. 2015.
262. M. Damjan, *Prodajna ali licenčna pogodba za računalniško programje?*, Pravnik, Nos. 1–3, 2005, 143, 148 et seq (2005).
263. M. Damjan, *Prodajna ali licenčna pogodba za računalniško programje?*, Pravnik, Nos. 1–3, 2005, 143, 149 (2005).
264. Articles 704–728 of the Obligations Code. These provisions are mainly of a dispositive nature. For more about licensing agreements in Slovenian law, *see*: M. Damjan, *O pravni naravi in predmetu licence*, Podjetje in delo 3-4/2006/XXXII, 631–665 (2006).
265. Articles 704–705 of the Obligations Code.
266. In accordance with Art. 83 of the Obligations Code. *See*: M. Damjan, *Prodajna ali licenčna pogodba za računalniško programje?*, Pravnik, Nos. 1–3, 2005, 143, 154 (2005).
267. *See, e.g.*, Judgment of the Higher Court of Ljubljana No. I Cpg 276/2016 of 31 May 2016. Also: B. Berčič, *Pregled tipičnih pogodb s področja informacijskih sistemov*, Pravna praksa, No. 32, 15–19 (2003).
268. Article 112 ZASP.
269. G. Peljhan, *Naročanje in izdelava programske opreme*, Pravna praksa No. 2, 13 (1996).

software. In such case, however, the principal does not acquire the source code, which usually results in a lower purchase price and brings a great deal of uncertainty and problems in the event of the author's bankruptcy.[270] In such cases, it is in the interest of the principal to negotiate and define the conditions for the future maintenance of the program, the requirements for subsequent changes to the program, and the fate of the source code in the event of the author's bankruptcy.

224. As far as consumer protection in the field of the supply of digital content is concerned, the Consumer Rights Directive contains certain provisions (transposed into Slovenian law by ZVPot) aimed at protecting consumers in contractual agreements for the supply of digital content. However, the protection established by the Consumer Rights Directive with regard to digital content is very limited.[271] For this reason, the EU adopted a new directive dealing particularly with the supply of digital content – the Digital Content Directive,[272] which was transposed into Slovenian law by the Consumer Protection Act (Zakon o varstvu potrošnikov (ZVPot-1)) in October 2022 and mostly follows the directive's wording. It brings a new level of protection for consumers entering into contracts for the supply of digital content. The Directive does not differentiate between different types of contractual agreements, e.g., purchase or licensing agreements, but encompasses all kinds of contractual agreements for the supply of digital content, including contracts for the development of digital content that is tailor-made to the specific requirements of the consumer.[273] It is limited to the relationship between consumers and traders, whereas other groups, such as small and medium-sized companies, are excluded.[274]

225. The Directive applies to digital content as defined by Article 2(1)(a): '"digital content" means data which are produced and supplied in digital form'. As follows from its preamble, 'the Directive should cover, *inter alia*, computer programs, applications, video files, audio files, music files, digital games, e-books or other e-publications, and also digital services which allow the creation of, processing of, accessing or storage of data in digital form, including software-as-a-service, such as video and audio sharing and other file hosting, word processing or games offered in the cloud computing environment and social media'.[275] However, the Directive does not apply to free and open source software, where the source code is openly shared and users can freely access, use, modify, and redistribute the software or modified versions thereof, provided that it is not supplied in exchange for a price and that the consumer's personal data are exclusively used for improving the security, compatibility, or interoperability of the software.[276] The reason behind this rule is that free

270. *Ibid.*
271. For more, *see*: M. Damjan, *Varstvo potrošnikov pri pogodbah o dobavi digitalnih vsebin*, Podjetje in delo, 6-7/2012/XXXVIII, 1462–1472 (2012).
272. Directive (EU) 2019/770 on certain aspects concerning contracts for the supply of digital content and digital services of 20 May 2019.
273. Recital 26 of the preamble to the Digital Content Directive.
274. G. Spindler, *Proposal for a Directive on the Supply of Digital Content*, 288 (S. Grundmann ed., *European Contract Law in the Digital Age*, Intersentia 2018).
275. Recital 19 of the preamble of the Digital Content Directive.
276. Recital 32 of the preamble of the Digital Content Directive.

and open source software can contribute to research and innovation in the market for digital content and digital services, whereas the European legislature aims to avoid imposing obstacles to such market developments.[277]

277. *Ibid.*

Chapter 4. Turnkey Contracts

226. A turnkey contract is a contract under which, when a computer system is delivered to the user, the user only has to 'turn a key' to have a fully operable computer system. This type of contract comprehensively regulates the analysis of user needs, software architecture development, solution programming, testing, transfer to use, implementation, and the maintenance of software for the client. The subject of such a contract is broader than that of a programming contract, which only contains certain solutions according to the client's needs. The Slovenian statutory law does not specifically address turnkey contracts in the area of information technology.

Chapter 5. Maintenance Contracts

227. A maintenance contract is a contract under which one party, the maintainer, undertakes to ensure the proper working order of the hardware or software indicated by the other party, the user.[278] Contracts for the maintenance of software or hardware are governed by the rules of contracts for services[279] as laid down in the Obligations Code[280] or the rules of labour contracts as laid down in the Employment Relationships Act.[281] Maintenance contracts are mainly concluded for a longer period of time and executed on a continuing basis. It is one of the main characteristics of long-term contracts for services concluded for an indefinite time that each party may at any time terminate the contract by giving notice to its contractual partner (with the exception of termination given at an inappropriate time, which is not allowed).[282]

228. If the maintenance is based on a contract for services, the maintainer can outsource the work to another contractor (a subcontractor) unless otherwise agreed by the parties. In such case, the Obligations Code determines that the subcontractor has a direct claim against the principal (i.e., the user) for the payment of services rendered in his or her favour (as agreed in the maintenance contract). The subcontractor will succeed with the '*actio directa*' if his or her claim is due and has been recognized by his or her contract partner (i.e., the maintainer).[283]

229. The main obligation of a maintainer arising from such contract is to keep the hardware or software of the user in sound working order. The maintenance can be of a preventive or curative character. A maintainer is generally obliged to achieve a specific result – the sound working order of the hardware or software. This means that the mere fact of not having achieved such result can result in his or her liability.

230. The main obligation of a user arising from a maintenance contract is to pay the fee stipulated in the contract. It may be agreed as a lump sum or per service (for each time such is rendered). Usually, a combination of both forms is agreed upon. The user also has the duty to cooperate: he or she must give the maintainer access to the equipment and must refrain from carrying out maintenance work by him- or herself or that it be performed by others, unless explicitly allowed by the maintainer.

---

278. A. Marchili, *The Maintenance Contract*, Journal of Media Law and Practice 5(2), 151 (1984).
279. *See also*: B. Berčič, *Pregled tipičnih pogodb s področja informacijskih sistemov*, Pravna praksa, No. 32, 15–19 (2003).
280. Articles 619–648.
281. *Zakon delovnih razmerjih* – ZDR-1, Official Gazette of the Republic of Slovenia, No. 21/13, last amendment No. 203/20.
282. Article 333 of the Obligations Code.
283. Article 631 of the Obligations Code.

231. A maintenance contract usually sets a time frame in which the maintainer is available to carry out maintenance and lays down the conditions and availability for emergency repairs.

232. It should be noted that maintenance contracts are steadily improving in practice on the basis of – mostly foreign – contract templates, while they have been rather neglected in the past decades from a theoretical point of view. The limited amount of Slovenian literature on this issue supports this view.

Part IV. Electronic Transactions

Chapter 1. The Legal Status of Electronic Transactions

§1. Introduction

233. In order to provide solutions to legal questions arising from technological developments and the accelerated introduction of electronic commerce into the business and public sectors, in 2000, the Slovenian legislature adopted the Electronic Commerce and Electronic Signature Act (*Zakon o elektronskem poslovanju in elektronskem podpisu* – ZEPEP).[284,285] By doing so, the legislature took into account the Model Law on electronic commerce of the United Nations' Commission of International Trade Law (UNCITRAL) and the relevant European legislation[286] (Directive 1999/93/EC of the European Parliament and of the Council of 13 December 1999 on a Community framework for electronic signatures[287] and Directive 2000/31/EC of the European Parliament and of the Council of 8 June 2000 on certain legal aspects of information society services, in particular electronic commerce, in the Internal Market – the e-Commerce Directive). Since it is one of the main features of electronic commerce that it is global and not limited to national territories, the legislature pointed out that this field should be regulated uniformly on the European and international levels.[288] It follows from the proposed draft of the Act that its purpose is not to keep pace with the development of information communication technology, which is extremely fast and brings revolutionary novelties on an almost regular basis but to remain technologically neutral and not focused on specific types of technology.[289]

---

284. Official Gazette of the Republic of Slovenia, No. 57/2000, last amendment No. 121/21.
285. Until 2000, e-commerce and electronic signatures were not regulated in Slovenian law.
286. Government of the Republic of Slovenia, Centre for informatics, Electronic commerce and electronic signature (available at: http://unpan1.un.org/intradoc/groups/public/documents/UNTC/UNPAN015724.pdf, accessed 31 Mar. 2019).
287. Later repealed by Regulation (EU) No. 910/2014 of 23 Jul. 2014 on electronic identification and trust services for electronic transactions in the internal market.
288. This was stated by the legislature in the proposed draft of the Electronic Commerce and Electronic Signature Act. *See*: Predlog Zakona o elektronskem poslovanju in elektronskem podpisu, Poročevalec, No. 15, 14 Mar. 2000, p. 7 (available at: http://www.sistory.si/cdn/publikacije/39001-40000/39169/Porocevalec_2000-03-14_015.pdf, accessed 31 Mar. 2019).
289. Predlog Zakona o elektronskem poslovanju in elektronskem podpisu, Poročevalec, No. 15, 14 Mar. 2000, p. 7.

234. Adopting ZEPEP was indispensable for the integration of Slovenia into the global information society, since the hitherto law was only adapted to classic paper forms. Therefore, one of the main purposes of the Act was to remove the obstacles in the Slovenian legislation that could threaten the progress of electronic forms of business and judicial or other proceedings.[290]

235. The Act is based on modern principles, such as the principle of the non-discrimination of electronic forms, the principle of openness, the principle of the contractual freedom of the parties, the principle of duality, the principle of the protection of personal data and of consumers, and the principle of international recognition.[291] In 2021 ZEPEP was partly replaced by the Electronic Identification and Trust Services Act (*Zakon o elektronski identifikaciji in storitvah zaupanja* (ZEISZ))[292] that follows the requirements set out in the Electronic Identification and Trust Service Regulation.[293]

236. According to the principle of the non-discrimination of electronic forms, which is considered to be one of the essential purposes for the adoption of new legislation, paper forms and electronic forms are equalized, where this is possible and reasonable. Thus, in the evaluation of evidence, courts and state organs cannot refuse evidence solely on the grounds of it being in electronic form.

237. Since the technology is changing faster than the legislature can keep up with, the principle of openness or technological neutrality ensures that legislation does not refer to only one kind of technology or just to current solutions, but that it remains general and thus useful in the long term and adaptable to new technologies.

238. The principle of duality allows the use of different technological solutions of different reliability and different legal consequences of the use of such solutions. It is related to the principle of excluding prior authorization, set out in the e-Commerce Directive, according to which 'Member States shall ensure that the taking up and pursuit of the activity of an information society service provider may not be made subject to prior authorization or any other requirement having equivalent effect.'[294]

239. In general, the provisions of the ZEPEP are *ius dispositivum*, which means that the solutions proposed by the Act are capable of modification by the agreement

290. Predlog Zakona o elektronskem poslovanju in elektronskem podpisu, Poročevalec, No. 15, 14 Mar. 2000, p. 7.
291. Government of the Republic of Slovenia, Centre for Informatics, Electronic Commerce and Electronic Signature, p. 5.
292. Official Gazette of the Republic of Slovenia, Nos. 121/21 and 189/21.
293. Regulation (EU) No. 910/2014 of the European Parliament and of the Council of 23 Jul. 2014 on electronic identification and trust services for electronic transactions in the internal market and repealing Directive 1999/93/EC, OJ L 257 of 28 Aug. 2014.
294. Article 4(1) of Directive 2000/31/EC of the European Parliament and of the Council of 8 Jun. 2000 on certain legal aspects of information society services, in particular electronic commerce, in the Internal Market – the e-Commerce Directive.

between the parties. This is in line with the principle of contractual freedom. However, some provisions are *ius cogens*, when this is necessary for the protection of the public interest.

240. The principles of the protection of personal data and consumer protection also play an important role. Since personal data are even more exposed to possible abusive practices in the electronic world, it is one of the priorities of ZEPEP to offer adequate protection in this field. The principle of consumer protection refers to an average consumer, who usually does not have sufficient technical knowledge. Thus, it is even more difficult for consumers to implement their rights in electronic commerce. Due to this problem, the Act imposes on service providers several duties pertaining to e-commerce in order to protect consumers.[295]

241. The principle of international recognition enables the mutual recognition of electronic documents and signatures from EU and non-EU states. In 2014, the Electronic Identification and Trust Services Directive (910/2014/EC) was adopted on the EU level, which took effect on 1 July 2016, establishing a new legal structure for electronic identification, signatures, seals and documents throughout the EU. It introduced a single, standardized regulation for all EU Member States.

242. In 2009, the Slovenian legislature adopted the Electronic Commerce Market Act (*Zakon o elektronskem poslovanju na trgu* (ZEPT)),[296] which regulates certain aspects of e-commerce and the liability of providers of electronic services.

§2. Contracts Concluded by Electronic Means

I. Introduction

243. The Electronic Commerce and Electronic Signature Act introduced the principle of the full validity of contracts concluded by electronic means. The conclusion of a contract by electronic means is based on the general rules of contract law, as contained in the Obligations Code, which are supplemented by the rules of ZEPEP and ZEPT.

244. According to the general rules of Slovenian contract law, a contract is concluded if the parties reach an agreement on the terms that are essential to the type

295. According to the Slovenia Country Commercial Guide of 2019 (available at: https://www.export.gov/article?id=Slovenia-E-Commerce, accessed 31 Mar. 2019) 'online sales of consumer goods have grown substantially in Slovenia in recent years, as has the use of credit cards for in-person and online transactions. Approximately 90% of Slovenians aged 10–74, as well as almost all companies with ten or more employees, have broadband internet access. According to recent statistics, more than 48% of Slovenian internet users make monthly web purchases, while the average amount per purchase has doubled. E-commerce growth has been most pronounced in the food and beverage, automotive, and pet food and product markets.'

296. Official Gazette of the Republic of Slovenia, No. 61/2006, last amendment No. 189/21.

of transaction involved.[297] However, the conclusion of a contract by electronic means raises specific issues pertaining to the formation and conclusion of a contractual agreement with regard to its content and form, as well as to the identification of the time and place of the conclusion of the contract.

245. Contract law in Slovenia is based on the principle of consensuality, which means that a contract is concluded by the mere consent of the parties, whereas no particular form is required unless otherwise stipulated by law. If the law requires a written form, that requirement is met by an electronic message if the information contained therein is accessible and usable for a subsequent reference.[298] In order to fulfil the requirement of a written form, a contract must be signed by the parties.[299] According to the principle of the non-discrimination of the electronic forms, an advanced electronic signature verified with a qualified certificate is equal to an autographic signature. However, the rule of non-discrimination does not apply to contracts that must be made in the form of a notarial note. In such cases, the form of a notarial note cannot be replaced by an electronic form.

246. However, a variety of agreements cannot be validly concluded online. According to the Electronic Commerce and Electronic Signature Act, the following contracts cannot be concluded in electronic form:

(1) contracts regulating the transfer of property or other rights on immovables;
(2) testaments;
(3) contracts regulating property relationships between spouses;
(4) contracts on the disposal of property belonging to persons who have been dispossessed of legal capacity;
(5) contracts on the conveyance and division of property *inter vivos*;
(6) contracts of life-subsistence and agreements of the waiver of heirship prior to inheritance;
(7) contracts of donations and contracts on donations *mortis causa*;
(8) contracts of sale with the retention of ownership.[300]

247. One of the problems that arises from the fact that parties are not simultaneously physically present at the time of concluding a contract is that they are not able to identify with certainty their contracting partner. For such cases, the Electronic Commerce and Electronic Signature Act establishes the presumption that an electronic message originates from a sender if '(i) it is sent by the sender, or (ii) it is sent by a person authorized by the sender, or (iii) it is sent by an information system programmed by the sender him- or herself, or programmed by an order of the sender to operate automatically, or (iv) the recipient established the origin of the message by the application of a procedure or technology that was previously agreed

---

297. Article 15 of the Obligations Code.
298. Article 13 (1) ZEPEP.
299. Where a written form is required for a mutual contract, it is sufficient that each party signs the version of the document intended for the other party.
300. Article 13 (2) ZEPEP.

upon by the sender and recipient'.[301] However, this rule does not apply to cases where (i) the recipient has received notice from the sender that the electronic message is not that of the sender and had reasonable time to act accordingly or (ii) if the recipient knew or should have known, had he or she exercised reasonable care or used any agreed technology and procedure, that the electronic message was not that of the sender.[302]

II. The Formation of Contracts

248. Regarding the formation of online contracts, there are different ways that the agreement can be concluded. The contracting parties can reach an agreement through the exchange of electronic mail messages or online on a website. Situations wherein the contracting parties reach an agreement through the exchange of e-mails will be addressed first, followed by other ways to reach an agreement.

249. Since the Obligations Code does not contain specific provisions pertaining to contracts concluded by electronic means, the general rules on contracts concluded *inter absentes* apply. The fact that contracting parties are not in the presence of each other at the time of making the contract is also important in B2C relationships. ZVPot contains several provisions pertaining to the particularities of distance contracts.[303]

250. According to a general rule of the Obligations Code, a contract is concluded when the offeror receives a declaration by the addressee that he or she accepts the offer (the so-called receipt theory). The acceptance should reach the recipient's sphere of control so that one can expect that the recipient would become aware of it, based on a presumption of normal circumstances. Since the time of receipt is as a rule essential for the effect of an offer or its acceptance, ZEPEP defines the moment when an electronic mail message is deemed to have reached the addressee. Unless otherwise agreed, it is the time when the electronic message enters the recipient's information system.[304] However, if the recipient has designated the information system for the purpose of receiving electronic messages, receipt occurs at the time when the electronic message enters the designated information system, or, if the electronic message is sent to an information system other than the designated information system, at the time when the electronic message is retrieved by the recipient.[305]

251. Although the receipt theory is generally accepted in Slovenian law, ZEPEP contains a rule defining the moment when an electronic mail message is considered to be dispatched. According to this rule, the dispatch of an e-mail occurs when it

301. Article 5 (1) ZEPEP.
302. Article 5 (2) ZEPEP.
303. *See*: Articles 43–45a ZVPot.
304. Article 10 (1) ZEPEP.
305. Article 10 (2) ZEPEP.

enters an information system outside the control of the sender.[306] Since the so-called mailbox theory applies in general only to registered mail, this rule is not of great importance for electronic messages.

252. If the offeror has set a deadline for its acceptance, the offer must be accepted within this period. If no such deadline has been set, then an offer not made in the presence of the other party may be accepted only until such time as the offeror might expect to receive acceptance under normal circumstances.[307] Since the transmission speeds over the internet are high, the periods necessary for the transmission of the offer or acceptance decrease significantly, so that the acceptance deadline depends mostly on the time necessary for processing and deciding on the offer. Thus, in the case of electronic offers, the acceptance period is usually very short.

253. If the recipient has received several electronic mail messages, he or she is entitled to regard each electronic message as a separate electronic message and to act on that assumption, except to the extent that the electronic message was duplicated and the recipient knew or should have known of it had he or she exercised reasonable care or used any agreed technology and procedure.

254. In general, the recipient is under no obligation to confirm to his or her contracting partner the receipt of an electronic message therefrom. However, according to the Electronic Commerce and Electronic Signature Act, contracting parties might agree that the validity of an electronic message is conditional on the confirmation of receipt.[308] Where the parties have reached such an agreement, the electronic message is treated as though it has never been sent until the sender receives acknowledgement of receipt. Where the sender does not state that the electronic message is conditional on receipt of the acknowledgement, and the acknowledgement has not been received within the time specified or agreed or a reasonable time, the sender may give notice to the recipient stating that no acknowledgement of the receipt has been received and specifying a reasonable time by which the acknowledgement must be received. If the acknowledgement is not received within the time specified, following previous notification of the recipient, the sender may treat the electronic message as though it had never been sent. Where the sender has not agreed with the recipient as to a particular form of acknowledgement of the receipt of the electronic message, an acknowledgement may be given by any confirmation by the recipient, automated or otherwise, or any conduct of the recipient sufficient to indicate to the sender that the electronic message has been received.[309]

---

306. Article 9 ZEPEP.
307. Article 26 of the Obligations Code.
308. *See also*: M. Pavliha et al., *Zakon o elektronskem poslovanju in elektronskem podpisu s komentarjem* (GV Založba 2002), 53.
309. Article 7 ZEPEP.

255. Where the sender receives the recipient's acknowledgement of receipt, it is presumed that the related electronic message was received by the recipient. However, this presumption does not imply that the electronic message sent corresponds to the electronic message received.

256. Regarding the place of the conclusion of a contract, the Electronic Commerce and Electronic Signature Act stipulates that unless otherwise agreed, an electronic message is deemed to be dispatched from the place where the sender has his or her place of business or permanent residence at the time of sending the electronic message and is deemed to be received at the place where the recipient has his or her place of business or permanent residence at the time of receipt. If the sender or the recipient does not have a permanent residence, an electronic message is deemed to be dispatched from the place or received at the place of their habitual residence at the time of sending or receiving the electronic message.[310]

257. A contract may also be concluded online. Under Slovenian law, notice of goods or services on a website does not constitute an offer. Instead, it is merely an invitation to make an offer (a so-called *invitatio ad offerendum*). In Slovenian law, websites are treated differently than shop windows. Namely, exhibiting items for sale in the window of a brick-and-mortar store is considered to be an offer.[311] Differently, when concluding a contract online an offer is only made when a customer gives notice of his or her intention to buy an item from the website, and the seller is free to accept or reject that offer. However, the seller's invitation to make an offer constitutes a precontractual obligation, a violation of which may, where applicable, provide grounds for compensatory damages claims on the part of the customer (*culpa in contrahendo*). According to ZEPT, a provider of goods or services is under the obligation to provide a prompt electronic confirmation of receipt of a user's order. An order and confirmation of receipt are deemed to be received when the parties to whom they are addressed are able to access them.[312]

258. A contract may also be concluded at an online auction (e.g., via platforms such as eBay, etc.). Bids made in online auctions are binding on the buyer and the seller. By offering the goods, the seller makes a binding offer.[313] The seller must later recognize the highest bidder as a contractual partner. The prospective buyer makes an offer within the auction period. If he or she is the highest bidder in the end, then he or she becomes an official contractual partner of the merchant. The transfer of the maximum bid serves as binding acceptance of the offer, and a further declaration of consent is not necessary. This means that when the time of the online auction runs out, the seller and the highest bidder form a contract.

310. Article 11 ZEPEP.
311. According to Art. 23 of the Obligations Code. The contract is concluded when the buyer enters the shop and says that he or she would like to buy the item in the window.
312. Article 7 (4), (5) ZEPT.
313. *See, e.g.*, Judgment of the Supreme Court of Slovenia II Ips 650/2008 of 26 Jan. 2012.

Chapter 2. The Regulation of Electronic Signatures and Certification Services

259. Electronic signatures in Slovenian law are regulated by the Electronic Identification and Trust Services Act (*Zakon o elektronski identifikaciji in storitvah zaupanja* – ZEISZ),[314] which was adopted in 2021 and is based on the Electronic Identification and Trust Service Regulation.[315] The new legislation brought some changes in comparison to the old Electronic Commerce and Electronic Signature Act (*Zakon o elektronskem poslovanju in elektronskem podpisu* – ZEPEP).[316]

260. The new legislation is based on the principle of the non-discrimination of electronic forms, according to which advanced electronic signatures that are based on a qualified certificate are equivalent to hand-written signatures and are admissible as evidence in legal proceedings (they have the same probative value as hand-written signatures). According to the principle of mutual recognition, which is explicitly recognized in the Electronic Identification and Trust Service Regulation, qualified electronic signatures are mutually recognized as valid by all the EU Member States. It was also explicitly determined in the former ZEPEP that qualified certificates issued in another EU Member State are equal to those issued in Slovenia. Such mutual recognition is considered to be crucial for maintaining a single digital market across the entire EU.

261. The Slovenian Information Technology Directorate (*Direktorat za informatiko*), under the auspices of the MJU, maintains a list of qualified trust service providers in the Republic of Slovenia, which are responsible for issuing qualified certificates for electronic signatures. In order to be included in such a list, service providers must meet the conditions laid down in the Electronic Identification and Trust Service Regulation. The body responsible for supervision of the activity of qualified trust service providers is the Information Society Inspection Service (*Inšpekcija za informacijsko družbo*), under the auspices of the MJU.

262. Besides the Electronic Identification and Trust Service Regulation, which is directly applicable in the Republic of Slovenia, ZEISZ provides some further guidelines in the field. It contains a detailed list of information that should be contained in the records of holders of qualified certificates for electronic signatures and electronic stamps maintained by qualified trust service providers.[317] Such information should be kept by qualified trust service providers for ten years after the expiration date of an issued qualified certificate.[318] ZEISZ also lays down detailed rules on the procedure for issuing an electronic signature, which mostly deal with the

314. Official Gazette of the Republic of Slovenia, No. 121/21 and 189/21.
315. Regulation (EU) No. 910/2014 of the European Parliament and of the Council of 23 Jul. 2014 on electronic identification and trust services for electronic transactions in the internal market and repealing Directive 1999/93/EC, OJ L 257 of 28 Aug. 2014.
316. Official Gazette of the Republic of Slovenia, No. 98/04, last amendment No. 121/21.
317. Articles 25 and 26 ZEISZ.
318. Article 27 ZEISZ.

identification of applicants (*see* Articles 29–32 thereof). There are also some further rules on the revocation and temporary loss of the validity of a qualified certificate (Articles 34–36 thereof). It is explicitly determined in the Act that a qualified certificate is valid for a maximum of ten years from the date of issuance.[319]

263. In order to ensure an adequate number of qualified trust service providers, the Government Office for Digital Transformation calls on the public at least every two years to express the interest in the certification of qualified signature creation devices.[320]

319. Article 39 ZEISZ.
320. Article 43 (1) ZEISZ.

Chapter 3. The Protection of Users of Electronic Services

264. Internet-specific consumer protection related to distance contracts[321] can be found in the Consumer Protection Act (ZVPot), in which the Distance Selling Directive[322] (subsequently replaced by the Consumers Rights Directive)[323] was transposed. ZVPot requires that a trader provides consumers certain information, such as the main characteristics of the goods or services, the identity of the trader, etc., in a clear and comprehensible manner before the consumer is bound by the contract.[324] If the trader is selling products on a website, it shall indicate clearly and legibly, at the latest at the beginning of the ordering process, whether any delivery or payment restrictions apply.[325] ZVPot also imposes on the trader the obligation to provide the consumer with confirmation of the contract concluded, on a durable medium within a reasonable time after the conclusion of a distance contract, and at the latest at the time of the delivery of the goods or before the performance of the service begins.[326] One of the characteristics of distance contracts is also a 'cooling-off period' – a period of fourteen days for a consumer to withdraw from a contract, without the need to give any reason and without incurring any costs (with the exception of the costs of returning the goods).[327]

265. As far as the protection of users of electronic signatures and certification services is concerned, the Electronic Commerce and Electronic Signature Act (ZEPEP) used to establish the liability of the certification service provider to every person who relied on a qualified certificate, *inter alia*, for the accuracy of the data listed in the certificate and for the revocation of the certificate (if the requirements for its revocation are met). If the certification service provider breached its duties imposed by law, it was liable for damages, unless it proved that the damage occurred without its fault. However, these provisions of ZEPEP were annulled by the ZEISZ, which, however, remains silent on this issue. Thus, rules on the liability of trust service providers as contained in the Electronic Identification and Trust Service Regulation apply.[328]

---

321. Contracts concluded online are considered to be distance contracts and are, on the European level, regulated by Directive 2011/83/EU (the so-called Consumers Rights Directive).
322. Directive 97/7/EC of the European Parliament and of the Council of 20 May 1997 on the protection of consumers in respect of distance contracts.
323. Directive 2011/83/EU of the European Parliament and of the Council of 25 Oct. 2011 on consumer rights, amending Council Directive 93/13/EEC and Directive 1999/44/EC of the European Parliament and of the Council and repealing Council Directive 85/577/EEC and Directive 97/7/EC of the European Parliament and of the Council.
324. Article 43c (1) ZVPot.
325. Article 43c (3) ZVPot.
326. Article 43c (6) ZVPot.
327. D. Možina, *Razdor, odpoved in odstop od pogodbe*, Pravni letopis, 57, 68 (2011). For more *see*: D. Možina, A. Vlahek, *Contract Law in Slovenia* (Kluwer 1st ed. 2019).
328. Article 13 of the Electronic Identification and Trust Service Regulation.

Part V. Non-contractual Liability

Chapter 1. The Concept of Non-contractual Liability

266. Non-contractual liability for damage caused to another (delictual liability) is in Slovenian law primarily based on the principle of fault, meaning that the person who caused the damage intentionally or negligently is liable to the person who suffered legally relevant damage.[329] To be compensated, the plaintiff must demonstrate the unlawful conduct, the occurrence of legally relevant damage, and the causal link between them.

267. The factual causality (*conditio sine qua non*) is usually too broad to provide adequate results in order to establish delictual liability. Therefore, the theory of adequate causality is generally used in order to determine the causal link between the unlawful conduct and the occurrence of damage. According to this theory, the unlawful conduct is considered to be a cause of the damage if it typically leads to such damage.[330] Thus, untypical damage may not be attributed to unlawful acts according to this theory. However, this doctrine can be overridden by the eggshell skull rule, according to which a person who causes damage is liable for all consequences resulting from his or her unlawful acts leading to an injury to another person, even if the injured party suffers unforeseeable or untypical damage (e.g., due to a pre-existing vulnerability or medical condition).[331]

268. The peculiarity of the Slovenian regime of non-contractual liability is a general reversal of the burden of proof of fault. This means that a person who causes damage to another person shall be relieved of liability if he or she is able to prove that he or she acted without fault.[332] The reversal of the burden of proof explicitly follows from the general clause, according to which 'a person who causes damage to another person shall be liable for such damage, unless he or she proves that the damage occurred without his or her fault'.[333] There are different levels of fault: ordinary negligence (*culpa levis*), gross negligence (*culpa lata*), and intent. While ordinary negligence is the failure to use the level of care and caution that a diligent person would use in similar circumstances, gross negligence is the failure to use the

329. Article 131 (1) of the Obligations Code.
330. *See, e.g.*, Judgment of the Supreme Court of Slovenia III Ips 69/2014 of 20 Jan. 2015.
331. *See, e.g.*, Judgment of the Supreme Court of Slovenia II Ips 133/2016 of 16 Nov. 2017.
332. M. Juhart et al. eds., *Uvod v civilno pravo* (Uradni list 1st ed. 2011), 241.
333. *Ibid.*

level of care and caution that even inattentive or thoughtless persons would exercise under all circumstances. In the recent theoretical discussions, it has been stressed that the reversal of the burden of proof only applies to ordinary negligence, while gross negligence and intent have to be proven by the plaintiff.

269. There are also instances of strict liability (liability without fault), such as liability for dangerous objects and dangerous activities, the liability of parents for damage caused by their minor children; the liability of employers for their employees; the liability of legal persons for their representatives; the liability of an owner of a building for damage suffered by another due to falling objects or other defects of the building; liability for damage caused by animals, etc.

270. An employer is liable for a loss suffered by a third party caused by an employee when performing his or her work or caused in relation to his or her work, unless he or she proves that the employee acted with due care.[334] The injured party may claim damages directly from the employee if he or she acted intentionally.[335] In such cases, employers and employees are jointly and severally liable for a loss suffered by a third party. In all other cases, when the employee acted negligently, the injured party can claim compensation only from the employer. An employer who paid damages to an injured party would have a recourse claim towards the employee if the employee acted with intent or gross negligence.[336]

271. Slovenian law recognizes pecuniary losses and certain types of non-pecuniary losses, which should be compensated for if non-contractual liability is established. A reduction in the value of property (*damnum emergens*) and a loss of profit (*lucrum cessans*) are legally relevant pecuniary losses. Although compensation in kind is primarily foreseen in order to compensate for pecuniary loss,[337] monetary compensation is much more frequent in practice. The scope of legally relevant non-pecuniary losses is limited, since only certain types of losses are recognized by law. These are the following: physical distress, fear, mental distress suffered due to a reduction in life activities, disfigurement, a violation of one's good name or reputation, a violation of personal rights or freedoms, mental distress suffered by close relatives due to the death or severe disability of the injured party, the loss of holiday enjoyment, damage to the reputation of a legal person, or mental distress suffered by the author due to an infringement of his or her moral copyright. Pecuniary damages are awarded in order to compensate the injured party for the non-pecuniary losses he or she suffered.

334. Article 147 of the Obligations Code.
335. Article 147 (2) of the Obligations Code.
336. Article 147 (3) of the Obligations Code.
337. Article 164 (1) of the Obligations Code.

Chapter 2. The Liability of Network Operators

272. According to the Slovenian Electronic Communications Act (*Zakon o elektronskih komunikacijah* – ZEKom-1), 'operator' means an undertaking providing a network or service.[338] The definition encompasses both network operators and service providers. Since the liability of service providers is examined in the following chapter, this chapter deals with network operators as those who monitor and maintain the operation of the infrastructure of a communications network. Network operators remain completely neutral with respect to the content of the information transferred. According to the definition of a 'network operator' in ZEKom-1, a network operator is a natural person or legal entity that provides public communications networks or associated facilities.[339]

273. In order to prevent abuse of the possible dominant position of a network operator on the electronic communications services market, administrative authorities, more precisely AKOS, can order that a price control of an operator be carried out. If AKOS finds that a relevant market is insufficiently competitive, it may determine in its decision the undertaking or undertakings with significant market power. In such a decision, AKOS may impose on a specified network operator with significant market power several obligations with regard to cost recovery and price controls.[340] If a network operator breaches the rules of competition law, it may be held liable for the damage caused according to the general rules of non-contractual liability.[341] Since it is usually difficult for the plaintiff to prove the amount of loss suffered, it can be determined by the judge by exercising his or her judicial discretion.[342]

274. With regard to the non-contractual liability of network operators, no specific rules have been established, and the general regime of tortious liability of the Obligations Code applies. When acting in the course of its professional activity, a network operator shall fulfil its obligations according to the rules and customs of the profession. Thus, the decisive criterion for determining its due care is the diligence of a good expert.[343]

338. Article 3, No. 41 ZEKom-1. However, a natural person or legal entity that enables free-of-charge access to the internet with no profitable intent, where internet service provision is not part of its profitable activity, does not fall into the definition of operator in ZEKom-1.
339. Article 3, No. 42 ZEKom-1 .
340. *See*: Art. 106 ZEKom-1.
341. *See*: Art. 62 ZPOmK-1.
342. Judgment of the Supreme Court of Slovenia No. III Ips 98/2013 of 23 May 2014.
343. Judgment of the Higher Court of Ljubljana No. II Cp 584/2011 of 24 Aug. 2011.

Chapter 3. Liability of Intermediary Service Providers

275. Intermediary service providers (also referred to as 'ISPs') generally only have a limited degree of knowledge about the data they transmit or store. Therefore, the allocation of liability between them and the persons who originally put such information online can be problematic. Nevertheless, service providers are an attractive target for legal action, as they are visible and well known, and their financial strength is likely to be greater than that of their customers or users.[344] In order to protect them from liability for the illegal activities of their users, the European legislature introduced a legal framework in the e-Commerce Directive,[345] which aims at limiting their liability. The exemption of service providers from liability for the illegal activities of their users has different rationales: promoting the activity of such intermediaries, preserving their business models, and preventing excessive collateral censorship (i.e., preventing intermediary service providers from censoring the expressions of their users).[346]

276. The liability regime of ISPs as contained in the EU e-Commerce Directive was adequately transposed into Slovenian law by the Electronic Commerce Market Act (ZEPT).[347] It does not establish a general liability regime for ISPs, but instead provides for a system of specific liability exemptions. This means that in cases where ISPs provide a specific service (mere conduit, caching, and hosting) and comply with a series of requirements, they will not be held liable for the services performed (within some limitations).

277. While the legislation aims to limit the liability of ISPs for the illegal activities of their customers or users, they remain fully responsible for the data and information provided by themselves.[348] The liability of service providers for their own content is governed by the general principles of civil and criminal law.[349]

278. However, the liability of ISPs for user-generated content is very limited. It is a general principle that service providers are not obliged to monitor the information which they transmit or store or to actively seek facts or circumstances indicating illegal activity.[350] Thus, a general obligation to monitor information cannot be imposed on providers, which is in line with the e-Commerce Directive.[351] This solution is reasonable since such an obligation could render it almost impossible to provide services in a realistic and commercial way if providers were obliged to check

344. I. J. Lloyd, *Information Technology Law* (Oxford University Press 2008), 572.
345. Directive 2000/31/EC of the European Parliament and of the Council of 8 Jun. 2000 on certain legal aspects of information society services, in particular electronic commerce, in the Internal Market.
346. Directorate General for Internal Policies, Providers Liability: From the eCommerce Directive to the Future, 2017, p. 6.
347. Articles 8–11 ZEPT.
348. Article 8 (2) ZEPT.
349. Article 8 (2) ZEPT. *See also*: M. Damjan, *Odgovornost ponudnikov storitev informacijske družbe in spletnih medijev za uporabniške vsebine*, Pravosodni bilten, No. XXXVIII, 153, 157 (2017).
350. Article 8 (3) ZEPT.
351. *See*: Art. 15 (1) of the Directive.

and control all the information that flows through their networks.[352] It should also be borne in mind that this general rule aims not only to relieve ISPs of the obligation to monitor user-generated content but also to prohibit such activity in order to protect the privacy of users.[353] However, a court can require a service provider that provides services of mere conduit, caching, and hosting to terminate or prevent an infringement, to remove illegal content, or to disable access to it, in order to detect or prevent crime or to protect privacy or classified information and business secrets. Administrative authorities may, in accordance with sector-specific legislation, propose that a court issues such an order if this is in the public interest. If a court so requires, the ISP must provide it with the information required to identify its users within three days.

279. If ISPs provide a service that consists of the transmission in a communications network of information provided by a recipient of the service or the provision of access to a communications network ('mere conduit'), they are not liable for the information transmitted if they do not initiate the transmission, do not select the receiver of the transmission, and do not select or modify the information contained in the transmission.[354] For instance, if a bar owner allows his or her guests to use its Wi-Fi, it will not be liable for the content generated by them unless the abovementioned conditions are fulfilled.

280. The service of caching differs from mere conduits as data are not only transmitted but also temporarily stored.[355] Therefore, a caching provider has a greater technical possibility of control over data.[356] According to ZEPT, a caching provider will not be liable for the automatic, intermediate, and temporary storage of that information performed for the sole purpose of making more efficient the information's onward transmission to other recipients of the service upon their request, if:

(a) the provider does not modify the information;
(b) the provider complies with the conditions on access to the information;
(c) the provider complies with the rules on real-time updating of data set out in generally recognized and applied industry standards;
(d) the provider does not interfere with the lawful use of technology widely recognized and used by industry in order to obtain data on the use of the information; and
(e) the provider acts expeditiously to remove or to disable access to the information it has stored upon obtaining actual knowledge of the fact that the information at the initial source of the transmission has been removed from the network,

352. *See also*: P. Baistrocchi, *Liability of Intermediary Service Providers in the EU e-Commerce Directive*, Computer & High Technology Law Journal, Vol. 19, 126 (2002).
353. M. Damjan, *Odgovornost ponudnikov storitev informacijske družbe in spletnih medijev za uporabniške vsebine*, Pravosodni bilten, No. XXXVIII, 153, 157 (2017).
354. *See*: Art. 12 (1) ZEPT.
355. M. Damjan, *Odgovornost ponudnikov storitev informacijske družbe in spletnih medijev za uporabniške vsebine*, Pravosodni bilten, No. XXXVIII, 153, 159 (2017).
356. *Ibid.*

or access to it has been disabled, or that a court or an administrative authority has ordered such removal or disablement.[357]

281. If these requirements are met, caching remains a substantively neutral procedure and the ISP's liability for damages is excluded.

282. In comparison to mere conduit and caching, hosting is a service that enables the provider to carry out more permanent storage of user data. Some examples of hosting services are website hosting, blog hosting, cloud hosting, platforms, etc. Hosting providers are not liable for illegal activity or information placed on their systems by a user, so long as they do not gain actual knowledge of the activity or information. Upon obtaining such knowledge, they must act expeditiously to remove or disable access to the information ('notice and takedown').[358] A host provider is not obliged to (actively) search for illegal content or to verify the veracity of information, but should take measures against illegal content if it gains knowledge of thereof.[359] Measures against illegal content should be taken as soon as the host provider gains knowledge of the illegal content and not only when the illegality is established by an injunction or a judgment.[360] Since the requirement of an 'expeditious act' is rather abstract, it should be interpreted in the light of the circumstances of each case.

283. It should be kept in mind that limited liability protection for mere conduit, caching, and hosting providers applies only to liability for damages, whereas they may still be required by a court or administrative authority to terminate or prevent known infringements.

284. Since the transposition of the e-Commerce Directive into domestic law, Slovenian courts have given some guidelines for the interpretation of the statutory provisions on the liability of online hosts. It follows from the case law that a host provider that does not act expeditiously in order to remove or disable access to illegal information and by doing so breaches the duty of notice and takedown is not automatically liable for the illegal content. Instead, liability can be established according to the general rules of civil and criminal liability.[361] Although not explicitly provided for by ZEPT, the non-contractual liability of a host provider is based on fault.[362] Namely, instances of strict liability can be established only when explicitly provided for by law.

357. *See*: Art. 10 (1) ZEPT.
358. *See*: Art. 11 (1) ZEPT.
359. This has also been stressed in Slovenian case law, *see, e.g.*: Judgment of the Higher Court of Ljubljana No. I Cp 3097/2016 of 12 Apr. 2017.
360. Judgment of the Higher Court of Ljubljana No. I Cp 252/2014 of 19 Mar. 2014.
361. Judgment of the Higher Court of Ljubljana No. I Cp 289/2017 of 12 Jul. 2017.
362. Article 131 (1) of the Obligations Code. *See*: Judgment of the Higher Court of Ljubljana No. I Cp 289/2017 of 12 Jul. 2017. M. Damjan, *Odgovornost ponudnikov storitev informacijske družbe in spletnih medijev za uporabniške vsebine*, Pravosodni bilten, No. XXXVIII, 153, 163 (2017).

285. The civil liability of host providers is considered to be liability for its own acts (omissions) and not liability for the acts of others.[363] However, it is not entirely clear under what circumstances it can be attributed to a host provider that it should have known about illegal information.[364] According to the e-Commerce Directive, Member States can require host providers to apply the duty of care that can reasonably be expected of them and which are specified by national law in order to detect and prevent certain types of illegal activities.[365] As follows from Slovenian case law, the courts apply the standard of reasonable conduct when deciding on the liability of host providers.[366] Thus, the host provider can be held liable for damages if it could reasonably be expected from it to prevent or stop the illegal conduct.[367]

286. As far as the liability of online hosts for providing access to hyperlinks leading to illegal content is concerned, this issue has not yet been addressed by the Slovenian legislature. However, it has been suggested by scholars to refer in such cases to the general rules on the liability of host providers and use them by analogy, taking into consideration all the relevant circumstances of the case.[368]

287. Online portals can also be held liable according to the Mass Media Act (*Zakon o medijih* (ZMed)).[369] An online portal falls within the definition of media according to ZMed if it is a daily or periodic publication of editorially designed programme content accessible to the public.[370] However, the liability of an online portal operator under ZMed is not stricter than the one under the Electronic Commerce Market Act (ZEPEP). Thus, an online portal operator has no general obligation to monitor, but must act accordingly as soon as it gains knowledge of illegal content. However, ZMed offers more precise guidance as to the 'notice and takedown' obligation of the operator. Influenced by the Judgment of the ECtHR in *Delfi AS v. Estonia*,[371] it is explicitly required that the operator of an online portal allowing audiences to post comments must establish the rules on commenting and make them publicly available.[372] A breach of this duty shall be punished by a fine.[373] A comment which is not in line with the operator's rules must be removed as soon as possible but not later than one working day after the infringement was reported.[374]

---

363. M. Damjan, *Odgovornost ponudnikov storitev informacijske družbe in spletnih medijev za uporabniške vsebine*, Pravosodni bilten, No. XXXVIII, 153, 163 (2017).
364. M. Damjan, *Odgovornost ponudnikov storitev informacijske družbe in spletnih medijev za uporabniške vsebine*, Pravosodni bilten, No. XXXVIII, 153, 160 (2017).
365. Rec. 48 of the Preamble of the Directive.
366. Judgment of the Higher Court of Ljubljana No. I Cp 289/2017 of 12 Jul. 2017, para. 12.
367. Judgment of the Higher Court of Ljubljana No. I Cpg 862/2013 of 9 Oct. 2013.
368. M. Damjan, *Odgovornost ponudnikov storitev informacijske družbe in spletnih medijev za uporabniške vsebine*, Pravosodni bilten, No. XXXVIII, 153, 156 (2017).
369. Official Gazette of the Republic of Slovenia, No. 110/06, last amendment No. 67/19.
370. Article 2 ZMed.
371. Judgment of the European Court of Human Rights, *Delfi AS v. Estonia*, No. 64569/09 of 16 Jun. 2015.
372. Article 9 (3) ZMed.
373. Article 148a (3) ZMed.
374. Article 9 (3) ZMed.

It follows from the case law that the liability imposed by ZMed may be established only for an online portal organizer and not its owner.[375]

375. Judgment of the Higher Court of Ljubljana No. II Cp 2096/2018 of 23 Jan. 2019, which dealt with the liability for an unauthorized publication of the author's work in the media.

Chapter 4. Product Liability

288. Product liability is one of the first areas that was harmonized at the European level. The Slovenian product liability regime is in line with the European regime as established by the Product Liability Directive,[376] which was transposed into Slovenian law by the Consumer Protection Act (ZVPot).[377] Since the Product Liability Directive is a means of full harmonization, the level of protection in Slovenia does not deviate from that of Europe. Already before the implementation of the Directive, product liability was addressed by the Obligations Code.[378] The liability regime under the Obligations Code was considered to be very progressive and was friendlier to injured parties than that of the Directive. However, as potential claimants under the Product Liability Directive are not only consumers but 'injured parties' in general,[379] the liability regime under ZVPot takes precedence over the general regime under the Obligations Code due to the principles *lex specialis derogate legi generali* and *lex specialis derogate legi priori*.[380] This position has also been confirmed in the case law.[381]

289. Product liability under ZVPot is based on the concept of liability without fault (i.e., strict liability). This means that a producer is liable where a product is defective regardless of its fault. It is for the claimant to prove the existence of the defect, the damage, and the causal relationship between them. A product is considered to be defective when it does not provide the safety that a person is entitled to expect. When assessing the public's legitimate expectations as to the safety of a product, all relevant circumstances have to be taken into account, including the presentation of the product, the use thereof which could reasonably be expected, and the time when the product was put into circulation.[382] The defectiveness of the product should be interpreted in line with EU law, thereby taking into consideration of the extensive case law of the Court of Justice of the European Law (CJEU) on this issue.

290. Potential tortfeasors, i.e., 'producers' within the meaning of the Directive, are manufacturers of products or raw materials (including those who present themselves as producers by putting their name, trademark, or distinguishing feature on a product) and EU importers. If the producer cannot be identified or if the supplier

376. Directive 85/374/EEC of 25 Jul/ 1985 on the approximation of the laws, regulations and administrative provisions of the Member States concerning liability for defective products.
377. Official Gazette of the Republic of Slovenia, No. 98/04, last amendment No. 31/18. *See*: Articles 4–11a of the Consumer Protection Act.
378. Article 155 of the Obligations Code.
379. As explicitly stated in ZVPot, protection under the product liability regime is not limited to consumers (Art. 11a ZVPot).
380. D. Možina, *Odgovornost proizvajalca za proizvod z napako: evropsko obligacijsko pravo izpodriva nacionalno pravo*, Podjetje in delo, Vol. 33, No. 1, 71–86 (2007).
381. *See, e.g.*, Judgments of the Higher Court of Ljubljana No. I Cpg 287/2017 of 19 Mar. 2019 and No. I Cpg 664/2017 of 20 Jul. 2017.
382. Article 6 (1) ZVPot.

fails to inform the injured party of the identity of the producer, the supplier of the product may be held liable according to the rules of product liability.[383]

291. The product liability regime applies to all movables even though incorporated into another movable or into an immovable, including electricity ('products'). However, the technological development and ubiquity of digital products and services have brought many challenges as to the application of the Product Liability Directive. With regard to software, the Slovenian courts have not yet had a chance to examine whether such falls within the definition of a product as enshrined in the Directive. This issue is still rather controversial and is not the only one when it comes to digital content. For this reason, the Internal Market and Consumer Protection Committee suggested in its Draft Opinion on Civil Liability Regime for Artificial Intelligence of 28 April 2020, addressed to the Committee on Legal Affairs, to scrutinize whether it is necessary to include software in the definition of 'products' under the Product Liability Directive and to update concepts such as 'producer', 'damage', and 'defect'.[384] The Committee also stressed the importance of ensuring a fair liability system that would make it possible for consumers to prove that a defect in a product caused damage, even if third-party software is involved or the cause of a defect is hard to trace.[385] Thus, it might be expected that the Product Liability Directive will be amended accordingly in the future.

292. The liability regime under the Directive does not apply to all types of damage but only to material damage caused by death or personal injury and material damage to any item of property other than the defective product itself.[386] Other types of damage caused by the defective product, such as non-material damage, pure economic loss, damage to or the destruction of business property, and damage to the product itself, are left to national law. This means that other causes of action must be used to recover such losses. In Slovenia, these types of damages are subject to the general regime of civil liability. It should also be mentioned that the Slovenian legislature did not use the opportunity provided by the Directive to limit the producer's total liability for damage to an amount that may not be less than EUR 70 million.

293. The compensation claim of an injured party is subject to a two-tier prescription regime that combines a three-year subjective period and a ten-year long stop period. While the subjective limitation period runs from the day on which the plaintiff became aware, or should reasonably have become aware, of the damage,

383. Article 4 (3) ZVPot.

384. Draft Opinion of the Committee on the Internal Market and Consumer Protection for the Committee on Legal Affairs on Civil Liability Regime for Artificial Intelligence of 28 Apr. 2020, p. 3 (available at: https://www.europarl.europa.eu/doceo/document/IMCO-PA-648381_EN.pdf accessed 28 Feb. 2021).

385. *Ibid.*, p. 4.

386. The liability for damage to other products is limited with a threshold of EUR 500 and two further requirements: (i) that the item of property is of a type ordinarily intended for private use or consumption, and (ii) that it was used by the injured person mainly for his or her own private use or consumption. (Art. 9 of the Product Liability Directive).

the defect, and the identity of the producer, the objective period starts to run on the date on which the producer put into circulation the product that caused the damage. By missing the three-year limitation period, the Slovenian legislature failed to transpose the Directive correctly.[387] However, it has been stressed by scholars that the liability regime should be interpreted in line with the Directive, meaning that both limitation periods should apply accordingly.[388]

294. Once it has been established that a particular product is defective, the producer may raise one of the Directive's defences that were transposed into Slovenian law. A producer may argue that:

(a) it did not put the product into circulation; or
(b) having regard to the circumstances, it is probable that the defect which caused the damage did not exist at the time when the product was put into circulation by the producer or that this defect came into existence afterwards; or
(c) the product was neither manufactured by the producer for sale or any form of distribution for economic purpose nor manufactured or distributed by the producer in the course of its business; or
(d) the defect is due to the compliance of the product with mandatory regulations issued by public authorities; or
(e) the state of scientific and technical knowledge at the time when the producer put the product into circulation was not such as to enable the existence of the defect to be discovered (so-called development risk defence);[389] or
(f) in the case of a manufacturer of a component, that the defect is attributable to the design of the product in which the component has been fitted or to the instructions given by the manufacturer of the product.[390]

387. Article 9 ZVPot only applies to an objective ten-year limitation period.
388. D. Možina, *Odgovornost proizvajalca za proizvod z napako: evropsko obligacijsko pravo izpodriva nacionalno pravo*, Podjetje in delo, Vol. 33, No. 1, 71–86 (2007).
389. Although Member States were given the option to exclude the development risk defence, Slovenia did not use this chance and, by transposing it into ZVPot, it acted in favour of producers.
390. Article 10 of the Consumer Protection Act.

Part VI. Privacy Protection

Chapter 1. Regulation of Personal Data Processing

§1. INTRODUCTION

295. Article 37 of the Constitution of the Republic of Slovenia protects the privacy of correspondence and other means of communication, while Article 38 guarantees the protection of personal data. Pursuant to the latter, the processing of personal data contrary to the purpose for which it was collected is prohibited. Any interference with the right to the protection of personal data (e.g., the collection and use of personal data) as well as the purposes of its processing, supervision, and protection of the confidentiality of personal data shall be provided by law. Additionally, Article 38 guarantees the right of access to personal data and judicial protection in case the rights of the data subjects are infringed.

296. Although Slovenia has a longstanding tradition of the protection of personal data, which dates back to the Social Information System Act (*Zakon o družbenem sistemu informiranja*),[391] enacted in 1983 when Slovenia was still a part of the Socialist Federal Republic of Yugoslavia, today it lags behind other European countries as it remains the only EU Member State that has not harmonized its national data protection legislation with the General Data Protection Regulation (hereinafter: the GDPR).

297. The main legislative instrument governing the protection of personal data in Slovenia is the GDPR, which is directly applicable. However, the Personal Data Protection Act (*Zakon o varstvu osebnih podatkov* (ZVOP-1)),[392] which was enacted in 2004 to transpose Directive 95/46/EC on the protection of individuals with regard to the processing of personal data and on the free movement of such data, remains in force as far as it does not contravene the GDPR. Its provisions still govern sectoral arrangements of data protection regarding biometrics, video surveillance, direct marketing, records of entry and exit from premises, public books, the linking of personal data and expert supervision.

298. Several proposals for a new Personal Data Protection Act (*Zakon o varstvu osebnih podatkov* (ZVOP-2)) have been considered in the past few years. The latest

391. Official Gazette of the SRS, No. 10/83.
392. Official Gazette of the Republic of Slovenia, No. 94/07, last amendment No. 177/20.

version of the ZVOP-2 was presented in February 2022 (Doc. No. 007-87/2019) and as of June 2022 it has not yet been adopted.

299. Data protection in the police sector is regulated by the Act on the Protection of Personal Data in the Area of the Treatment of Criminal Offences (*Zakon o varstvu osebnih podatkov na področju obravnavanja kaznivih dejanj* (ZVOPOKD)),[393] which transposes Directive (EU) 2016/680 on the protection of natural persons with regard to the processing of personal data by competent authorities for the purposes of the prevention, investigation, detection or prosecution of criminal offences or the execution of criminal penalties, and on the free movement of such data, and repealing Council Framework Decision 2008/977/JHA (hereinafter: Directive 2016/680) into the national legislation.

300. Apart from the GDPR, the Personal Data Protection Act and the Act on the Protection of Personal Data in the Area of the Treatment of Criminal Offences, several laws govern the protection of personal data in specific fields, e.g., telecommunications (the Electronic Communications Act, *Zakon o elektronskih komunikacijah* – ZEKom-1), patient rights (the Patients' Rights Act, *Zakon o pacientovih pravicah* (ZPacP), employment (the Employment Relationships Act, *Zakon o delovnih razmerjih* (ZDR), banking (the Consumer Credit Act, *Zakon o potrošniških kreditih* (ZPotK-2), and travel documents (the Travel Documents Act, *Zakon o potnih listinah* (ZPLD-)1; the Identity Card Act, *Zakon o osebni izkaznici* (ZOIzk-1).

§2. The Personal Data Protection Act

I. Definitions

301. The definitions of the GDPR are directly applicable. Slovenian data protection legislation uses the term 'an individual' (*posameznik*) when referring to a data subject.[394] There are some additional terminological discrepancies between the Personal Data Protection Act and the GDPR: e.g., the Personal Data Protection Act uses the terms data processor (*upravljavec osebnih podatkov*) and contractual controller (*pogodbeni obdelovalec*) instead of processor and controller, and the protection of personal data (*zavarovanje osebnih podatkov*) refers to measures ensuring the security of personal data. The proposal for a new data protection act applies the terminology of European data protection legislation.

II. Personal and Territorial Scope

302. The Personal Data Protection Act applies to the processing of personal data if (1) the controller is established, has its registered office or is registered in the Republic of Slovenia; (2) a branch of the controller is registered in the Republic of

393. Official Gazette of the Republic of Slovenia, No. 177/20.
394. Article 6(2) ZVOP-1.

Slovenia;[395] or (3) the controller processes personal data by using automated or other equipment located in the Republic Slovenia. The latter provision does not apply if the equipment is only used to transmit personal data over the territory of the Republic of Slovenia.[396]

303. The provisions of the ZVOP-1 do not apply to the processing of personal data by individuals performed for purely personal use, in connection with their family life or other solely domestic activity.[397] Some provisions of the Act are not binding on political parties, trade unions, and religious communities in the course of the processing of the personal data of their members.[398] The media are also exempted from the application of certain provisions when processing personal data for the purpose of informing the public.[399]

III. The Prohibition of Discrimination

304. The Personal Data Protection Act guarantees the protection of personal data to any individual irrespective of nationality, race, colour, religion, ethnic origin, sex, language, political or other opinion, sexual orientation, property, birth, education, social status, citizenship, place or type of residence, or any other personal circumstance.[400]

IV. Data Protection of Deceased Individuals

305. The personal data of deceased individuals may be disclosed if the law authorizes the controller of personal data to disclose such.[401] In any event, the controller may disclose the data to the individual‘s heirs of first and second order if they demonstrate legitimate interest in the processing of such personal data and the deceased individual did not prohibit such further processing in writing.[402] The processing of the personal data of a deceased individual is also allowed for historical, statistical, or scientific research purposes.[403] A deceased individual may prohibit the processing of his or her personal data for such purposes; the restriction of such further processing must be stipulated in written form and may be also required by the individual‘s heirs of first and second order.[404]

395. Article 5(1) ZVOP-1.
396. Article 5(2) ZVOP-1.
397. Article 7(1) ZVOP-1.
398. Article 7(2) ZVOP-1.
399. Article 7(3) ZVOP-1.
400. Article 4 ZVOP-1.
401. Article 23(1) ZVOP-1.
402. Article 23(2) ZVOP-1.
403. Article 23(3) ZVOP-1.
404. Article 23(4) ZVOP-1.

V. Sectoral Arrangements

A. *Direct Marketing*

306. Articles 72 and 73 of the ZVOP-1 regulate the processing of personal data for direct marketing; however, this provision only applies as far as marketing is conducted by post and not by any other (electronic) means, e.g., e-mail, SMS, or MMS. The latter is governed by *lex specialis*, namely the Electronic Communications Act (*Zakon o elektronskih komunikacijah* – ZEKom-1).

307. Pursuant to the provisions of the ZVOP-1, a controller may use personal data collected (1) from publicly available sources or (2) while lawfully carrying on its activity, to offer goods, services, employment, or the temporary performance of work. The ZVOP-1 stipulates the categories of personal data which may be processed by the controller for the purpose of direct marketing and obliges the controller to obtain consent from the individual concerned if his or her data are to be transmitted to a third party.[405] The controller must stop the processing of personal data for direct marketing purposes if an individual so requests in writing or in any other agreed form. Such a request may be given anytime.[406]

B. *Video Surveillance*

308. Video surveillance may be introduced in the public or private sector. An individual who is subjected to video surveillance shall, pursuant to the Personal Data Protection Act, be informed that video surveillance is being carried out and provided with information about the state authority or legal person conducting such surveillance and provided the telephone number of a contact person to obtain information about the retention period and the location of the recordings of the video surveillance system.[407] The notice containing this information must be made visible and published in plain sight in order to enable individuals to obtain information about the circumstances of data processing at the latest when video surveillance begins. Additionally, the provisions of the GDPR regarding the right to information fully apply in all cases of video surveillance – the controller shall therefore provide individuals subjected to video surveillance the information stipulated in Articles 13 and 14 of the GDPR.
The Personal Data Protection Act also stipulates some additional requirements for video surveillance regarding:

(1) access to business premises;
(2) multi-apartment buildings; and
(3) working spaces.

---

405. Article 72 ZVOP-1.
406. Article 73 ZVOP-1.
407. Article 74(3) ZVOP-1.

1. Video Surveillance of Access to Business Premises

309. Video surveillance of access to business premises may be used in the public and private sectors, if it is necessary in order (1) to ensure the safety of people or property; (2) to ensure the monitoring of entries to or exits from official or business premises; (3) where there exists a potential threat to employees due to the nature of the work. Video surveillance measures may be introduced pursuant to a written decision which stipulates the reasons for its introduction, or prescribed by law. All employees subjected to video surveillance must be informed in writing that the business premises are under surveillance. Recordings of a video surveillance system as well as some additional categories of personal data may be retained for up to one year.[408]

2. Video Surveillance of Working Spaces

310. Video surveillance of a working space may be implemented if certain strict conditions are fulfilled: (1) surveillance must be necessary in order to ensure the safety of people or property or to protect classified information and trade secrets; (2) the objective pursued cannot be achieved by other less invasive means; (3) the surveillance must be spatially limited to areas of the working space where the harm to protected interests could actually occur; monitoring of changing rooms, restrooms, and elevators can never be permitted.[409]

3. Video Surveillance in Apartment Buildings

311. Video surveillance may also be introduced in apartment buildings if the measure is necessary in order to ensure the safety of people or property. Areas that may be covered by video surveillance system include entrances, exits, and common areas of buildings. Monitoring of entrances into apartments is strictly forbidden.[410]

C. Biometrics

312. Pursuant to Article 78 of the Personal Data Protection Act, **a biometric measure** is defined as a process of comparing and determining the biometric characteristics of an individual with the aim of identifying the individual or verifying his or her identity.

313. A biometric measure may be introduced in **the public sector** only if it is prescribed by law, it is necessary in order to ensure the safety of people or property

408. Article 75 ZVOP-1.
409. Article 77 ZVOP-1.
410. Article 76 ZVOP-1.

or to protect classified information and trade secrets, and the objective pursued cannot be reached by other less invasive means. However, if the use of biometrics is prescribed in an international treaty or is necessary for the purpose of identifying individuals when crossing international borders, the last two conditions shall not apply.[411]

314. Biometric measures may also be introduced **in the private sector**, but under different conditions. In addition to ensuring the safety of people or property or protecting classified information and trade secrets, biometric measures can be imposed if they are strictly necessary for the performance of a business activity. Employees must receive a written notice informing them of the biometric measures imposed. Biometric measures in the private sector do not have to be prescribed by law, but in such cases the controller has to obtain the prior authorization of the national data protection authority, the Information Commissioner.[412]

D. Records of Entry to and Exit from Premises

315. In order to ensure the safety of people or property or to maintain order on the premises, individuals entering or exiting premises may be required to provide their personal data and the reason for entering such. The categories of personal data that can be processed for this purpose are strictly limited to the categories stipulated in Article 82 of the Personal Data Protection Act and can be retained for up to three years. If necessary, the identity of an individual may be verified by examining his or her identity document.[413]

E. Public Registers and the Linking of Filing Systems

316. Personal data included in a public register regulated by law may be further processed according to the purpose for which they were collected or are processed.[414]

317. Official records and public registers containing personal data may only be linked if such is prescribed by law. If the personal data in official records and public registers to be linked are processed for different purposes, the controller shall notify the Information Commissioner of the linking. The linking of databases containing special categories of personal data is only allowed if the Information Commissioner

411. Article 79 ZVOP-1.
412. Article 80 ZVOP-1.
413. Article 82 ZVOP-1.
414. Article 83 ZVOP-1.

authorizes such and the controllers ensure the adequate protection of such personal data,[415] while the linking of personal data relating to criminal convictions and minor offences is prohibited.[416]

§3. Act on the Protection of Personal Data in the Area of the Treatment of Criminal Offences

318. The Act on the Protection of Personal Data in the Area of the Treatment of Criminal Offences (*Zakon o varstvu osebnih podatkov na področju obravnavanja kaznivih dejanj* – ZVOPOKD) transposes Directive (EU) 2016/680 of the European Parliament and of the Council of 27 April 2016 on the protection of natural persons with regard to the processing of personal data by competent authorities for the purposes of the prevention, investigation, detection or prosecution of criminal offences or the execution of criminal penalties, and on the free movement of such data, and repealing Council Framework Decision 2008/977/JHA (hereinafter: Directive 2016/680) and Directive (EU) 2016/681 of the European Parliament and of the Council of 27 April 2016 on the use of passenger name record (PNR) data for the prevention, detection, investigation and prosecution of terrorist offences and serious crime in the part that regulates the competences of data protection officers in Slovenian national legislation. It was adopted in November 2020 and has been valid since 31 December 2021.

I. Definitions

319. The definitions pursuant to Article 4 of the ZVOPOKD (e.g., personal data, processing, profiling, controller, processor, etc.) are in line with the definitions in Directive 2016/680.[417] However, the Slovenian data protection legislation uses the term *individual* (*posameznik*) when referring to a data subject, and the ZVOPOKD is no exception. There are some additional terminological peculiarities: when referring to a controller, the ZVOPOKD uses the term competent authority (*pristojni organ*).

II. Personal and Territorial Scope

320. The ZVOPOKD applies to the processing of personal data processed by the police, public prosecutors' offices, the Probation Administration of the Republic of Slovenia, the Prison Administration of the Republic of Slovenia, and other authorities for the purposes of the prevention, investigation, detection, or prosecution of criminal offences or the execution of criminal penalties.[418] The ZVOPOKD also

415. Article 84 ZVOP-1.
416. Article 85 ZVOP-1.
417. Article 4 ZVOPOKD.
418. Article 1(1) ZVOPOKD.

stipulates when its provisions apply to the processing and access to personal data by criminal courts when they perform the judicial function by adjudicating criminal cases.[419]

321. The ZVOPOKD applies to the processing of personal data (1) which is (wholly or partly) performed by automated means; (2) for the processing of personal data forming a part of a filing system or intended to form part of a filing system which is not performed by automated means.[420]

III. Principles Relating to the Processing of Personal Data

322. There are no specific principles unique to national law in Slovenia; the same principles apply as set out in Directive 2016/680:

- *Lawfulness, fairness, and transparency*: personal data must be processed lawfully, fairly, and in a transparent manner.[421]
- *Purpose limitation*: personal data are collected for specified, explicit, and legitimate purposes and are not processed in a manner that is incompatible with those purposes.[422]
- *Data minimization*: personal data must be adequate, relevant, and limited to what is necessary in relation to the purposes for which they are processed.[423]
- *Accuracy and currency*: personal data must be accurate and, where necessary, kept up to date; every reasonable step must be taken to ensure that personal data that are inaccurate, having regard to the purposes for which they are processed, erased or rectified without delay.[424]
- *Storage limitation*: personal data are kept in a form that permits the identification of data subjects for no longer than is necessary for the purpose for which the personal data are processed.[425]
- *Integrity, confidentiality, availability*: personal data are processed in a manner that ensures the appropriate security of the personal data, including protection against unauthorized or unlawful processing and against accidental loss, destruction, or damage, using appropriate technical or organizational measures.[426]

IV. The Rights of Individuals

323. The provisions of the ZVOPOKD referring to the rights of individuals are harmonized with Directive 2016/680. An individual (data subject) has the (1) right

419. Article 1(2) ZVOPOKD.
420. Article 3 ZVOPOKD.
421. Article 5(1) ZVOPOKD.
422. Article 5(2) ZVOPOKD.
423. Article 5(3) ZVOPOKD.
424. Article 5(4) ZVOPOKD.
425. Article 5(5) ZVOPOKD.
426. Article 5(6) ZVOPOKD.

of access to data, and (2) the right to the rectification or erasure of personal data and the restriction of processing.

324. The right of access to data: an individual has the right to obtain from a controller the confirmation of (1) whether the controller is processing the individual's personal data and to (2) access a copy or extract of the personal data being processed. The right of access may be, wholly or partly, restricted to the extent that, and for as long as, such partial or complete restriction constitutes a necessary and proportionate measure in a democratic society with due regard for the fundamental rights and legitimate interests of the natural person concerned, in order to (1) avoid obstructing official or legal inquiries, investigations, or procedures from the field of the prevention, investigation, or prosecution of criminal offences or the execution of criminal penalties, (2) protect public security, (3) protect national security, or (4) protect the rights and freedoms of others.[427]

325. The right to the rectification or erasure of personal data and the restriction of processing: an individual has the right to: (1) obtain from the controller without undue delay the rectification of inaccurate personal data relating to him or her; (2) have incomplete personal data completed, and (3) to obtain from the controller the erasure of personal data concerning him or her without undue delay where processing infringes the provisions adopted pursuant to Article 5, 6, or 7 of the ZVOPOKD.[428]

326. The possibility to limit the right of access to data fully complies with the Directive.[429]

V. The Obligations of Controllers, Processors, and Joint Controllers

327. There are no special variations from the Directive regarding the role, competences, or obligations of controllers, processors, and joint controllers.

328. Controllers are obliged to implement appropriate technical and organizational measures to ensure and to be able to demonstrate that processing is performed in accordance with the ZVOPOKD. If two or more controllers jointly determine the purposes and means of processing, they are considered *joint controllers*. Joint controllers must determine their respective responsibilities regarding the processing of personal data for compliance with the provisions of the ZVOPOKD in a transparent manner.[430] A controller may only use processors providing sufficient guarantees to implement appropriate technical and organizational measures in such a manner that the processing will meet the requirements of the ZVOPOKD and

427. Article 24 ZVOPOKD.
428. Article 26 ZVOPOKD.
429. Article 25 ZVOPOKD.
430. Article 43 ZVOPOKD.

ensure the protection of the rights of the individual. Pursuant to Article 44, processing by a processor is to be governed by a contract that is binding on the processor with regard to the controller and that sets out the subject matter and duration of the processing, the nature and purpose of the processing, and the type of personal data.

VI. Data Protection Officers

329. In full compliance with Directive 2016/680, the ZVOPOKD provides that a controller is obliged to designate one of its employees as a data protection officer, who independently advises and assists the controller in ensuring that the processing complies with the ZVOPOKD and other relevant data protection legislation.[431]

VII. Special Provisions

330. In addition to transposing the provisions of Directive 2016/680 into Slovenian national law, the ZVOPOKD regulates some specific data processing operations.

A. *Linking of Personal Data*

331. The linking of personal data held in official records and public registers is only allowed if it is prescribed by law. The controller or the processor must inform the supervisory authority (the Information Commissioner) of its intention to link the data along with a detailed description of the legal basis for the linking, the technical and organizational measures taken in order to safeguard the rights of the individuals, and a data protection impact assessment.[432]

B. *The Transmission of Personal Data*

332. The ZVOPOKD stipulates the conditions under which it is permissible for a controller to transmit personal data (1) to another public sector authority or vice versa (2) to legal or natural persons in the private sector. The procedure for the transfer of personal data is specified in detail, as well as the exceptions when the procedure does not apply.[433] An applicant who requests the transmission of personal data must provide the controller the following data: information about the applicant, the legal basis for obtaining the requested personal data, and the purpose of processing; the applicant must also specify the scope and categories of the

431. Article 55 ZVOPOKD.
432. Article 62 ZVOPOKD.
433. Articles 67–69 ZVOPOKD.

requested data and provide information on how the data will be obtained. If the request for the transmission of personal data is denied, the applicant has the right to appeal to the competent court.[434]

§4. The National Data Protection Authority

333. The Information Commissioner of the Republic of Slovenia (*Informacijski pooblaščenec* – the Information Commissioner) is the national data protection authority in Slovenia. It was established on 31 December 2005 pursuant to the Information Commissioner Act (*Zakon o informacijskem pooblaščencu* – ZInfP)[435] by merging two previously independent state bodies – the Inspectorate for Personal Data Protection and the Commissioner for Access to Public Information. As a consequence, in addition to its competences in the field of data protection, it is also entrusted with ensuring respect for the right to access public information.

334. The Information Commissioner is an independent and autonomous state body that is led by the state official bearing the same name (the Information Commissioner),[436] who is appointed by the National Assembly of the Republic of Slovenia for a five-year term and may be reappointed once.[437] When carrying out his or her tasks, he or she is supported by his or her deputies, advisors, and researchers. Inspection supervision over the implementation of data protection legislation is carried out by state supervisors for personal data protection.[438]

I. Competences

335. The Information Commissioner acts as an appeals body, an inspection authority, and a minor offences authority and has various competences stipulated by the Information Commissioner Act, the GDPR, the Personal Data Protection Act, the Electronic Communications Act, and other legislation governing data protection in various domains (e.g., healthcare, banking, public administration).

336. Pursuant to Article 2 of the Information Commissioner Act, the Information Commissioner has the following competences in the field of data protection:

(a) Exercising **inspection supervision** over the implementation of legislation governing the protection or processing of personal data.
(b) **Deciding on appeals** of individuals as regards the exercise of their rights pursuant to the provisions of the Act governing personal data protection.

434. Article 69 ZVOPOKD.
435. Official Gazette of the Republic of Slovenia, No. 113/05, last amendment No. 51/07 – ZUstS-A.
436. Article 2 ZInfP.
437. Article 6 ZInfP.
438. Article 8 ZInfP.

(c) Acting as a **minor offence authority** in relation to violations of the Information Commissioner Act and legislation governing personal data protection.

Additionally, the Information Commissioner has other competences stipulated in the Personal Data Protection Act:

(a) it acts as an **advisory body** by giving preliminary opinions to ministries, the National Assembly, local authorities, and other state bodies regarding the compliance of legislative and other policy proposals with the data protection regime;[439]
(b) it performs various tasks in order to raise awareness of data protection and to inform the public of the tasks it performs, e.g., it can issue non-binding opinions, instructions and guidelines, publish important judicial decisions relating to data protection on its website, hold press conferences, and issue statements;[440]
(c) it has competences regarding data transfers to third countries;[441]
(d) it has competences in the field of sectoral arrangements, e.g., regarding the introduction of biometric measures; and
(e) it ensures the uniform implementation of data protection measures.

Pursuant to Article 23a(1) of the Constitutional Court Act (*Zakon o ustavnem sodišču* – ZUstS),[442] the Information Commissioner has the competence **to file a request before the Constitutional Court of the Republic of Slovenia** if a question of the constitutionality or lawfulness of regulations or general acts issued for the exercise of public authority arises in connection with a procedure it is conducting.

II. Inspection Procedure

337. During an inspection procedure, the Information Commissioner shall verify compliance with data protection regulations; in particular, it monitors:

(a) the lawfulness and transparency of the processing of personal data;
(b) the appropriateness of organizational and technical measures and procedures implemented in order to ensure the security of the processing of personal data;
(c) implementation of the principle of accountability;
(d) the transfer of personal data to third countries and international organizations; and
(e) compliance with other provisions of the GDPR and the Personal Data Protection Act as far as they are still in force.[443]

439. Article 48 ZVOP-1.
440. Article 49 ZVOP-1.
441. Art 64 ZVOP-1.
442. Official Gazette of the Republic of Slovenia, No. 64/07, last amendment No. 92/21.
443. Article 51 ZVOP-1.

338. Inspection procedures are regulated by the relevant provisions of the Personal Data Protection Act, the GDPR, the Inspection Act (*Zakon o inšpekcijskem nadzoru* (ZIN))[444] and the General Administrative Procedure Act (*Zakon o splošnem upravnem postopku* (ZUP)).[445]

339. In the event of a violation of the provisions of the Personal Data Protection Act, the GDPR, or any other regulation governing the protection of personal data, the Information Commissioner may order the irregularities and omissions to be rectified, prohibit the processing of personal data, or the transfer of personal data to a third state or an international institution or order any other measure stipulated in the Inspection Act.[446]

340. If the violation meets the legal requirements for a criminal offence or a minor offence, a criminal complaint shall be filed or a procedure in accordance with the Minor Offences Act (*Zakon o prekrških* (ZP-1))[447] shall be carried out by the Information Commissioner acting as a minor offence authority.[448]

341. However, the competence of the Information Commissioner to impose fines has been greatly affected since 2018 by the fact that Slovenia has still not enacted a new Personal Data Protection Act (ZVOP-2) that is in line with the provisions of the GDPR. In 2021 the Supreme Court of the Republic of Slovenia[449] and the Higher Court in Ljubljana[450] finally resolved this anomalous situation, which had arisen after two lower courts decided that the Information Commissioner could not impose sanctions even for violations of the ZVOP-1 that are still in force. The Information Commissioner can therefore impose fines for infringements of valid provisions of the ZVOP-1; however, violations of the GDPR still result in impunity.

§5. Data Protection Reform: The Personal Data Protection Act (ZVOP-2)

342. Data protection law in Slovenia is still not aligned with the EU data protection framework. In February 2022 the Ministry of Justice presented the newest proposal for a reformed Personal Data Protection Act (*Zakon o varstvu osebnih podatkov*, ZVOP-2),[451] which will (if adopted) constitute the core of data protection legislation in Slovenia along with the General Data Protection Regulation and the

444. Official Gazette of the Republic of Slovenia, No. 43/07 – official consolidated text, last amendment No. 40/14.
445. Official Gazette of the Republic of Slovenia, No. 24/06 – official consolidated text, last amendment No. 3/22– ZDeb.
446. Article 54(1) ZVOP-1.
447. Official Gazette of the Republic of Slovenia, No. 29/11 – official consolidated text, last amendment No. 5/21 – Odl. US.
448. Article 54(3) ZVOP-1.
449. Decision of the Supreme Court of Slovenia No. IV Ips 2/2021, 16 Mar. 2021.
450. Decision of the Higher Court in Ljubljana No. PRp 215/2021.
451. Ministry of Justice, Personal Data Protection Act – Ordinary Procedure – Proposal for reading – New material No. 4 (Doc. No. 007-87/2019), 21 Feb. 2022.

ZVOPOKD. At the time of writing (June 2022), the ZVOP-2 has not yet been adopted and may be further amended, therefore only key developments and changes are presented below.

343. In addition to substantive changes aimed at harmonizing data protection law throughout the EU, the ZVOP-2 also adopts terminology of European data protection legislation (e.g., processor, controller, joint controller, data protection officer, the security of personal data, etc.).

344. The proposal stipulates additional requirements for lawful processing in public and private sectors to be in compliance with points (c) and (e) of paragraph 1 of Article 6 of the GDPR. Further processing of personal data for purposes other than that for which personal data have been collected is allowed if it satisfies the conditions set in the GDPR. Intelligence and counterintelligence authorities may process personal data if processing is strictly necessary for the performance of their tasks and competences.

345. Pursuant to the proposal, personal data relating to criminal convictions and minor offences are considered to be special categories of personal data.

346. Minors older than 15 years may validly consent to the processing of their personal data in relation to information society services.

347. The proposed ZVOP-2 also contains provisions regarding the processing of the personal data of deceased individuals. The data protection regime is similar to the one currently in force; however, it will only apply to the personal data of the deceased twenty years after his or her death.

348. The procedure for exercising the rights of individuals (data subjects) will be regulated in more detail in the ZVOP-2, including the procedure by the supervisory authority, the Information Commissioner (*Informacijski pooblaščenec*) and judicial remedies.

349. The Information Commissioner will remain the single supervisory authority for the protection of personal data in the Republic of Slovenia, competent for supervision of the processing of all personal data except for the cases which are exempt from its oversight under the provisions of the Constitution or other legislative acts. The competences of the Information Commissioner and the procedural provisions for the exercise of its supervisory authority will remain governed by the ZVOP-2, the Information Commissioner Act, as well as the ZVOPOKD.

350. Based on the requirements of the GDPR, the ZVOP-2 will introduce a new regime for the persons who will be competent for the protection of personal data within processors and controllers, namely data protection officers and their deputies. It will stipulate the conditions that individuals have to fulfil in order to be designated as data protection officers in the public and private sectors; they are required to have knowledge and experience in the field of personal data protection. Special attention is devoted to potential conflicts of interest. The proposal provides the possibility of some institutions (e.g., courts and public prosecutor offices) and professions (e.g., lawyers and notaries) designating a joint data protection officer taking into account their organizational structure and size.

351. The second part of the ZVOP-2 proposal will contain sector-specific regimes for protecting personal data. In addition to sectoral arrangements, which are regulated in the ZVOP-1 (e.g., video surveillance, biometrics, records of entry into and exit from premises) and in the new act are harmonized with the GDPR, the ZVOP-2 will also govern the processing of personal data for scientific and historical research purposes, statistical and archiving purposes, as well as the relationship between the protection of personal data and freedom of expression and the right to access public information.

352. National penalties applicable to the infringements of the GDPR and the ZVOP-2 are stipulated in the third part of the proposal, which provides that administrative fines pursuant to the GDPR are to be considered minor offence in the Republic of Slovenia. In addition to determining the range of the imposed fines, it also provides guidelines to determine the exact amount of a fine.

Chapter 2. The Protection of Telecommunications Privacy

§1. Introduction

353. Article 37 of the Constitution of the Republic of Slovenia guarantees the privacy of correspondence and other means of communication. Any interference with the privacy of correspondence and other means of communications must be (1) prescribed by law; (2) authorized by a court order; (3) limited in time; (4) necessary for the initiation or conduct of criminal proceedings, or for reasons of national security.

354. Constitutional protection of the confidentiality of communication is reiterated in the Electronic Communications Act (*Zakon o elektronskih komunikacijah* – ZEKom-1),[452] which on the other hand stipulates the conditions and procedures for permissible interferences with the right to privacy in the electronic communications sector.
Interferences with the confidentiality of communications for the purpose of initiating and conducting criminal proceedings are governed by the Criminal Procedure Act (*Zakon o kazenskem postopku* (ZKP)),[453] while the Slovenian Intelligence and Security Agency Act (*Zakon o Slovenski obveščevalno-varnostni agenciji* (ZSOVA))[454] regulates the measures interfering with the privacy of correspondence and other means of communications imposed by the Slovenian Intelligence and Security Agency.

§2. The Electronic Communications Act

355. Slovenia transposed Directive 2002/58/EC of the European Parliament and of the Council of 12 July 2002 concerning the processing of personal data and the protection of privacy in the electronic communications sector (hereinafter: the Directive on Privacy and Electronic Communications) into national law by enacting the Electronic Communications Act. The processing of personal data and the protection of the privacy of electronic communications is regulated in detail in Part XII of the ZEKom-1, while the relevant definitions are stipulated in Article 3 and are harmonized with the definitions pursuant to the Directive on Privacy and Electronic Communications.

356. In May 2022 a reformed Electronic Communications Act was submitted to the legislative procedure, but has not yet been adopted. Only minor changes are foreseen in the section addressing the processing of personal data and protection of the privacy of electronic communications.

452. Official Gazette of the Republic of Slovenia, No. 109/12, last amendment No. 189/21 – ZDU-1M.
453. Official Gazette of the Republic of Slovenia, No. 176/21.
454. Official Gazette of the Republic of Slovenia, No. 81/06.

I. The Confidentiality of Communications

357. In order to safeguard the reasonable expectation of privacy when using electronic communications and to ensure freedom of communication and freedom of expression, the ZEKom-1 protects the confidentiality of communications, which relates to: (1) the content of communications; (2) traffic and location data; and (3) facts and circumstances related to the interruption of a connection or a connection not being established.[455] In general, all forms of the surveillance or interception of communications, such as listening to, intercepting, recording, storing, and forwarding communications without the consent of the users concerned, is prohibited, unless permitted by the provisions of the ZEKom-1 or unless such form of surveillance or interception is strictly necessary for the purpose of the transmission of such communications.[456]

358. Recording and storing communications without the prior consent of all participants in the communication is also prohibited for other participants if they do not and cannot expect that their communication is being recorded.[457]

359. Data protected by the confidentiality of communications may nevertheless be processed by **operators**, which are defined as **service providers and network operators**,[458] as well as anyone involved in the performance of their activities, which may only process the data if and to the extent necessary for the provision of publicly available communications services. Operators must inform users of their data being processed at the time of the signing of the contract between the subscriber and the operator or when the provision of the public communications service commences. As soon as it is technically feasible to erase the data and they are no longer necessary for the provision of the public communications service, the data must be erased.[459]

360. Communications and related traffic data may also be recorded in **the course of lawful business practices** for the purpose of providing evidence of a commercial transaction or of any other business communication, provided that the parties to the communication are informed in advance of the recording and its purpose and retention period.[460]
Interference with the confidentiality of communications is also permitted:

(a) in order to protect the life and limb of an individual;[461]
(b) to enable lawful interception of communications following an order issued by a competent authority;[462]

---

455. Article 147(1) ZEKom-1.
456. Article 147(5) ZEKom-1.
457. Article 147(6) ZEKom-1.
458. Article 3(41) ZEKom-1.
459. Article 147(3,4) ZEKom-1.
460. Article 147(7) ZEKom-1.
461. Article 153 ZEKom-1.
462. Article 160 ZEKom-1.

(c) for organizations and public authorities responsible for law enforcement, defence, protection and rescue, as well as intelligence and security services; callers must be notified in advance that the call is being recorded, and provided information about the purpose of processing the collected data and its retention period;[463] and
(d) for other public authorities if provided by law.[464]

II. Security of Processing

361. In Article 145 and 146, the ZEKom-1 regulates the security of the processing of personal data. Providers of publicly available electronic communications services are obliged to take appropriate technical and organizational measures in order to ensure a level of security appropriate to the risk presented, taking into account technological developments and the cost of their implementation.[465] Risk is defined as any action, service, or product that interferes with the secrecy, confidentiality, and security of an electronic communications network or an electronic communications service by altering the availability, content, price, or quality of the service, and which can be effectively prevented by the operator alone or jointly with other operators.[466]

362. The provider of a publicly available electronic communications service has to inform subscribers of a particular risk of a breach of the security of the network and of any possible remedies.[467] The provider is also obliged to notify subscribers without undue delay in the event of a personal data breach (*kršitev varstva osebnih podatkov*), if it is likely it will adversely affect the personal data and privacy of the subscriber or the individual concerned.[468] An exception to the obligation to notify subscribers of a personal data breach are cases in which the provider of a publicly available electronic communications service has implemented appropriate technical safeguards that ensure that such measures render the data unintelligible to anyone who is not authorized to access such.[469] Even in such cases, the Communications Networks and Services Agency of the Republic of Slovenia (*Agencija za komunikacijska omrežja in storitve Republike Slovenije* – AKOS) may require the provider to do so.[470] Additionally, AKOS must be notified without undue delay of every personal data breach by the provider of a publicly available electronic communications service.[471] The minimum content of such notice to subscribers, individuals, and AKOS is stipulated in Article 159(5) ZEKom-1.

463. Article 147(9) ZEKom-1.
464. *Ibid.*
465. Article 145(1) ZEKom-1.
466. Article 145(2) ZEKom-1.
467. Article 146 ZEKom-1.
468. Article 159(2) ZEKom-1.
469. Article 159(3) ZEKom-1.
470. Article 159(4) ZEKom-1.
471. Article 159(1) ZEKom-1.

III. Directories of Subscribers

363. Pursuant to Article 150 ZEKom-1, subscribers have to be informed free of charge and before they are included in the printed or electronic directory of its purpose and the potential further processing of their personal data. They must be given the opportunity to determine whether and which personal data will be included in the directory. If a subscriber wants his or her data to be included in the directory, the entry of some categories of personal data is mandatory (e.g., personal name, address). Subscribers have the right to verify, correct, or delete their data from the directory free of charge.[472] All categories of personal data relating to subscribers that service providers may process are stipulated in Article 148 ZEKom-1, which also stipulates for which purposes data may be processed (e.g., the conclusion, performance, monitoring, or termination of the contract) and for how long (the data retention period).

364. In addition to the above-mentioned requirements, which are also stipulated in Article 12 of the Directive on Privacy and Electronic Communications, the ZEKom-1 in Article 150 additionally regulates the use of the personal data of subscribers for commercial or research purposes. Subscribers must be given the opportunity to prohibit the use of their personal data for such purposes either at the time of the entry of their personal data in the directory or any time thereafter.[473]

IV. Traffic Data

365. The provisions relating to the processing and storing of traffic data in the ZEKom-1 mostly reiterate the obligations of service providers stipulated in Article 6 of the Directive on Privacy and Electronic Communications. Traffic data relating to subscribers and users which are processed and stored by the operator must be erased or anonymized as soon as they are no longer necessary for the transmission of a communication.[474] The operator may nevertheless store and process traffic data necessary for the purposes of subscriber billing and interconnection payments. The processing of traffic data for such purposes is only permitted until the payment for the service has been made in full, but at the latest until the expiry of the limitation period.[475] Service providers must inform their subscribers and users in their general terms and conditions which traffic data will be processed and for how long such will be retained.[476] Only authorized persons performing certain tasks and duties under the control of the operator (e.g., billing, responding to customer enquiries, fraud detection) may access and process traffic data. Processing must be limited to what is necessary for the purposes of such activities.[477]

---

472. Article 150(2) ZEKom-1.
473. Article 150 ZEKom-1.
474. Article 151(1) ZEKom-1.
475. Article 151(2) ZEKom-1.
476. Article 151(4) ZEKom-1.
477. Article 151(5) ZEKom-1.

366. The provider of a publicly available electronic communications service may process traffic data for the purpose of marketing electronic communications services or for the provision of value-added services to the extent and for the duration necessary for marketing or services. The processing of traffic data for such purposes may only be based on the consent of the subscriber or user, who must be informed of the categories of personal data processed, the purpose of the processing, and the data retention period. Users or subscribers can at any time withdraw their consent for the processing of traffic data.[478]

367. In addition to the cases stipulated in the Directive on Privacy and Electronic Communications in which traffic data may be stored for a longer period of time, the ZEKom-1 also permits longer retention periods in the following situations:

(a) to monitor and control the use of data services;
(b) emergency number calls;
(c) internal procedures;
(d) to trace malicious or nuisance calls;
(e) when traffic and location data are needed for the protection of life and limb;
(f) to enable the lawful interception of communications.[479]

V. Location Data Other than Traffic Data

368. The requirements of the ZEKom-1 regarding the processing of location data other than traffic data are identical to those of the Directive on Privacy and Electronic Communications without any national specificities and derogations.

VI. The Processing of Traffic and Location Data in Special Circumstances

369. In order to protect the vital interests of an individual, the operator must, on the basis of a written request from the police, provide the information necessary to establish the last location of the mobile communication equipment of a missing individual, if the circumstances of a particular case so require and this information is necessary in order to:

(a) prevent the death of or serious bodily harm to an individual, if there is a reasonable likelihood that the life or limb of that individual is in imminent danger;
(b) locate an individual without or with limited legal capacity or who is diagnosed with a medical condition indicating a risk to his or her life or limb and who has been reported missing;
(c) locate a child who has been reported missing by his or her parents or legal guardians; and

478. Article 151(3) ZEKom-1.
479. Article 151(1) ZEKom-1.

(d) the missing person is, or is believed to be, in possession of mobile communication equipment.[480]

VII. The Presentation of Calling and Connected Line Identification

370. The regulation of the presentation of calling and connected line identification in the ZEKom-1 is identical to the provisions of the Directive on Privacy and Electronic Communications without any national specificities and derogations. If the possibility of the presentation of calling and connected line identification is offered, the service provider must inform the public thereof in its general terms and conditions.[481]

VIII. The Tracing of Malicious or Nuisance Calls

371. On the basis of a written application, a subscriber (a requesting subscriber) can request the operator to trace malicious or nuisance calls. The operator may for a limited period of time of up to three months record the origin of all calls to the subscriber.[482] The subscriber who requested the tracking of malicious or nuisance calls must be informed in writing of the result of the tracking, i.e., data identifying the calling party (e.g., the telephone number).[483] However, the operator may only disclose the identity of the calling subscriber to the requesting subscriber if the latter is able to demonstrate a legal interest in bringing proceedings for the protection of his or her rights before a court. If the data on the calling subscriber are disclosed to the requesting subscriber, the operator must inform the calling subscriber and the Information Commissioner.[484] Data collected for the purpose of tracing malicious or nuisance calls must be retained by the operator for three years after the data have been forwarded to the requesting subscriber.[485]

IX. Unsolicited Communications

372. Article 158 ZEKom-1 directly transposes Article 13 of the Directive on Privacy and Electronic Communications in Slovenian national legislation, with the only addition being the possibility to use the e-mail address of a natural person, if a legal person publicly publishes this e-mail address as its contact e-mail address.[486]

---

480. Article 153 ZEKom-1.
481. Article 154(6) ZEKom-1.
482. Article 155(1) ZEKom-1.
483. Article 155(2) ZEKom-1.
484. Article 155(3) ZEKom-1.
485. Article 155(4) ZEKom-1.
486. Article 155(6) ZEKom-1.

X. Cookies

373. Article 157 ZEKom-1 stipulates that the storing of information or gaining of access to information already stored in the terminal equipment of a subscriber or a user is permitted if the subscriber or user concerned consented to the processing of this information after being provided beforehand with clear and comprehensive information about the controller and the purposes of processing in accordance with the law governing the protection of personal data.[487] Technical storage or access is nevertheless allowed without the consent of the individual if the data is processed for the sole purpose of carrying out the transmission of a communication over an electronic communications network, or it is strictly necessary in order for the provider of an information society service to provide a service the subscriber or user explicitly requested.[488]

374. Pursuant to the same article, a user may consent to the processing of his or her personal data by using the relevant settings in the browser or other applications if it is technically feasible, efficient, and in accordance with the law governing the protection of personal data.[489] However, this provision of the ZEKom-1 is not aligned with the GDPR and its stricter requirements for valid consent; therefore, the provisions of the GDPR must prevail and be applied directly. A user or a subscriber must therefore validly consent to the installation of cookies in accordance with the requirements of the GDPR.

XI. The Lawful Interception of Communications

375. Article 160 ZEKom-1 regulates the conditions and procedure the operator must follow upon receiving an order from a competent authority authorizing the interception of communications. The operator has to enable the lawful interception of communications as soon as it receives a copy of the order of the competent authority that specifies: (1) the point of the public communications network at which the lawful interception of communications is to be carried out, (2) the duration of the measure, and (3) other information relating to the manner and scope of the measure.[490] In exceptional cases, the operator must enable the interception of communications on the basis of a verbal order issued by the competent authority, provided that the law allows for the issuance of a verbal order and stipulates the conditions and circumstances under which a verbal order may be issued.[491]

487. Article 157(1) ZEKom-1.
488. Article 157(2) ZEKom-1.
489. Article 157(3) ZEKom-1.
490. Article 160(1) ZEKom-1.
491. Article 160(2) ZEKom-1.

376. Records about every lawful interception of communications, which include the information contained in the order of the competent authority and the information on the execution of the order (who executed it and the duration of the interception) must be kept by the operator for a period of thirty years.[492]

492. Article 160(5) ZEKom-1.

Part VII. Computer-Related Crime

Chapter 1. General Legal Development

377. In 1995, Slovenia introduced a new Criminal Code[493] and a new Criminal Procedure Act.[494] Both already contained provisions on criminal offences and investigative measures aimed at investigating and punishing computer-related crimes. In the years to come, both have been amended to comply not only with developments in the nature of computer-related crime but also with the constitutional requirements of privacy protection.

§1. Developments in the Field of Substantive Criminal Law

378. The level of protection of privacy through substantive criminal law has been stable and sufficient. From 1995 onwards, the criminal codes in force provided protection of the right to privacy by including offences on unlawful eavesdropping and audio recording, unlawful video recording, violations of the secrecy of communications, and the abuse of personal data.

379. Other trends in substantive criminal law reflect the increasingly widespread use of IT technologies in everyday life. The text of the Criminal Code of 1995 laid the ground for the subsequent development of computer-related offences. It already included the core of the offences falling within the three categories of computer-related crime later recognized by the Budapest Convention.[495]

380. Within integrity-related offences, the Criminal Code (Kazenski zakonik (KZ)) of 1995 introduced:

- the offence of the misuse of personal data (Article 154 KZ), which included violating a computerized personal data collection;
- the offence of damaging computer data and programs (Article 225 KZ);

493. Official Gazette of the Republic of Slovenia, No. 63/94 with subsequent amendments.
494. Official Gazette of the Republic of Slovenia, No. 63/94 with subsequent amendments.
495. Ratified by Slovenia in 2004. *See*: the Act Ratifying the Convention on Cybercrime and Additional Protocol to the Convention on Cybercrime Concerning the Criminalization of Acts of a Racist and Xenophobic Nature Committed through Computer Systems, Official Gazette of the Republic of Slovenia, – International Treaties No. 17/04.

- the offence of illegal entry into a computer system (Article 242 KZ), which was limited to illegal entry while engaged in economic activities with the aim of obtaining illegal proceeds or causing damage to other persons; and
- the offence of the illegal production of accessories and tools for the purpose of illegally entering a computer system (Article 309 KZ).

381. Regarding computer-related crimes, the Criminal Code of 1995 declared 'computer capabilities' equivalent to movable property (Article 126 KZ). The illegal appropriation of computer capabilities, in this way, could amount to theft (Article 211 KZ), robbery (Article 213 KZ), misappropriation (Article 215 KZ), or embezzlement (Articles 245 and 263 KZ). Similarly, the term 'document' was defined from the very start to include any 'data carrier or other object appropriate and intended to produce evidence of any fact relevant to legal relations' (Article 126 KZ), thus allowing the application of the offence of counterfeiting in the realm of computer-related crime.

382. The Criminal Code of 1995 made no specific reference to content-related offences. However, the wording was broad enough to apply the wording of relevant provisions when responding to computer-related crime. For example, the offence of manufacturing and presenting pornographic materials extended to 'any acts that made pornographic material available' to a person under 14 years of age (Article 187 KZ).

383. Later amendments to the Criminal Code of 1995 resulted in the redrafting of the two integrity-related offences. In particular, Article 225 KZ was redrafted to include: (i) illegal entry into an information system (penalizing illegal interception of non-public data transfer within or from an information system) and (ii) the illegal manipulation and destruction of computer data, the illegal hindrance of data transfer, and the disruption of the system's functioning. The offence under Article 242 was renamed as the offence of intrusion into an information system and redrafted to penalize illegal entry into an information system in pursuit of economic activities with the aim of acquiring illegal proceeds or causing damage to others.

384. The Criminal Code of 2008 (*Kazenski zakonik* (KZ-1))[496] and subsequent developments show increasing awareness of the need to respond to computer-related crime. The number of offences that clearly envisage a computer-related dimension has grown significantly. For example, a computer-related dimension has been introduced or strengthened in provisions on:

- terrorism (Article 108 KZ-1);
- stalking (Article 134a KZ-1);
- the abuse of personal data (Article 143 KZ-1), which additionally penalizes the publication of personal data on the internet (in the case of victims of crime and protected witnesses);

496. Official Gazette of the Republic of Slovenia, No. 55/08, with subsequent amendments.

- the solicitation of persons under 15 years of age for sexual purposes, known as grooming (Article 173a KZ-1); and
- the presentation, manufacture, possession, and distribution of pornographic material (Article 176 KZ-1).

385. The integrity-related offences have been renamed. Article 221 KZ-1 now governs the offence of an attack on an information system, which essentially corresponds to illegal entry into an information system under KZ from 1995, with the added penalization of an attempt. The offence of the misuse of an information system (Article 237 KZ-1) corresponds to the previous intrusion into an information system.

386. The latest amendments of the KZ-1 have also responded to the need to redraft some of the criminal sanctions to make them more effective. In this way, the sentence of suspended probation may include an instruction for the perpetrator 'to observe a prohibition on establishing direct and indirect contacts with one or more specific persons, including the use of electronic means of communication' (Article 65 KZ-1). Article 71a KZ-1 introduced a new precautionary measure, the prohibition on communicating with the victim of a criminal offence, which includes a prohibition 'on establishing direct and indirect contacts or communicating with the victim or the victim's relatives, including by electronic means of communication'. The same restriction may be imposed in the case of conditional release (Article 88 KZ-1).

§2. Developments in the Field of Criminal Procedure Law

387. In the field of criminal procedure law, the need to adapt the text of the Criminal Procedure Act (*Zakon o kazenskem postopku* – ZKP) originated mostly from the need to provide a sufficient statutory basis for investigative measures and electronic evidence. The ZKP of 1995 did provide some basis for conducting covert investigative measures, such as the interception of electronic communication. These provisions were, however, struck down in 1997 by the Constitutional Court,[497] only to be replaced in 1998[498] by the solutions that are still largely in place today.

388. Soon, however, the need for additional solutions became evident. First, the gap in providing an adequate statutory basis for access to communications traffic data was recognized. The amendments to the ZKP in 2004[499] filled the gap by introducing Article 149b ZKP, which enabled access to communications traffic data and subscriber data. In 2007, the shortcomings of the previous arrangements were laid

497. Decision of the Constitutional Court of the Republic of Slovenia No. U-I-25/95, 27 Nov. 1997.
498. Act Amending the Criminal Procedure Act, Official Gazette of the Republic of Slovenia, No. 72/98.
499. Act Amending the Criminal Procedure Act, Official Gazette of the Republic of Slovenia, No. 43/04.

bare by the Supreme Court of the Republic of Slovenia.[500] The provision was later significantly expanded,[501] five years after the abolition of mandatory data retention in 2014.[502]

389. Second, the ZKP – until 2009 – did not provide any specific statutory basis for the search of electronic devices. Until 2009, the courts relied on the rules governing the use of experts in criminal procedure, while the police felt justified to browse the data on seized electronic devices without a specific statutory basis, relying on judicial authorizations for the search of premises or persons. No special provisions existed on for the preservation of electronic evidence. The amendments to the ZKP in 2009 were motivated by another decision by the Constitutional Court.[503] The court clearly refused to accept that the police may freely browse call logs and messages when they seize a cell phone. The court found that such actions amounted to a violation of the right to communication privacy. The legislature was required to provide a clear statutory framework that included the judicial authorization (or, alternatively, consent) to allow the inspection of electronic data. The 2009 amendments to the ZKP[504] also included provisions on the preservation of data stored on electronic devices, incorporating the basic principles of digital forensics.

390. The third gap was revealed in 2004, again due to an intervention of the Constitutional Court. In 2016, the court found that the ZKP does not sufficiently protect client-lawyer privilege.[505] The legislature responded in 2019[506] by introducing a sifting procedure that would prevent disproportionate processing of confidential data, either in the case of the interception of communications or in the case of inspecting electronic devices.

391. These developments in criminal procedure were mostly motivated by the need to secure compliance with the right to communications privacy. However, the need to provide adequate tools for combating serious cybercrime has not yet been met. Specifically, there is a great reluctance to introduce tools that may aid in overcoming encryption. With the exception of a legislative proposal of 2013,[507]

500. Decision and Judgment No. II Ips 473/2005, II Ips 474/2005, 10 Oct. 2007.
501. Act Amending the Criminal Procedure Act, Official Gazette of the Republic of Slovenia, No. 22/19.
502. Decision of the Constitutional Court of the Republic of Slovenia U-I-65/13, 3 Jul. 2014.
503. Decision of the Constitutional Court of the Republic of Slovenia No. Up-106/05, 2 Oct. 2008.
504. Act Amending the Criminal Procedure Act, Official Gazette of the Republic of Slovenia, No. 77/09.
505. Decision of the Constitutional Court of the Republic of Slovenia No. U-I-115/14-28, Up-218/14-45, 21 Jan. 2016.
506. Act Amending the Criminal Procedure Act, Official Gazette of the Republic of Slovenia, No. 22/19.
507. An attempt to introduce so-called interception at the source. Proposal of the Act Amending the Criminal Procedure Act No. EVA 2013-2030-0106. *See*: Opinion of the Slovenian DPO No. 007-57/2013, 12 Dec. 2013, available at https://www.ip-rs.si/fileadmin/user_upload/Pdf/pripombe/MP.pdf__novela_ZKP-M.pdf__dec_2013.pdf, accessed 14 Jul. 2022.

there have been no attempts to introduce a statutory basis for the use of software that would allow for the remote and covert inspection of devices, the surveillance of their users' activities, or the interception of encrypted communications.

Chapter 2. The Application of Substantive Criminal Law in the Area of ICT

§1. Evolution of the Legislation

392. We can *see* from the provisions of the European Council's 2001 Convention on Cybercrime (*the Budapest Convention*) and Directive 2013/40/EU on attacks against information systems, that the provisions on cybercrime law in the Criminal Code (*Kazenski zakonik* – KZ-1)[508] are scattered throughout various chapters.
'Real' cybercrimes include, in addition to the offences under Article 221 KZ-1, the provisions of the KZ-1 on:

(1) breaking into a computer-controlled database (Misuse of Personal Data, Article 143 KZ-1), where the legislature emphasized, through placement, the meaning of personal data before the ways they are compromised by breaking into a database;
(2) information system abuse (Article 237 KZ-1) by similar prohibited conduct in business operations and by causing an unlawful material benefit or damage to property; and
(3) the prohibited conduct of the manufacture, sale, putting to use, importation, exportation, or making available in any other manner, as well as the status of possession under property law, instruments intended for the intrusion or illegal access to an information system with the intention of committing a criminal offence (Manufacture and Acquisition of Weapons and Instruments Intended for the Commission of a Criminal Offence, paragraph 3 of Article 306 KZ-1).

393. A consequence of these scattered provisions is that descriptions of prohibited conduct in various offences in the KZ-1 are inconsistent, such as 'breaking in or entering without authorization' (Article 143), 'breaking in or illegal access' (Articles 221 and 306), and 'unauthorized use of a system' in Article 237 (while the latter is not included in the description of criminalization under Article 221).[509]

§2. Types of Offences

394. 'Real' cybercrime offences are, by the elimination test, those that would disappear if modern telecommunications networks and the internet stopped existing.

508. Official Gazette of the Republic of Slovenia, Nos. 50/12, 6/16, 54/15, 38/16, 27/17, 23/20, 91/20, 95/21, and 186/21.
509. The analysis is made regarding the original Slovenian version of the Criminal Code (KZ-1), which contains plural and singular verbs, while the officially translated version of the KZ-1 does not contain the relevant differences, e.g. the translated version uses plural *data* throughout the text, while the original uses both plural *data* and singular *datum*.

Such is the group of cybercrimes against the confidentiality, integrity, and availability of computer data and systems, i.e., confidentiality, integrity and availability (CIA) offences, which are criminalized under Article 221 KZ-1. Other cybercrimes include: (1) content-related cybercrime, which includes: (a) sexual content-related criminal offences, (b) violent content-related criminal offences, and (c) criminal offences related to violations of intellectual property rights; and (2) computer-related cybercrime, which includes various types of fraud and other (mainly) property offences, which have merely gained a new opportunity in the cybernetic 'space' and would exist without telecommunications networks and the internet.

I. Confidentiality, Integrity, and Availability Cybercrimes

A. *Attacks on Information Systems*

395. The criminalization of attacks on information systems (Article 221 KZ-1) covers the set of cybercrimes against the confidentiality, integrity, and availability of computer data and systems, i.e., CIA offences. The protected good is, namely, the security of the information system and data that are the object of attack in the form of compromising the confidentiality, integrity, or availability of computer data or an information system.

396. Historically, prohibited conduct under the Criminal Code (*Kazenski zakonik* from 1995 – KZ) (and its two amendments, the KZ-A and the KZ-B) and the KZ-1 (and its subsequent amendments) changed significantly, which is undoubtedly a consequence of attempts to manage the rapidly changing societal reality. The title of the provision also changed: 'Damage to Computer Data and Programmes' (Article 225 KZ, 1994), 'Unauthorized Access to a Secure Computer Database' (Article 225 KZ-A, 1999), 'Unauthorized Access to an Information System' (Article 225 KZ-B, 2004), and finally 'Attacks on Information Systems' (Article 221 KZ-1, 2008) (the differences between individual prohibited acts are described below). The term *attack* on an information system is a hypernym that combines all the various forms of prohibited conduct against an information system's confidentiality, integrity, and availability.

397. The prohibited conduct under *paragraph 1* of Article 221 KZ-1 has a tumultuous history. Under the *KZ* from 1995 was prohibited to 'illegally change, delete, or in any other way render useless data or programmes intended for computer processing or use' (paragraph 1 of Article 225), and only the *KZ-A* amendment criminalized 'illegal access' to another person's protected computer database for the purpose of becoming acquainted with any data. By the *KZ-B* amendment, the legislature kept the prohibited conduct of 'illegally accessing' an information system and added the newly prohibited conduct of 'illegally intercepting' data in paragraph 1 of Article 225. In the *KZ-1*, the legislature at first changed the prohibited conduct under paragraph 1 and removed 'illegal access' and added 'intrusion' into an information system (and kept the 'illegal interception of data') – paragraph

1 of Article 221. Apparently, it thought that 'mere'[510] illegal access is either the same as or less dangerous than intrusion and does not merit a criminal legal response. But the 2011 *KZ-1B* amendment once again restored the previously prohibited conduct of 'illegal access' and also kept the previously prohibited conduct of 'intrusion' into an information system – paragraph 1 of Article 221 KZ-1. Just 'mere' access was never criminalized.

398. The difference between illegal access and intrusion into an information system is that illegal access means gaining insight into an information system without right, whereas intrusion entails accessing by bypassing, disabling, and otherwise blocking security mechanisms or by violating an information system's security measures or by using technical means. Intrusion is therefore always without right. But to fulfil the elements of a criminal offence, access must also be without right. Where to search for the right to access?

399. In the KZ-1, the legislature uses the term *illegal*,[511] which primarily means to commit an act without right (Budapest Convention). The right to access can have various legal grounds. Illegal access is access that the perpetrator does not have permission for.

400. Access means accessing an information system or only part thereof. As the Explanatory Report to the European Council's Convention on Cybercrime explains, accessing part of a system does not also mean that this element will be fulfilled just by sending an electronic message to the system (point 46 of Article II). The question may arise whether such an interpretation is justified in cases of intentionally spamming with infected attachments (e.g., attachments containing ransomware, computer viruses and worms, spyware). But in such a case, the criminalization under paragraph 3 of Article 306 KZ-1 is applicable.

401. Accessing another system can be the result of ordinarily used communications protocols and programs, and in such case, we cannot say that the access was illegal. A typically misunderstood case is the installation of cookies and other similar programs, which are installed automatically on terminals and store data on the user's activities or gain access to data that are stored on the subscriber's or user's terminal (e.g.,, Flash cookies or Local Shared Objects, web beacons, bugs, or clear GIFs).[512] The Electronic Communications Act (hereinafter 'ZEKom-1') permits the technical retention of data or access thereto exclusively (paragraph 2 of Article 157 ZEKom-1):

510. As referred to by M. Šepec (2015), pp. 77–81.
511. Similarly, Art. 147 KZ-1 'illegal interference in another author's work', Art. 305 'illegally bearing the insignia of an official or member of the military', Art. 234 'illegal use of another's invention', Art. 136 'illegally search another or his objects', Art. 141 'illegal entry into another's apartment or closed premises' and Art. 186 'illegal production and trafficking of illicit drugs'.
512. Information Commissioner (2013).

(1) for the purpose of transmitting a message via an electronic communications network, or
(2) if this is strictly necessary to provide an information society service explicitly requested by the subscriber or user.

402. In these cases, not even the user's consent is required. But from a criminal legal standpoint, it is important that accessing an information system is technically illegal if there is no consent from the user or subscriber, which is a violation of the ZEKom-1, which allows for fines (Article 235 ZEKom-1). However, this is not a criminal offence; it is a violation of the rules of cookie installation, and is therefore a minor offence. That is why, in this context, the Explanatory Report to the European Council's Convention on Cybercrime states[513] that the application of specific technical tools that results in access does not automatically mean that the access is without right per se (point 48).

403. Similar *entry into* or *accessing an information system*, as with cookies, is done in many other activities in connected information systems, for example, the installation of another computer code, such as JavaScript, HTML, and an operating system or program fixes. If such access of a user's information system is seen as a common commercial practice and the use of standard protocols and programs (which only the court can decide on in specific cases), then the accessing of the information system is not *without right.* If the sectoral legislation demands the user's permission, as the ZEKom-1 does for the installation of cookies (Article 157), then, with the absence of consent, the elements of a minor offence are fulfilled, and not those of a criminal offence under Article 221 KZ-1, because it is a common operating or commercial practice (which was conducted incorrectly; hence, liability for a minor offence is triggered in accordance with the appropriate sectoral law).

404. There are possible exceptions defined by the Budapest Convention, which allows countries a wide margin of discretion by defining illegal access as punishable only if it is executed with additional elements:

(1) by violating security measures; or
(2) with the accompanying intent of the perpetrator to acquire computer data; or
(3) with some other dishonest intent of the perpetrator; or
(4) in relation to connected computer systems (this means that the state can exclude the criminalization of accessing unconnected computers).

405. A similar caution is expressed in Directive 2013/40/EU on attacks against information systems, which stipulates that Member States should criminalize illegal access only when it is executed: (1) by infringing a security measure and (2) in cases that are not minor (the diction of a 'minor' case should be understood in the sense of criminal policy in relation to point 11 of the preamble to the Directive).[514]

---

513. Point 48.
514. A case may be considered minor, for example, where the damage caused by the offence and/or the risk to public or private interests, such as to the integrity of a computer system or to computer data,

406. The Slovenian legislature decided to take up a more repressive stance with regard to this issue and criminalized (illegal) access to an information system itself and does not demand the existence of any additional (objective or subjective) circumstances.

407. In accordance with the general rules (paragraph 1 of Article 34 KZ-1), however, the attempt at illegal access or intrusion is not punishable. Nonetheless, the criminalization of *attempting to illegally access* an information system would be problematic because it is an attempt to execute an act which is in and of itself preparatory for other prohibited conduct under Article 221 KZ-1.

408. The criminal offence does not contain explicit references to other regulations; it is not a blanket norm. However, it does contain a few 'implicit' *blanket norms*, as some elements of the offence have to be interpreted through other regulations. Such are the terms, 'data' and 'information system'. In accordance with the Electronic Commerce and Electronic Signature Act (ZEPEP), electronic data are data that are formatted, stored, sent, received, or exchanged electronically (point 1 of Article 2); an information system is software, hardware, communications, and other equipment that operates independently or in a network and is intended for collecting, processing, distributing, using, and other forms of processing data in electronic form (point 11 of Article 2). The concept of the information system is thus in line with the concept of a 'computer system' in the Budapest Convention, under the subsequent explanation of this term, which was given by the explanatory Cybercrime Convention Committee in the 2006 guidelines. The concept of an information system is also in line with Directive 2013/40/EU on attacks against information systems.

409. The blanket provisions, in this case, are the provisions in the ZEKom-1 under which traffic data are any data processed for the purpose of the conveyance of a communication over an electronic communications network or for the purpose of its billing (point 45 of Article 3 ZEKom-1).

410. The term 'data' should be interpreted broadly, because the previous differentiation between ('more' important and protected) content data and ('less' important and protected) traffic data does not carry any contextual weight in the information society. Like content data, traffic data can also reveal (sensitive) personal data.[515]

---

or to the integrity, rights, or other interests of a person, is insignificant or is of such nature that the imposition of a criminal penalty within the legal threshold or the imposition of criminal liability is not necessary.

515. Sensitive personal data are data on racial, national or ethnic origin, political, religious or philosophical beliefs, trade union membership, health status, sexual life, the entry in or expungement from criminal records or records of minor offences that are kept on the basis of a statute that regulates minor offences (hereinafter: minor offence records); biometric characteristics are also sensitive personal data if their use makes it possible to identify an individual in connection with any of the aforementioned circumstances. From point 19 of Art. 6 of the Personal Data Protection Act (ZVOP-1).

The Constitutional Court of the Republic of Slovenia decided on the nature of traffic data in Judgment Up-106/05 from 2 October 2008 (point 8):

> The case law of the European Court of Human Rights (hereinafter referred to as ECHR) stipulates that information on telephone numbers dialled is considered an integral element of telephone communications [reference to the judgment in the case *Malone v. the United Kingdom*, dated 2 August 1984, A 82, point 84]. In the opinion of the ECHR, the release of that information to the police without the consent of the subscriber amounts to an interference with the right guaranteed by Article 8 of the Convention for the Protection of Human Rights and Fundamental Freedoms (Official Gazette RS, No. 33/94, IT, No. 7/94) [reference to the judgment in the case *Malone v. the United Kingdom*, point 84]. In view of the above-mentioned, the scope of the protection of communication privacy must be interpreted more broadly such that it also includes information on telephone calls, which are an integral element of communication. Data in the telephone memory record must be, considering their nature, regarded as an integral element of communication privacy. Therefore, obtaining data on the last dialled and last unanswered calls as well as the examination of the content of short text messages entail an examination of the content and circumstances of the communication and consequently an interference with the right determined by the first paragraph of Article 37 of the Constitution.

411. That is why the provision in question protects several types of data:

(1) the content of communications;
(2) traffic data and location data related to the communication referred to in the point above; and
(3) the facts and circumstances surrounding the termination of the connection or the connection not being established (compare with Article 147 ZEKom-1).

412. The primary good protected by the criminalization of Article 221 KZ-1 is the security of an *information system and data*, which covers the *accessibility*, *confidentiality*, and *integrity* of an information system and data (the prohibition of transfer, damage, deletion, degradation, changing, and obstruction). But there are more secondary interests that are protected by this criminalization. These include, for example, an individual's privacy, the protection of business secrets, the protection of intellectual property rights, the good and smooth functioning of information communications networks, and data transfer.

413. In terms of the possible perpetrator, an offence under Article 221 KZ-1 can be committed by anyone (*delictum commune*, *delictum non-proprium*). While the criminalization under paragraphs 1 and 2 of Article 221 KZ-1 is primarily dependent on active conduct, it can also be executed through *commission by omission*. In case of perpetration through commission by omission, the offence is *continuous* and has two points of completion: formal completion, where the perpetrator causes an unlawful state by the omission of due action, and material completion, when the unlawful state is terminated.

414. Communication privacy is directly protected by criminal law through the criminalization of a violation of the secrecy of means of communication (Article 139 KZ-1), which criminalizes the unlawful viewing of a message that is transferred through traditional means of communication (a letter, telegram, or any other closed document or consignment) (paragraph 1 of Article 139 KZ-1) or by telephone or some other electronic means of communication (point 2, paragraph 2 of Article 139 KZ-1). The criminalization under Article 221 KZ-1, however, refers to electronic data, i.e., the interception of data. The main difference between the offence under Article 139 and the offence under Article 221 KZ-1 is in this part then in line with the difference between information (a message) and data. The former refers to the general protection of communication privacy, while the latter refers to the confidentiality and integrity of electronic data. The criminalization under Article 139 KZ-1 protects messages (communication that is understandable by, or rather, intended for people), whereas the criminalization under Article 221 KZ-1 protects data transferred between machines.

415. The object of protection of the criminalization of *illegal interception* is the *confidentiality* of an information system, or rather the electronic data during non-public transfer to or from the information system. The protected good is *communication privacy*, as is defined by Article 8 of the European Convention on Human Rights and Article 37 of the Constitution of the Republic of Slovenia, by which this protection is expanded to all forms of electronic communications (telephone, fax, e-mail, the protocol for the transfer of hypertext, and graphic, audio, and other media content online, or the *HyperText Transfer Protocol* or http). *Historically***,** the act of 'illegally intercepting data' was added by an amendment to the Criminal Code (the KZ-B from 2004).

416. The KZ-1 uses merely the element '*interception*', without any further definition of the nature of interception. Under the Budapest Convention (Article 3 of the Convention and point 53 of the Explanatory Report to the Convention) and Directive 2013/40/EU (Article 6), the fundamental element of such criminalization is interception by *technical means*. The Slovenian legislature does not require the involvement of technical means, and in this regard, expands the scope of criminality – in terms of criminal policy, the consideration of the drafters of the Budapest Convention was precisely to criminalize only interception by technical means and thus prevent over-criminalization. Interception must refer to *non-public* transmissions of computer data, which refers to the nature of the communication process, and not the nature of the data transmitted. *The transmission of* (electronic) data differs from communication and is possible between devices, whereas communication occurs only between people.[516] Transmission means any direction that data travel in: to or from a computer system, or, with the diction of the referenced provision,

516. M. Šepec (2015), p. 101.

'transfer *to or from* the information system' (paragraph 1 of Article 221 KZ-1, emphasized by A. Z.). The significance of transfers *within* an information system is that it also protects data transferred between the central processing unit, on one side, and, for example, a screen or printer, on the other. Under Article 221 KZ-1, the interception of such data is not criminalized then, but only when data that 'travel' from the information system are intercepted.

417. Interception refers to *data*. The Slovenian legislature has (similarly as with illegal access, mentioned above) chosen a version that expands the scope of criminality and does not define additional elements of illegal interception. That is why this can be: 1. also executed by non-technical means, and 2. without additional elements defined by the Budapest Convention, namely (a) without the perpetrator's dishonest intent, or (b) in relation to connected computer systems (i.e., the state can also choose not to criminalize access to unconnected computers) (Article 3). From this standpoint, the Slovenian legislature did not transpose the provisions of the Convention consistently, which is why the criminalization under Article 221 is broader than the Convention demands. But compared to Directive 2013/40/EU, such criminalization is broader in one part (regarding 'technical' interception) and narrower in another, because interception 'within' a system is not criminalized.

418. Interception under international law includes the listening to, monitoring, or surveillance of the content of communications and the procuring of the content of data either *directly*, through access and use of information systems, or *indirectly*, through the use of electronic eavesdropping or tapping devices by technical means. The last case means intercepting data indirectly through the *electromagnetic radiation* of devices or electromagnetic emissions from an information system.[517] The KZ-1 does not have such expansions of the scope of criminality and limits this scope merely to direct interception. Interception must be *without right*.

419. An attempt to illegally intercept data is not punishable in line with general rules (paragraph 1 of Article 34 KZ-1). Under the Budapest Convention, an attempt can be punishable if such is the criminal policy of the legislature of the signatory State (paragraph 3 in conjunction with paragraph 2 of Article 11 of the Convention). The Slovenian legislature did not opt for criminalizing an attempt of this prohibited conduct, because it should, considering the low fine prescribed, explicitly define the punishability of the attempt.

420. The objects of protection under *paragraph 2 of Article 221* KZ-1 are the *integrity* and accessibility of an information system. *The relation between paragraphs 1 and 2* of Article 221 KZ-1 concretely means that, in case of illegal access, intrusion, or the interception of data without further manipulation thereof or an interference with the system or data (use, changing, transfer, deletion, adding, etc.), the perpetrator will commit an offence under paragraph 1. But if he or she *continues* to 'manipulate' the data, for instance by installing malicious computer code, he

517. For example, point 9 of the preamble to Directive 2013/40/EU on attacks against information systems.

or she will commit an offence under paragraph 2. This means that the conduct in paragraph 2 originates from (previously committed) conduct under paragraph 1, but can also be committed independently of the conduct under paragraph 1.

421. Paragraph 2 includes several alternative types of prohibited conduct. The prohibited conduct of illegal use, changing, reproduction, transmitting, and destroying data apply to *data integrity*.

422. When describing types of prohibited conduct, the KZ-1 uses *perfective* verbs, which means an offence is committed with a single action. However, an exception is made for data transfer, for which the KZ-1 uses imperfective verbs and criminalizes multiple instances of transferring data. In line with the legality principle, criminalization in this latter case needs to be interpreted as a cumulative offence, when one act does not suffice. Why the legislature used the imperfective form is unclear (whether it is a deliberate decision or a lapse), since the Budapest Convention uses the perfective form 'the transmitting' (in the sense of merely one transmission) of data (e.g., Article 5). We emphasize this for two reasons: first, there is no criminal offence if there is no subjective element present in the perpetrator that links the perpetrator's individual acts. Second, the use of perfective verbs causes the systemic incoherence of the KZ-1 despite the warnings of domestic as well as foreign criminal law theory that this use is inappropriate and obsolete. Similarly, the legislature used sometimes the plural form of *data* and sometimes singular *datum* in Article 221 KZ-1. This goes to show that it is very likely another legislative lapse.

423. All prohibited conduct in *paragraph 2 of Article 221* KZ-1 constitutes a *data and system interference* (Articles 4 and 5 of the Convention and Directive 2013/40/EU) (the Slovenian translation of the term *interference* is not consistent in KZ-1 as several Slovene words are used to translate this English term, which is confusing for practitioners).

424. Data interference under the KZ-1 incorporates five forms of conduct that only partly (in the first two types of prohibited conduct cited in Table 11) correspond to the prohibited forms of conduct in the Budapest Convention and Directive 2013/40/EU on attacks against information systems.

Table 11 Prohibited Forms of Conduct of Data Disruption or Data Interference

	KZ-1 2nd Paragraph (Article 221)	*Convention Data Interference (Article 4)*	*Directive 2013/40/EU Illegal Data Interference (Article 5)*
1	Destroys	Deletion	Deleting
2	Changes	Changing	Changing
3	–	Deterioration	Deteriorating
4	–	Damaging	Damaging

	KZ-12nd Paragraph (Article 221)	*Convention Data Interference (Article 4)*	*Directive 2013/40/EU Illegal Data Interference (Article 5)*
5	Uses	–	–
6	Transmits	–	–
7	Reproduces	–	–
8	Obstructs the transfer of data	Data interference	Rendering data inaccessible

Source: Author's own.

425. Deteriorating and *damaging* partially overlap in international acts. They refer to negative changes in the integrity or content of data and are included in the prohibited conduct of 'changing' data according to the criminalization under paragraph 2 of Article 221 KZ-1.

426. The question is why merely '*using*' and '*transmitting*' data in paragraph 2 of Article 221 KZ-1 are criminalized, since they expand the scope of criminality greatly compared to international acts.

427. Reproducing data in practical terms means to duplicate, copy, or multiply data, which expands the scope of criminality greatly. There is no equivalent term to be found in international acts.

428. The obstruction of data transfer only partly corresponds to the prohibited conduct of 'rendering data inaccessible' (Directive 2013/40/EU), as data transfer is a broader term than access.

429. Regarding data interference, the Convention allows Member States to reserve the right to criminalize an interference only if it results in 'serious harm'. Directive 2013/40/EU, on the contrary, binds Member States to also criminalize an *attempt at such,* which the KZ-1 transposes in paragraph 3 of Article 221. Here we have to emphasize that an offence in the part describing data transfer is a cumulative offence. But due to the incompatibility of the concepts of cumulative crime and an attempt, an attempt at this form of conduct is not possible and therefore not punishable, despite the provision of paragraph 3. Despite this, the KZ-1 is in line with Directive 2013/40/EU, because the latter does not require the criminalization of data transfer. An attempt at an offence under paragraph 4 of Article 221 KZ-1 is punishable according to the general rules on punishability.

430. The second part of paragraph 2 of Article 221 KZ-1 applies to the integrity and accessibility of an *information system* (also called 'computer sabotage').[518] This is an interference with the lawful use of an information system.

518. *See*: Council of Europe Recommendation No. R (89) 9 On Computer-Related Crime, 13 Sep. 1989.

431. Illegally *entering data* is a form of an interference with an information system‘s functioning, which has the peculiarity that accessing a single datum suffices (the provision of Article 221 KZ-1 uses the plural form for other prohibited conduct).

432. *Hindrance* (or *obstruction*) constitutes acts that disrupt an information system‘s normal functioning. Under the Convention, such an act can only be executed in six ways.[519] Only *serious* hindering should be criminalized, but the criminalization under paragraph 2 of Article 221 KZ-1 does not contain this additional condition, by which the Slovenian legislature expanded the scope of criminality greatly. Theory is critical of such a scope because an overlap with minor offences and collisions with legislation in the field of direct marketing by means of electronic communications (and consequentially the field of unwanted electronic messages and unsubscribed advertisements) may occur.

433. Because the scope of the criminalization of (any sort of) hindrance is too broad, *spamming* can be a criminal offence under paragraph 2 of Article 221 KZ-1, as well as a minor offence under two special laws (the Electronic Communications Act – ZEKom-1 and the Electronic Commerce on the Market Act – ZEPT) and the systemic law (the Personal Data Protection Act – ZVOP-1). Theory states that, *de lege ferenda,* it would be more appropriate to specify the prohibited conduct of *hindrance* not only according to severity, but to duration (continuous or temporary) and scope (partial or complete) as well. More specifically, hindrance then constitutes e-mail flooding or spamming, hindrance with a distributed denial-of-service (*DDoS attack)*, which involves the cooperation of several computers, or with computer viruses and worms, which slow down a system‘s functioning, etc.[520] Because the verb ‘to hinder’ does not have a perfective form in Slovene language, we have to determine, through teleological interpretation, whether a single act suffices to fulfil this prohibited conduct, which is why the crime in this part is not a cumulative offence.

434. From the set of forms of prohibited conduct that apply to information system interferences under the compared international acts (*see* Table 11), paragraph 2 of Article 221 KZ-1 defines only two forms of prohibited conduct: *entering data* into an information system and *hindering the functioning* of an information system. This changes the criminalizing focus: international acts on the criminalization of data and information system interference focus on the hindrance (or obstruction) of the functioning of an *information system* (under the Convention, ‘hindering’ a system; under Directive 2013/40/EU, ‘illegal system interference’), and the referenced provision focuses on *data.* In other words, the Slovenian legislature focused on data

519. Explanatory Report to the European Council’s Convention on Cybercrime, point 66.
520. The difference between a virus and a worm is that a virus requires the participation of a user who, through his or her normal use, triggers its operation and infects files, whereas a worm operates automatically.

interference, not on the hindrance of information systems. Which offence hindering the functioning of an information system constitutes is still to be determined by case law.

435. If data or information system interference (by the forms of prohibited conduct referred to in paragraph 2) causes *great damage,* this is a more serious form of a criminal offence (the more severe sentence of imprisonment for a term of three months to five years is prescribed). The term great damage means damage exceeding EUR 50,000 (point 3 of paragraph 3 of Article 99 KZ-1).

436. As a result, the scope of criminalization in the KZ-1 is broader compared to international documents. In the case of data *transfer*, this means that the KZ-1 expanded the scope of criminality, since data transfer suffices regardless of whether it seriously hinders or interrupts the functioning of an information system or if it even has any effect on a system at all. In the case of data *use*, this means that merely using such data suffices, regardless of whether this use also constitutes an information system interference.

437. The place of committing (locus delicti) a criminal offence under Article 221 KZ-1 is, under the general rules, the place where the perpetrator was acting or should have acted and the place where the unlawful consequence occurred (Article 19 KZ-1). Theory states that the 'location' of data is increasingly difficult to assess, e.g., due to the development of cloud computing. The inability to define the location of data will lead to traditional international legal aid, which is tied to the definition of 'location', i.e., where the cloud computing service provider is based.[521] How to reconceptualize the meaning of the 'location' of data, for example in determining jurisdiction, remains a major challenge.

438. The Convention does not explicitly define *criminal penalties*, while Directive 2013/40/EU on attacks against information systems sets the minimums of prison sentences, which are in some parts *higher* than those prescribed in the KZ-1 and KZ-1 does not comply with the Directive. For a criminal offence under Article 221 KZ-1, a prison sentence of up to one year is prescribed (paragraph 1), up to two years (paragraph 2), and for a term between three months and five years for the aggravated form by causing great damage (paragraph 4). Directive 2013/40/EU is stricter. For illegal data and system interference, for example (paragraph 2 of Article 221 KZ-1), the Directive prescribes a maximum term of imprisonment of at least five years (paragraph 4 of Article 9 of Directive 2013/40/EU) if the acts are committed as part of a *criminal organization*[522] and when committed against a *critical infrastructure* information system. General rules on the liability of members and

521. For more on this, *see*: UNODC, p. 216.

522. A criminal organization is defined by Framework Decision 2008/841/JHA as a structured association, established over a period of time, of more than two persons acting in concert with a view to committing offences which are punishable by the deprivation of liberty or a detention order of a maximum of at least four years or a more serious penalty, to obtain, directly or indirectly, a financial or other material benefit (point 1 of Art. 1). Structured association means an association that is

leaders of a criminal organization do not apply, because there is no serious punishment prescribed for this case (Article 41 KZ-1). Of particular importance is the protection of critical information infrastructure, which is not adequately covered by the provision of Article 221 KZ-1.

439. A legal person may also be liable for a criminal offence (Article 25 of the Law on the Liability of Legal Entities for Criminal Offences, Article 12 of the Budapest Convention, and Articles 10 and 11 of Directive 2013/40/EU on attacks against information systems). *The set of criminal sanctions against legal persons* is more diverse under Directive 2013/40/EU, e.g., it includes exclusion from the entitlement to public benefits or aid.

440. Concurrence of offences: When committing a criminal offence under Article 221 KZ-1, there can be a concurrence with some other criminal offences. In relation to the criminal offence of the abuse of personal data (paragraph 2 of Article 143 KZ-1), the criminalization in question is a general one, since the special paragraph 2 of Article 143 regulates unauthorized access to or intrusion into a computer-controlled database in order to obtain personal data (and not any other data); therefore, there is no concurrence. The criminal offence of information system abuse (Article 237 KZ-1) is special (*lex specialis*) in relation to Article 221 KZ-1, as it applies to economic business operations. There is a special relation to the criminal offence of the manufacture and acquisition of weapons and accessories intended for crime (paragraph 3 of Article 306 KZ-1): this entails the criminalization of preparatory acts and conditions (regarding possession, manufacture, sale, putting to use, import, export or other provision) related to malicious computer programs and devices. The problem with interpreting paragraph 3 of Article 306 KZ-1 can come to light when the case involves the manufacture (and other prohibited conduct and state of possession) of accessories that are not intended only for intrusion or illegal access, but also for other prohibited conduct under the provision in question. It seems that this is a legislative lapse, since the provision of Article 306 KZ-1 was not changed concurrently with the changes to Article 221, as the KZ-1 criminalizes prohibited conduct related to accessories intended only for illegal access and intrusion, and not, for instance, accessories for illegal data interception. The criminal offence in question is special in relation to the criminal offence of damage to another's object (Article 220 KZ-1). Similarly, the criminal offence of terrorism with the prohibited conduct of information system interference or data interference within the information system of critical infrastructure is special (*lex specialis*) in relation to the provision in question (indents 4 and 5 of paragraph 1 of Article 108).[523]

---

not randomly formed for the immediate commission of an offence, nor does it need to have formally defined roles for its members, continuity of its membership, or a developed structure (point 2 of Art. 1).

523. *See*: T-CY Guidance Note No. 11, from 15 Nov. 2016, on the aspects of terrorism included in the Budapest Convention.

B. Information System Abuse

441. The criminal offence of information system abuse (Article 237 KZ-1) is an economic and material offence, which is otherwise similar to the criminal offence of an attack on an information system under Article 221 KZ-1, but the criminal offence in question criminalizes only conduct in economic business operations with the intent of gaining an unlawful material benefit or causing damage to property (the perpetrator's intent is elevated to the constituent element of the crime in question). The normative construction of the criminal offence in question consists of a basic offence, which is criminalized under paragraph 1, and an aggravated criminal offence, which occurs when the act referred to in paragraph 1 has resulted in a large material benefit or a large loss of property, and is criminalized in paragraph 2.

442. Criminalization signifies a form of 'true' cybercrime and belongs to a special area of crime called cybercrime in the *narrower sense*: the protected good is the security of the information system and data that are attacked in the form of compromising either the *confidentiality* of computer data or an information system or their *integrity* or *accessibility*.

443. But at the same time, the criminal offence of information system abuse is classified as an economic criminal offence, so the protected legal good of the criminal offence in question is, in addition to the security of the information system, also the *property of the company* and thus indirectly the economic system.

444. A criminal offence under Article 237 KZ-1 pursues various objectives. The primary goods that are protected by the criminalization under Article 237 KZ-1 are an *information system and data* security, which includes the accessibility, confidentiality, and integrity of the information system and data (the prohibition of transfer, damage, deletion, deterioration, alteration, and obstruction), and *the assets of the company or the economic system*. Secondary goods protected by such criminalization are, for example, the individual's privacy, business secrets, intellectual property rights, the good and smooth functioning of information and communications networks and data transmission, etc.

445. The prohibited forms of conduct according to the criminalization under Article 237 KZ-1 are the same as with the criminal offence of an attack on an information system, which is criminalized under Article 221 KZ-1, but for such to be a criminal offence under Article 237, two additional conditions are required: 1. the perpetrator acts in the performance of business operations, and 2. the perpetrator has the specific intention of either procuring an unlawful material benefit for him- or herself or a third person or causing damage to the property of another.

446. In relation to the criminal offence of an attack on an information system referred to in Article 221 KZ-1, the criminal offence of information system abuse is a special (*lex specialis*) criminal offence.

447. A historical overview shows that the name of such offence has changed several times. During the validity of the KZ (1995), the offence was called intrusion into a computer system, while with the adoption of the KZ-1A this article was renamed 'Intrusion into Business Information Systems'. In addition to the amendments to the text of the article, by the KZ-1B the legislature also changed the article's name to 'Information System Abuse', which is unsuitable in terms of both the content of the criminalization and of the demarcation from the criminal offence of an attack on an information system under Article 221 KZ-1.

448. While the criminalization under Article 237 KZ-1 is primarily dependent on an action, it can also be executed through commission by omission. In the event of perpetration by commission by omission, the offence is *continuous* and has two points of completion: formal completion, where the perpetrator causes an unlawful state by the omission of due action, and material completion, when the unlawful state is terminated.

449. An analysis of the prohibited conduct demonstrates that it can be committed by anyone (*delictum proprium*), because it can only be executed by a person participating in economic business operations. The circle of possible perpetrators is therefore necessarily narrowed to persons who carry out this activity or participate therein.[524] Since the property of the perpetrator is a constitutive element of a criminal offence, it is a *true delictum proprium.*

450. Pursuant to point 9 of Article 25 of the Law on the Liability of Legal Entities for Criminal Offences (hereinafter: ZOPOKD),[525] a legal person may also be liable for a criminal offence (such a request is explicitly stipulated by international documents, namely Article 12 of the Budapest Convention and Articles 10 and 11 of the Directive on Attacks Against Information Systems). The range of criminal sanctions against legal persons is more diverse under the Directive, such as the exclusion from entitlement to state benefits or aid or the introduction of judicial review.

451. Article 237 KZ-1 criminalizes only illegal access, intrusion, or the use of an information system in 'economic business operations'. It is not controversial that the statutory element 'in economic business operations' can be regarded as a synonym for the statutory element 'in conducting economic activity'. Economic activity is defined in paragraph 10 of Article 99 KZ-1 as any activity carried out for payment on the market, and any activity carried out professionally or in an organized manner for an agreed or prescribed payment. Conducting an economic activity or economic business operations is defined in paragraph 11 of the same article as conducting, managing, decision-making, representation, running, and supervision as a part of an economic activity or the management of real estate, movable

524. Ljubljana High Court Judgment III Kp 6/2008 from 2 Apr. 2008.

525. Liability of Legal Persons for Criminal Offences Act (*Zakon o odgovornosti pravnih oseb za kazniva dejanja* – ZOPOKD), Official Gazette of the Republic of Slovenia, Nos. 98/04, 65/08, 57/12.

property, cash, income, receivables, capital investments, other forms of financial assets, and other assets of legal entities under public or private law, and the disposal of these assets and supervision over them.

452. The perpetrator's *intent* in the criminalization in question is an explicit statutory element of a criminal offence, which the legislature clearly expressed in the description of the offence ('Whoever, in the performance of business operations, without authority accesses or intrudes [...], in order to procure an unlawful material benefit for him- or herself or a third person or to cause damage to the property of another [...]'). The perpetrator of the criminal offence in question must therefore pursue the purpose of gaining an unlawful material benefit for him- or herself or a third person or to cause damage to the property of another.

453. Material benefit needs to be interpreted as any increase in assets or a net asset surplus, where it does not matter whether it is an increase of the perpetrator or another person, as long as there is a causal connection between the asset increase and the committed offence. Loss of property, on the other hand, is seen as any sort of decrease of assets or preventing an increase in the assets of the injured party that happens as a result of the perpetrator's prohibited conduct (Article 132 of the Obligations Code (*Obligacijski zakonik* – OZ)).

454. The criminal offence of information system abuse under Article 237 KZ-1 criminalizes all forms of conduct in a single paragraph, unlike the general criminal offence under Article 221 KZ-1, in which the legislature organized prohibited conduct differently according to whether such entails only acts that are essentially a preparatory phase of the prohibited conduct it criminalized in paragraph 2.

455. The difference between *illegal access* and *intrusion* into an information system is that illegal access means gaining insight into an information system without right, whereas intrusion is accessing by bypassing, disabling, and otherwise blocking security mechanisms or by infringing the information system's security measures or by using technical means. Intrusion is therefore always without right. But to fulfil the elements of a criminal offence, access must also be without right. So where to search for the right to access? The KZ-1 uses the term *illegal*,[526] which primarily means to commit an act without right (the Budapest Convention). The right to access can have various legal grounds. Illegal access is access that the perpetrator does not have permission for.

456. The relation to Article 306 KZ-1, in cases of intentionally spamming infected attachments with electronic messages, for example, attachments that contain ransomware, computer viruses and worms, spyware, and so on, the criminalization under paragraph 2 of Article 306 KZ-1 is applicable. By sending the

526. Similarly, Art. 147 KZ-1: 'illegal interference in another author's work', Art. 305 'illegally bearing the insignia of an official or member of the military', Art. 234 'illegal use of another's invention', Art. 136 'illegally search another or objects', Art. 141 'illegal entry into another's apartment or closed premises', and Art. 186 'illegal production and trafficking of illicit drugs'.

message, delivery was executed, but the perpetrator did not access another information system; running the infected attachment is done by the (scammed) victim itself.

457. It is interesting that the legislature criminalized accessing an information system without any additional elements in Article 221 KZ-1 and thus importantly expanded the scope of criminality in comparison with the Directive on Attacks Against Information Systems (the possibility of criminalizing the act if it is committed only in breach of a security measure, i.e., bypassing the obstacle, and in cases that are not minor) and the Budapest Convention (which stipulates that Member States can define illegal access as a criminal offence only if it is executed with additional elements). On the contrary, however, the legislature narrowed the scope of criminality, because in Article 237 KZ-1 it criminalized, in the performance of business operations, only illegal access to an information system, the purpose of which is procuring an unlawful material benefit for him- or herself or a third person or causing damage to the property of another.

458. The use of singular and plural presents again *inconsistencies*: regarding the criminalization in question, the legislature uses a singular and plural form, i.e., datum and data. Moreover, the perfective and imperfective forms of the verbs that define prohibited conduct are also used.[527] For example, in the prohibited conduct in the second part of paragraph 1 of Article 237 KZ-1 ('Whoever, in the performance of business operations [...] without authority inserts, alters, hides, deletes, or destroys any data or computer programme'), *perfective* verbal forms are used, which means that it is not a cumulative crime, except regarding data transfer, where the *imperfective* verbal form is used. In accordance with the legality principle, the criminalization of this form of conduct must be interpreted as cumulative, thus when one act does not suffice. In principle, a cumulative crime is not just an objective series of illegal activities combined into one crime. A subjective element that connects these illegal activities must also be demonstrated.[528] In cumulative crimes, it is important that the criminal offence is executed professionally or habitually, so that it is *a perpetrator's intentional activity*, consisting of repeated activities of the same sort.

459. All prohibited conduct from the second part of paragraph 1 of Article 237 KZ-1 (uses, changes, copies, transmits, destroys, enters, obstructs) constitutes data and system *interference* (Articles 4 and 5 of the Convention and Directive 2013/40/EU), or rather illegal *data and system interference* (the translation of Articles 4 and 5) (the Slovenian translation of the English term *interference* is *different* in the Convention and in Directive 2013/40/EU. The translation from the Directive, which we will be using below, is contextually more adequate.).

460. The question is why the mere *using* and *transmitting* of data are criminalized in Article 237 KZ-1, since they expand the scope of criminality compared to

527. While in English »conduct is a plural
528. Bavcon *et al.* (2014), p. 216.

international acts. The aim of criminalizing data disruption or an interference therewith under international acts is to provide computer data and computer programs with protection similar to that enjoyed by objects against the intentional infliction of damage.[529] But the prohibited forms of conduct of use and transmission under the referenced provision exceed this purpose. Transmission refers more to a form of system disruption (the transmission of data disrupts an information system's functioning), whereas mere data use protects against other forms of abuse.

461. The prohibited conduct of illegal data *entry, the obstruction of data transfer,* and *hindering an information system's functioning* under Article 237 KZ-1 apply to the integrity and accessibility of an *information system* (also called 'computer sabotage').[530] This is an interference with the lawful use of the information system. The interest of operators and users is protected, so that they may use computer capabilities or the capabilities of information systems without hindrance or interruption.

462. Under the Convention, this act can only be executed in six ways.[531] Only *serious* hindering should be criminalized, which means that the legislature should define: (1) the minimum amount of damage that the hindering (interruption) caused, or (2) a significant detrimental effect on the owner's or operator's ability to use the system or communicate with other systems.[532] The Slovenian legislature only partly respected the provisions of the Convention, because it determined the additional element of procuring an unlawful material benefit or causing damage to property (any sort of damage suffices, since the legislature did not define the minimum amount of damage that the criminal offence has to cause). Theory suggests that, *de lege ferenda,* it would be more appropriate to specify the prohibited conduct of *hindrance* not only according to severity, but to duration (continuous or temporary) and scope (partial or complete) as well.[533]

463. Article 237 KZ-1 defines only two prohibited forms of conduct from the arsenal of prohibited conduct that relate to *information system interference* under the compared international acts (*see* Table 11): *entering data* into the information system and *hindering the functioning* of the information system. This changes the focus of criminalization: international acts on the criminalization of data and information system interference focus on the hindrance (or obstruction) of the functioning of an *information system* (under the Convention, 'hindering' a system; under Directive 2013/40/EU, 'illegal system interference'), while the referenced provision generally focuses only on *data* (of all the prohibited conduct, only 'entering into a system' and 'hindering the functioning of a system' apply to systems). The consequence of this is a greater scope of criminality in the domestic regulation compared to international documents. In the case of data *transmission*, this means that the

---

529. Explanatory Report, point 60.
530. *See*: Council of Europe Recommendation No. R (89) 9 On Computer-Related Crime, 13 Sep. 1989.
531. Explanatory Report, point 66.
532. *Ibid.*, point 67.
533. *See*: *ibid.*, point 69.

KZ-1 expands the scope of criminality, because the transmission of data suffices regardless whether it seriously hinders or obstructs the functioning of an information system or whether it has any effect on the system at all. In the case of data *use*, this means that merely using such data suffices, regardless of whether it also constitutes an information system interference.

464. The object of protection of the offence of '*illegal interception*', which is criminalized in Article 237 KZ-1, is the *confidentiality* of an information system, or rather electronic data during non-public transfer to or from an information system. The protected good is *communication privacy*, as defined by Article 8 of the European Convention on Human Rights and Article 37 of the Constitution of the Republic of Slovenia.

465. Interception applies to data. The KZ-1 merely uses the element 'interception', without any further definition of the nature of the interception. Under the Budapest Convention[534] and the Directive,[535] the fundamental element of such criminalization is interception by *technical means*. The Slovenian legislature does not demand the involvement of technical means and in this regard expands the scope of criminality – in terms of criminal policy, the intent of the drafters of the Budapest Convention was precisely to criminalize only interception by technical means and thus to prevent over-criminalization.[536]

466. The transmission of (electronic) data differs from communication and may occur between devices, whereas communication only occurs between people.[537] As opposed to the usual interpretation of the term transmission, which signifies any direction that data travels in, transmission into, as well as out of, an information system (the legislature also accepted this meaning of transmission in the general criminalization under Article 221 KZ-1), the criminal offence in question is criminalized merely by 'entry *into* an information system'. The significance of transfers *within* an information system is that this also protects data transferred between the central processing unit, on one hand, and, for example, a screen, keyboard, or printer, on the other. The criminalization under Article 237 KZ-1 now does not contain the interception of such data.

467. A criminal offence under Article 237 KZ-1 can only be executed with *motivated intent* (*dolus coloratus*), as opposed to the general criminal offence under Article 221 KZ-1, which the perpetrator can also commit with conditional intent. It is precisely the perpetrator's intent that is the key characteristic of the crime. The perpetrator's intent must also include, in addition to the form of conduct, the intent to procure a (great) unlawful material benefit or to cause (great) damage to property.

534. Article 3 of the Convention and Explanatory Report, point 53.
535. Article 6 of the Directive on Attacks against Information Systems.
536. Explanatory Report, point 53 ('*The requirement of using technical means is a restrictive qualification to avoid over-criminalization.*').
537. M. Šepec (2015), p. 101.

468. The attempt at a criminal offence under Article 237 is punishable under the general rules of the KZ-1 due to the level of the sentence prescribed (*see* Article 34 KZ-1), except when the conduct is 'to transmit', so the part of the criminalization that is a cumulative crime, which cannot be punishable, as the concept of attempt is incompatible with the concept of a cumulative criminal offence.

469. We must emphasize that the criminalization of *attempting to illegally access* an information system is problematic because it is an attempt to execute an act that is in and of itself preparatory in relation to other prohibited conduct under Article 237 KZ-1.

470. The place of committing (*locus delicti*) a criminal offence under Article 237 KZ-1 is, under general rules, the place where the perpetrator was acting or should have acted and the place where the unlawful consequence occurred (Article 19 KZ-1). International documents do not regulate this separately; they only determine jurisdiction rules.[538]

471. Criminal sanctions for offences are not explicitly defined in the Convention, whereas the Directive on Attacks Against Information Systems defines the minimum of the prescribed terms of imprisonment, which the legislature considered only partly in the designation of criminal sanctions under Article 237 KZ-1. For the criminal offence under Article 237 KZ-1, the prescribed term of imprisonment is up to three years (paragraph 1) or up to five years for an aggravated offence with a great material benefit procured or great property damage caused (paragraph 2). The sanctions in Article 237 KZ-1 are partly inconsistent with the Directive in the part that applies to an illegal data or system interference (paragraph 2 of Article 221 KZ-1) and in which the Directive prescribes a maximum term of imprisonment of at least five years if the acts are committed as part of a *criminal organization*[539] and when they are committed against a *critical infrastructure* information system. A higher sentence is prescribed for an aggravated criminal offence that is criminalized under Article 237 KZ-1 only if the perpetrator's prohibited conduct has resulted in procuring a great material benefit or causing great property damage that is not in line with the regulation in the Directive, and, in particular, the maximum prescribed imprisonment sentence is up to five years, whereas the Directive prescribes a five year term of imprisonment as the minimum possible sentence.

472. It is especially problematic that the protection of critical infrastructure information systems is not adequately (more strictly) covered by the provision of Article 237 KZ-1. *Critical infrastructure* is generally understood as the Member States' capabilities or systems, or part thereof, that are essential for maintaining basic societal functions, health, security, protection, the economic or social wellbeing of people, such as electric power plants, traffic and government networks, the malfunction or destruction of which would have serious consequences in a Member

538. Article 22 of the Budapest Convention, Art. 12 of the Directive on Attacks against Information Systems.
539. A criminal organization is defined by Framework Decision 2008/841/JHA.

State due to the inability to maintain these functions.[540] An even more precise definition is provided by the NIS Directive, which does not mention 'critical infrastructure', but defines '*operators of essential services*'.

473. Concurrences: when committing a criminal offence under Article 237 KZ-1, there can be a concurrence with some other criminal offences. In relation to the criminal offence of an attack against an information system under Article 221 KZ-1, the criminal offence of information system abuse is a *special criminal offence* (*lex specialis*). Under the general principle that a specific rule overrides a general rule (*lex specialis derogat legi generali*), we are dealing with only one criminal offence (an apparent true concurrence),[541] even though the elements of both offences are met. There is also an apparent true concurrence in the relationship between the criminal offence of the manufacture and acquisition of weapons and instruments intended for the commission of a criminal offence under paragraph 3 of Article 306 KZ-1 and information system abuse. Paragraph 3 of Article 306 KZ-1 criminalizes preparatory acts and conditions (regarding possession, manufacture, sale, putting to use, import, export, or other provision) related to malicious computer programs and devices. If the criminal offence of information system abuse is committed or at least attempted with the instruments referred to in paragraph 3 of Article 306 KZ-1, the preceding phase loses its independence and becomes part of the committed offence (*lex primaria derogat legi subsidiariae*).[542]

474. In accordance with Article 25 of the Liability of Legal Persons for Criminal Offences Act (*Zakon o odgovornosti pravnih oseb za kazniva dejanja* – ZOPOKD), a legal person can also be liable for a criminal offence.

II. Content-Related Cybercrimes

A. *Grooming*

475. The offence 'Solicitation of persons under 15 years of age for sexual purposes' (Article 173a KZ-1) was added to the KZ-1 by the amendment KZ-1B (adopted 2 November 2011 and entered into force 15 May 2012).
It defines grooming as conduct comprising two elements:

(1) the intentional proposal or establishment of emotional contact between an adult and a child; and
(2) concrete acts that lead to the realization of sexual abuse.

540. Directive on Attacks against Information Systems (point 4 of the preamble) and Directive 2008/114/ES from 8 Dec. 2008 on the identification and designation of European critical infrastructures and the assessment of the need to improve their protection (point (a) of Art. 2).
541. Bavcon *et al.* (2014), p. 211.
542. Bavcon *et al.* (2014), p. 212.

The criminalization under Article 23 of the Lanzarote Convention includes the proposal of two criminal offences:

(1) sexual activities that constitute sexual abuse, which is analogous to the provisions of Article 173 KZ-1; and
(2) the production of child pornography (in the sense of the provision of Article 176 KZ-1), which is similar to the Slovenian offence under Article 173a KZ-1.

476. The object of protection of the criminalization under Article 173a KZ-1 is the *sexual integrity of a child*, which is protected by the aforementioned international criminalisations. All of these consider a child to be a human being under 18 years of age.[543] Because it is an *endangerment* crime, an *abstract risk* in relation to the protected interest suffices. The offence under Article 173a KZ-1 defines a child as someone under 15 years of age, which means that, for the demands of criminal law, a minor under this age limit is absolutely incapable of validly consenting to sexual intercourse or other sexual acts, regardless of his or her maturity or judgment. In this respect, the offence is in line with the age limit set for sexual self-determination in Article 173 KZ-1.

477. The question posed regarding the part of the description of the offence that reads 'and where this proposal has been followed by concrete acts leading to such a meeting' is whether this is an illicit consequence or an objective condition of criminality, and whether the perpetrator's relation also to subsequent concrete acts is required and assessed. Since the legislature does not have a clear approach to clearly indicate an objective condition of criminality, the answer must be sought with explanatory methods.

478. The Explanatory Report to the Lanzarote Convention[544] explains that the drafters felt that mere sexual chatting with a child, albeit as part of preparation of the child for sexual abuse, was insufficient in itself to incur criminal responsibility – a further element was needed. That is why the Lanzarote Convention requires contracting states to criminalize the wilful proposal of an adult to meet with a child with the intention of committing the criminal offences under the Convention. The proposal to meet with a child must be followed by concrete acts that lead to the meeting: this requires concrete actions, such as the fact of the perpetrator arriving at the meeting place (point 160 of the Explanatory Report to the Lanzarote Convention).

479. In light of the above, the justification for self-defence against this criminal offence is admissible under the general rules (of Article 22 KZ-1), despite the very unusual elements of criminalizing more forms of conduct and at the same time even the objective condition of criminality in the part stating 'and this proposal has been followed by concrete acts'.

---

543. Council of Europe (2007), p. 8.
544. Points 155–160.

480. The legislature defines a victim in Article 173a KZ-1 with the statutory element *person*. Considering communication by means of ICT, the question posed by this statutory element is the interpretation of *computer doubles*, also called digital avatars, which act as 'virtual victims' in communication in which no real person from a protected group is involved, since the perpetrator addresses a computer program.

481. Regarding a computer-generated persona (an avatar), the KZ-1 does not allow such an expansion of the statutory element 'person' to avatars as well. According to the linguistic interpretation, communication must take place with a person 'below 15 years of age'. Age only makes logical sense with a real person, not a virtual one. The solicitation of a digital double for sexual purposes constitutes an (inappropriate) attempt.

482. The term *grooming* generally means 'to prepare for a specific position or purpose'[545] or 'to prepare for a future role or function'.[546] There are difficulties with Slovenization of the term, which is done in several more or less adequate ways, e.g., it is also translated (into Slovenian) as 'zapeljevanje', i.e., 'seduction',[547] which is partially inappropriate as it is not seduction, but deception and manipulation in an interpersonal relationship, characterized by a significant disproportion of power and the psychological immaturity of one person.

483. The term 'solicitation of persons below fifteen years of age' that the Slovenian legislature chose in the title of grooming offence is not appropriate because of the use of the plural regarding victims, whereas the singular is used in the description of the offence, which should be changed to use the singular form in the title as well. In both cases, i.e., the title and the description, the imperfective verbal form is used, which, on this (linguistic) level raises the question of when a criminal offence is completed or the question of the crime being cumulative and consequently the possibility of violating the legality principle in the case of a one-time 'solicitation of a person below 15 years of age'.
The criminalization consists of two cumulatively defined *acts*:

(1) proposing through ICT to meet; and
(2) concrete acts that follow such proposal to meet (the objective condition of criminality).

484. The crime in question is *dependent on active conduct* and cannot be committed by omission due to the nature of the statutory element 'to propose'. The verb used for the prohibited conduct '*proposing*' has a perfective and an imperfective form. The legislature opted for the imperfective form, which raises the question of whether it is a cumulative crime. Since we know the perfective form ('to propose'), we could assume that one action does not suffice to fulfil this statutory element and

545. Oxford Dictionary, 1975.
546. *See* the table of definitions in N. Bennett and W. O'Donohue, p. 960.
547. N. Skvarča, 2015.

complete the act (assuming other statutory elements are fulfilled). But since an additional element needs to be fulfilled ('concrete acts that lead to the meeting'), we could, through an interpretation of intent, assume the opposite, i.e., that a one-time proposal is enough and that it is not a cumulative offence.

485. In terms of content, these are more than just general conversations, as the perpetrator's clearly evident intent that he or she wants to meet for the purpose of committing one of the two alternatively defined criminal offences has to be present, meaning: 1. to commit the criminal offence of sexual assault under paragraph 1 of Article 173 KZ-1, or 2. to produce pictures or audio-visual or other 'items of a pornographic or other sexual nature'.

486. The proposal must take place over *information and communications technologies* (ICT), which is why only this technologically mediated form of the solicitation of specifically aged children for sexual purposes is prohibited, but not also forms that take place without ICT, for example through personal contact only. This prohibition of only the ICT or online form of grooming is somewhat unusual because: 1. on a principled level, it disproportionately criminalizes conduct in the 'virtual' environment compared to equally vile conduct in the physical environment, and 2. it incriminates the relatively lesser endangerment of a child in the cyber form in relation to the 'traditional' (*off-line*) form, in which physical contact (meeting in person) has already taken place due to the nature of things, including communication, and the perpetrator's steps towards committing the criminal acts under Articles 173 and 176 KZ-1 can follow more quickly. The point of the provision in question is the criminalization of the independent preparatory act, which should prevent the sexual abuse of children more effectively. In this regard, it would be more consistent to criminalize virtual (through ICT) and physical solicitation of children for sexual purposes in equal measure, or neither of them.

487. The proposal to meet must be followed by (a cumulatively defined element) *concrete acts leading to a meeting*. These concrete acts are shown as an objective condition of criminality, which should block any criminality if such additional acts do not occur. What sort of concrete acts should follow that lead to a meeting is open to interpretation, but they must certainly materialize in social reality, so that they can be materially investigated and so that the meeting can really take place. The *plural* form ('acts') is used, which means that a single concrete act does not suffice for the meeting to be realized. This 'concreteness' means particularly the proposal or agreement on the time and place of the meeting. Surely this does not mean that the perpetrator and the victim should have already met in person or that they were already headed there (for instance, already on their way by bicycle), as this exceeds the purpose of the criminalization in question, which is to avert the sexual assault of a child or some other sexual abuse of a child.

488. The element of the criminal offence '*proposes a meeting for the purpose*' can be problematic because it ascribes some purpose to the meeting. The proposal will be provable if it is actively offered, which certainly will not be the rule, as proposing a meeting will only be able to be implicitly contained in an attempt to coax an invitation from the victim. The perpetrator's attempt to emotionally attach him- or herself to the victim or 'courting' and inducing sympathy in the victim will make proving this element difficult, as a situation may arise where the victim him- or herself invites the perpetrator to a meeting. In such cases it will have to be proven through other concrete acts that lead to a meeting, which will, along with the proposal, allow the construction of a complete picture of the facts, including motivated intent. The perpetrator's thoughts and motive typically do no suffice, but have to be provable by concrete facts.[548] Therefore, objective elements that are expressed clearly and express the perpetrator's intent are essential.

489. According to theory, an *attempt* should, in principle, not be possible in abstract endangerment crimes. In the case in question, an attempt would be conceptually possible if only the first element was fulfilled ('proposing to meet for the purpose', which would then not be followed by 'concrete acts that lead to a meeting'), which once again raises the question of the compatibility of the concept of an objective condition of criminality and the concept of attempt. But we do not have to deal with these dogmatically challenging questions on attempt, because even if the attempt was possible, it would not be punishable under the general rules on the punishability of an attempt due to the low penalty prescribed (*see* Article 34 KZ-1).

490. In the provision in question, the perpetrator must have the intent to commit either the criminal act under Article 173a or Article 176 KZ-1, which comprises 'to have sexual intercourse or perform any lewd act', where the question is how to interpret 'any lewd act'. The confusion with the descriptions of 'intercourse', 'sexual conduct', and 'any lewd act' in the KZ-1 is complete!

491. An attempt to commit a criminal offence under Article 173a KZ-1 is not possible (and would not be punishable due to the low sentence prescribed) nor is it an inappropriate attempt.

492. Direct motivated intent (*dolus directus coloratus*, i.e., intent characterized by a special intent or motive) for both of these elements of conduct must be present for *culpability* to be indicated. For the criminal offence to exist, the prosecutor will have to prove that the perpetrator was aware of his or her act and that he or she also wanted to commit it against a person under 15 years of age. Direct intent regarding a person's age means that the perpetrator was aware that he or she was talking to a person under 15 years of age. The intent to meet and make contact also has to be present. In doing so, he or she will have to have the (special) intention of committing one of two alternatively defined crimes (sexual assault or the production of items of a pornographic or other sexual nature), his or her actions will therefore have to be characterized by motivated intent (*dolus coloratus*). The intent has to be direct and motivated, i.e., to commit a subsequent act or acts. The intent (characterization) must be clearly expressed, otherwise we would be 'punishing a crime of the mind'.[549]

548. Skvarča 2015, p. 25.
549. Bavcon and Mozetič (2007), p. 187.

493. An offence is *common* in terms of the possible perpetrator (*delictum commune*), as it can be committed by anyone without any special characteristics, rights, or position.[550]
Under paragraph 2 of Article 173a, *illegality is excluded* if two conditions are cumulatively fulfilled:

(1) the act was committed for the realization of sexual assault on a person under 15 years of age (referred to in paragraph 1 of Article 173 KZ-1); and
(2) the act was committed with a person of comparable age and it corresponds to the mental and physical maturity of this person (referred to in paragraph 5 of Article 173 KZ-1).

494. In terms of criminal policy, the reason to exclude unlawfulness in paragraph 2 is sensible. It stipulates this in case if the act was committed with a person of comparable age and if it corresponds to the mental and physical maturity of this person (*see* Article 173a in relation to Article 173(5) KZ-1). This means that there is no criminal offence if the act was committed:

(1) with a person of comparable age; and
(2) it corresponds to the mental and physical maturity of this person (*see also* the commentary on Article 173 KZ-1).

495. Regarding the release of information from the *criminal record,* the criminal offence is included in the list of indelible offences. On the basis of a legally justified request by institutions or associations to which children or minors are entrusted to be educated, schooled, protected, or cared for, information on expunged convictions for the criminal offence in question is also released from the criminal record (compare with paragraph 2 of Article 84 KZ-1).

496. The sentence prescribed for grooming is a maximum of one year in prison. Considering the relevant international acts, this is the minimum. Directive 2011/93/EU, for instance, binds Member States to stipulate a maximum term of imprisonment of at least one year (point 1 of Article 6 of Directive 2011/93/EU of the European Parliament and of the Council of 13 December 2011 on combating the sexual abuse and sexual exploitation of children and child pornography).

B. Child Sexual Abuse Material ('Child Pornography')

497. The offence of the presentation, manufacture, possession, and distribution of pornographic material (Article 176 KZ-1) is intended to protect children from being exposed to others' sexuality and from child abuse by depiction in pornographic material. The criminal offence is part of a net of criminalization by which

550. Bavcon et al. (2014), pp. 110 and 199.

modern systems of sexual criminal law strive to protect children from sexuality.[551] Among the many forms of conduct in this 'net of criminalization' for the protection of children are the following, which are included in this provision:

(1) stricter protection of children from sexual conduct (a) through the abuse of position or dependence, and (b) a special form of sui generis criminalization of the abuse of the 'natural' dependence of children on older people (particularly parents);
(2) the criminalization of a child *being exposed* to pornographic material, including the criminalization of acts that constitute the concrete or abstract danger that a child will be enabled to be exposed to pornographic material;
(3) the criminalization of the prohibition of using a child for *depiction* in pornographic material or a similar pornographic activity;
(4) the criminalization of acts that can encourage the inclusion of a child in pornographic material or in a pornographic activity.

498. The Optional Protocol to the Convention on the Rights of the Child on the sale of children, child prostitution, and child pornography from the year 2000 defines child pornography as 'any representation, by whatever means, of a child engaged in real or simulated explicit sexual activities or any representation of the sexual parts of a child for primarily sexual purposes' (point c of Article 2). It demands that contracting States criminalize several prohibited forms of conduct: producing, distributing, disseminating, importing, exporting, offering, and selling child pornography, and it also demands the criminalization of the status of possession (point c of paragraph 1 of Article 3).

499. At the level of the European Union and the Council of Europe, a comprehensive body of rules has been created to protect children from sexual abuse, exploitation, and child sexual abuse material, and its core consists of the 2001 *Budapest Convention*, the 2007 *Lanzarote Convention*, and the 2011 *Directive on combating the sexual abuse and sexual exploitation of children and child pornography*. The Budapest Convention only included acts related to child sexual abuse material in 'content-related cybercrime',[552] whereas the newer acts expand the response of criminal law to *sexual abuse* and the *sexual exploitation of children.* The response of criminal law is also supplemented by the greater preventative activity and greater protection of those who have already become victims and their families.

---

551. If the sexual content depicts an adult and is published without his or her consent, the criminalization of the abuse of personal data under para. 6 of Art. 143 KZ-1 may apply.
552. Theory classifies three forms of content among content-related cybercrime that require intervention by criminal law: hate speech, infringements of intellectual property rights and sexual content (mainly material containing child abuse, in some jurisdictions also obscene material). Material containing instructions, etc., for committing criminal offences (such as the manufacture of weapons) can also be included in this group.

500. There are important differences between these international documents in:

(1) the definition of the term 'child';
(2) restrictions related to visual material;
(3) the exclusion of simulated sexual intercourse;
(4) the criminalization of prohibited conduct, for example, the vast majority of countries criminalize the production and distribution of child sexual abuse material, and there are greater differences between countries in the criminalization of access to such material; and
(5) the criminalization of the status of possession of child sexual abuse material under property law.[553]

1. The Prohibition of Exposing a Person under 15 Years of Age to Pornographic Material

501. The content of paragraph 1 of Article 176 KZ-1 protects the specifically defined group of people 'under 15 years of age' from being exposed to pornographic material. The criminal legislation of other European countries has a similarly designed criminalization, including the German criminal code (*Strafgesetzbuch* – StGB), the Swiss StGB, the Croatian, Serbian, and Spanish criminal codes, as well as the code of the Federation of Bosnia and Herzegovina, whereas the mentioned international legal acts that regulate the field of the protection of children from sexual abuse and exploitation do not have such criminalization. Theorists point out[554] that the criminalization of presenting and enabling access to pornographic material, regardless of the sexual motive (of the perpetrator), is so broad that it can even restrict sexual education. However, the *object protected* by the criminalization under paragraph 1 of Article 176 KZ-1 is the individual's freedom of choice as to when and how he or she will confront (others') sexuality as a reflection of the individual's right to sexual self-determination.[555] The criminalization protects only people under 15 years of age. This necessarily indicates the legislature's assumption (in terms of criminal policy) that minors under 15 years of age are harmed by any sort of exposure to pornographic material so seriously that it requires the state's strictest repressive response in the form of criminal sanctions, whereas the effect of such material on older, but still underage persons, does not require such a response.[556] This raises the question of the justification for such a strict response to the danger that exposure to pornographic material poses to the mental and moral development of persons under the age of fifteen. Modern

553. Comparative law analysis by the Expert Group, p. 6.
554. D. Korošec, p. 295.
555. *Ibid.*, p. 297.
556. *Ibid.*, pp. 305 and 306.

criminal law strives to criminalize empirically proven dangers, which is why criminalization without psychological and similar studies on the dangers posed to the development of an individual easily becomes merely a reflection of 'the legislature's ideological moralization'.[557]

502. The evolution of this provision is important in terms of the *age of the person* to whom the perpetrator enables access to pornographic material or presents a sexual or pornographic performance. The KZ (1995) determined the lower age of 14 years, which was in line with the provisions on the limitations of criminal liability regarding the age of the perpetrators. The provision on the limitation of criminal liability in the KZ-1 regarding the age of perpetrators remained the same, so that a person who commits an unlawful act under the age of 14 cannot be the perpetrator of a criminal act (Article 21 KZ1-1) – in a dogmatic context, the person does not have criminal capability (although, in terms of the essence of a crime and unlawfulness, he or she can commit a criminal offence), but the decision in terms of criminal policy was that the age limit of persons that possess (including other forms of conduct in the article in question) pornographic material must be raised to 15 years. This incoherence in the KZ-1 unusually indicates that a 14-year-old is regarded as already mentally and morally mature enough to be attributed responsibility for committing a criminal offence, but at the same time is not deemed to be mentally and morally mature enough for contact with pornographic material or sexual performances.

503. In relation to children as a special group that the legislature protects particularly strictly from (generally unwanted) sexual conduct, several questions arise regarding the sensibility (of the criminal policy) of such treatment and its congruence with ethical and constitutional norms. Part of dogmatic theory points out that the legislature's escalation of crimes according to the victim's age is ethically as well as legally problematic, and such escalations also act arbitrarily in the special part of the Slovenian Criminal Code (KZ-1).

504. Material, which is a statutory element of the provision in question, includes text formats (e.g., writings), image formats (e.g., photographs), and audiovisual material (e.g., films in various formats), or also just audio or visual material in various formats. The KZ-1 only lists the material as examples and adds the general clause 'other items', which is appropriate from the standpoint of including potential new formats. The KZ-1 does not define the statutory element *pornography*, but almost all similar systems of sexual criminal law accept that pornography is based on 'the depiction of sexual events in an exaggerated, drastic manner, without any sensible connection to other expressions of life'.[558]

505. The form of conduct of presenting sexual conduct '*equivalent to' sexual intercourse* importantly expands the prohibited material, as it expands it beyond pornography to the field of any sort of sexuality. This blurs conceptual edges, since

557. *Ibid.*, p. 307.
558. D. Korošec, p. 298.

pornography is already changeable as a concept in time and space, and a sexual performance can also be a performance without any nudity (e.g.,, a display window with artistic dancers in the physical world and their equivalent in an online environment). Here we also come across the clash with the regulation of occupations from the standard classification of occupations. Under the Decree on the Standard Classification of Occupations from 2008 (SKP-08), there are also, among other personal service workers, social escorts (No. 5162), which concretely means that merely enabling someone to see this legally recognized profession being exercised constitutes the commission of a criminal offence. Sexual performance, however, means that a static exhibition of sexual objects, such as accessories or clothing, does not suffice, but the question is how to interpret the performance of the cited occupational structures. Can such be performed, for example, on the street or in a bar, or can such just be dancing in a display window or a specific manner of walking? Theory points out that the legislature should consider removing the mention of sexual performance.

506. The fundamental *methods of committing* a criminal offence under paragraph 1 of Article 176 KZ-1 include selling, presenting, publicly exhibiting, and enabling access in any other manner to items of a pornographic nature and presenting pornographic and sexual performances.

507. *Enabling access* to pornographic material is deemed to be enabling sensory perception thereof through sight and hearing.[559] Describing the form of conduct '*enabling access in any other way*' with a general clause and analogy *intra legem* is a very appropriate way to include new forms emerging online and in other information society services. This includes, for example, enabling through websites (the World Wide Web), e-mail, online social networks (such as Facebook), audiovisual content-sharing platforms (such as Pinterest and YouTube, especially payable channels), the darknet, or internet 'remote access' (e.g.,, internet telephony, meaning *Voice-over-IP* – VoIP).

508. The range of places where minors are exposed to pornographic material and can access it freely has expanded greatly with the development of modern technologies. Modern sexual criminal law responded by developing security standards on the efficiency of technological obstacles in computer networks and signal distribution systems (cable television). A provider of cable television is required to develop and guarantee an adequately efficient system for personally checking the legal age of contractual partners e.g.,, personally handing a verified adult a decoder card or personal identification number that enables access to pornographic content). Merely encoding a pornographic program is not enough for the provider to be relieved of criminal liability for enabling minors' access to pornographic content.[560] A content provider in a computer network is also criminally liable if it does not

559. D. Korošec, p. 300; and UNODC, p. 101.
560. *Ibid.*, p. 301.

demand the personal verification of users' legal age for access to pornographic content, regardless of whether the user only accesses pornographic content (the user only views an image, reads a text, or listens to audio) or also downloads a file containing pornographic content.

509. Access providers and administrators of *proxy-cache* servers, browsers, or host service providers and other providers of similar services are not, in themselves, criminally liable for enabling a minor access to pornographic content.[561] But the question of how much criminal liability the providers of all 'information society services' – in the sense of the definitions of the Electronic Commerce on the Market Act (ZEPT), which implemented Directive 2000/31/EC on electronic commerce – should also have, has not yet been properly resolved in case law and theory. Directive 2000/31/EC and the ZEPT differentiate three categories of *intermediary service providers*: 1. mere conduit service providers, 2. caching service providers, and 3. host service providers (Articles 12, 13, and 14 of Directive 2000/31/EC). The field of civil law[562] is unanimous in that the first two are not liable (for damages) for content, as they have no control over the transmitted content, but the question of how liable (for damages) host service providers should be for illegal content (not only child sexual abuse material, but also hate speech, pirated content, etc.) remains open. Host service providers store data or enable third parties access and can exculpate themselves if they have no knowledge of the content or if they remove the content or disable access to it immediately upon obtaining knowledge thereof (*notice and takedown*).[563]

510. Theory points out that that the taxonomy of the activities of internet intermediation that Directive 2000/31/EC established is no longer entirely appropriate, since the services of the so-called Web 2.0 or user-created content did not yet exist at the time of its making.[564] The line between online host service providers and content providers (their responsibility for content is not limited) is becoming blurred. Attributing responsibility to the providers of Web 2.0 is evidenced by the EU Code of Conduct on countering illegal hate speech online from 31 May 2016, signed by the European Commission and the four largest providers (Facebook, Twitter, YouTube, and Microsoft).

511. The service provider's *guarantor duties*, including the guarantor duty due to having authority over the source of the danger, are unanimously recognized in modern sexual criminal law. A service provider that is aware of the existence of illegal content and remains passive, where direct intent (*dolus directus*) is demanded for its passivity, has the technical capabilities to act in a given moment, and can also be reasonably expected to do so, is criminally liable for complicity by omission for

561. *Ibid.*, pp. 303–304.
562. *See, e.g.*, M. Damjan, p. 22; and Š. Mežnar (2014), p. 43.
563. M. Damjan, pp. 21–22.
564. Web 2.0 includes collaborative projects (e.g. Wikipedia), online diaries (blogs), multimedia sharing websites (e.g. YouTube and Picasa), online social networks (e.g. Facebook), virtual social worlds (e.g. Second Life), and virtual game worlds (e.g. World of Warcraft).

enabling a child access to pornographic material.[565] Enabling access can, in addition to complicity, also include forms of conduct of commission by omission.[566]

512. Broadcasting content in real time (live streams) is a special issue that the criminal law of some foreign countries cannot cover in the context of traditional pornographic criminalization. But the criminalization under paragraph 1 of Article 176 KZ-1 is set broadly enough to include the prohibition of presenting or enabling a minor access to pornographic content that is broadcast in real time.

513. *An attempt* at a criminal offence under paragraph 1 of Article 176 KZ-1 is not punishable under the general rules of the KZ-1 due to the low sentence prescribed (*see* Article 34 KZ-1).

2. The Prohibition of Using a Child for Depiction in Pornographic Material

514. All modern systems of criminal law now criminalize using a child for depiction in pornographic material, as well as many broadly covered preparatory actions (proposing or inciting, soliciting, or encouraging a minor to produce pornographic material), and even more distanced supportive prior preparatory actions and the status of possession of such material as defined under property law.

515. By criminalizing child sexual abuse material, criminal law protects children from abuse. There are several arguments that explain abuse: (1) a psychological-developmental argument based on insights into a child's emotional and cognitive immaturity; (2) the argument of equal treatment that a child is considered incapable of giving free and reasonable consent in many relationships and that therefore this should also apply to the ability to consent to sexual intercourse; (3) the ethical argument that a child, as a sexually immature being in these relationships, is only a means of fulfilling the desires of another and we therefore cannot speak of reciprocity.

516. But the production of 'virtual' child pornography, as opposed to 'real' child pornography, is no longer tied to the abuse of an actual child, and the literature provides additional arguments to justify criminalizing the virtual version. Fictitious depictions of children, however, are not a novelty, since art history is full of drawings, statues, murals, and other depictions of boys and girls (e.g., the god Cupid). But previous depictions differ from modern digital depictions at least in that digital material can no longer be differentiated from material that was made by abusing an actual child. The legal nature of the goods in this crime is relatively poorly researched in Slovenian criminal law, as well as in criminal law theory and case law.

565. D. Korošec, p. 304.
566. *Ibid.*, p. 305.

517. The term *child pornography* is not defined in the KZ-1., Its content must therefore be filled in by case law, while taking into account the definitions contained in international documents. The doctrine on child abuse emphasizes that the naming thereof is inappropriate and should be replaced with the terms 'child sexual abuse material – CSAM' or 'child sexual exploitation material – CSEM'.[567]

518. In a broader sense, child sexual abuse material that is shared or forwarded on the internet covers several forms:

> *material ('real') child pornography*, which clearly and unambiguously communicates the committed act of abuse that an actual child was part of;
> *provocative depictions of children* that appear on the internet in the form of child beauty pageants and non-nude child sites and are generally not prohibited by criminal law;
> *cyber ('virtual') child pornography*, which does not show an actual (real) person, but three kinds of computer-generated images: (a) depictions that exist independent of cyberspace, which merely serves as a medium for new publications (for example, digitized drawings on paper), (b) digitally manipulated material, which, through the use of computer programs, enables the recombination of photographs of actual people that are altered to an extent that makes it impossible to determine who the person is, and (c) computer-generated material (so-called pseudo-photography), where the production of controversial material is no longer tied to the photography and digital manipulation of photographs of actual children; instead, the material is entirely produced using digital imaging techniques.

519. Acquiring, producing, distributing, selling, importing, exporting, providing, gaining access to *all forms of virtual child pornography*, and possessing it (as a status under property law) are covered by the legislature by the statutory element 'pornographic or other sexual material depicting *realistic images of minors*'. This includes computer-simulated images, i.e., realistic images of non-existent children (collages or entirely imaginary images). As opposed to some other foreign systems of sexual criminal law (such as the regulations under the German StGB), the KZ-1 does not criminalize conduct related to pornographic material that contains a real person who may look like a child but is de facto above 18 years of age.

520. *Material* that is part of the forms of conduct referred to in paragraph 2 of Article 176 KZ-1 includes image formats (such as photographs), various forms of audiovisual material (such as films), or even just audio (e.g., audio recordings of 'hotlines'), or just visual material, since the legislature only lists the forms of conduct as examples and quite appropriately adds the general clause 'other items'. As opposed to paragraph 1 of the article in question, part of the forms of conduct in paragraphs 2 and 3 are not only items of a pornographic nature, but also *items of any other sexual nature*. The forms of conduct of participating and being present in

567. T. Krone and R. G. Smith, p. 2.

a pornographic or other sexual performance are also criminalized, which importantly expands criminalization to more indirectly involved persons. There is a special emphasis on the person knowingly being present, which constitutes motivated intent (*dolus coloratus*).

521. The term *pornographic performance* is defined in Article 2 of Directive 2011/93/EU on combating the sexual abuse and sexual exploitation of children and child pornography. We interpret the statutory element 'pornographic performance', which the legislature used in Article 176 KZ-1, in accordance with this provision.

522. The legislature described a victim in paragraphs 2 and 3 of Article 176 KZ-1 with the statutory element *minor*. This means that criminal law protects all persons who are *tempore criminis* under 18 years of age. Although Directive 2011/93/EU allows Member States the discretion to decide whether to criminalize pornographic or sexual material or a pornographic performance that includes *consensual sexual intercourse between minors* that have already reached the age of sexual consent (or between peers who are close in age and degree of psychological and physical development or maturity) (Article 8), while taking into account a few additional conditions, the legislature did not choose this option, which can, in practice, cause a number of problems. According to the provision of Article 173 KZ-1, a person who has reached the age of 15 may validly consent to sexual conduct, but cannot validly consent to participation in pornographic or other sexual material or a pornographic or other sexual performance until the age of 18. The question arises as to how to treat minors who record or take pictures of their sexual intercourse or send sexually explicit pictures and videos to their partner by means of information technology (*sexting*).

523. *Paragraph 2* of Article 176 KZ-1 is about inciting, soliciting, or encouraging a minor to: 1. *produce items* of a pornographic or other sexual nature, or 2. to *participate* in a pornographic or other sexual *performance*.

524. The possible intents of the perpetrator, i.e., producing items and participating in a performance, relate to three forms of conduct: (1) *inciting*, which linguistically means to direct, urge, or persuade someone (to commit a criminal offence); (2) *soliciting*, and (3) *encouraging*. All three of these forms of conduct must be executed in a specific way:

(a) by force, threat, or deception;
(b) by exceeding or abusing powers;
(c) by recruitment or solicitation; or
(d) for the purpose of exploitation.

525. The forms of conduct under paragraph 2 of Article 176 KZ-1 also include *being present* in a pornographic or other sexual performance that includes minors (this must be done 'knowingly', i.e., the perpetrator must be aware that he or she is present for this).

526. The perpetrator of the criminal offence under paragraph 2 of Article 176 KZ-1 is responsible for *producing* pornographic material or merely *participating in* or merely *being present* (attending) at a (pornographic or other sexual) performance. If, at the same time, the perpetrator also knowingly participated in sexual intercourse or other sexual acts in the sense of rape (Article 170 KZ-1) or sexual violence (Article 171 KZ-1), then the perpetrator is also liable for *participating* in other crimes against sexual integrity.

527. The forms of conduct of the criminal offence under paragraph 3 of Article 176 KZ-1 include:

(1) *acquiring, producing, distributing, selling, importing, exporting, or supplying in any other way* pornographic or other sexual material depicting minors or their realistic images;
(2) *gaining access* to such material through information or communications technologies; and
(3) *disclosing* the identity of a minor in such material.

528. Paragraph 3 also criminalizes the *possession* of such material. The possession of material constitutes exercising sheer actual power over a thing (the objective conception of possession), where no specific purpose or attitude to the thing is required. From this standpoint it is very inappropriate for criminal law, as it criminalizes such status, which expands the scope of punishability excessively. The essence of criminal law is precisely the accusation of the prohibited conduct, which can be commission or omission, which fails when mere possession is criminalized.

529. A user can possess material without being aware of this (for example, in a computer's cache memory). In some jurisdictions, case law has determined that a user only possesses material if he or she is aware thereof or should be aware thereof, where the subjective level of the user's computer skills is taken into account.[568] Conduct related to digital material that is accessible only through the internet or other information society services will be harder to define in practice. A user can *provide* material in several ways and must be aware of this, for example by joining a P2P (*peer to peer*) networking architecture. Theory points out that, therefore, the question of the user's knowledge on how a P2P network works is essential.

530. Regarding *production and manufacture*, subsequent international acts foresaw exceptions that do not constitute the danger of child abuse (e.g., imaginary depictions for one's own use without the risk of distribution). Older international acts do not criminalize *viewing* without the possession of material (e.g., the 2001 Budapest Convention), whereas newer acts (e.g., Directive 2011/93/EU on combating the sexual abuse and sexual exploitation of children and child pornography) also prohibit *accessing* and *viewing* such material and thereby avoid the difficult issue of determining the existence of the possession of the material. In this regard, the KZ-1

568. M. Ambrož, 2007.

was amended accordingly with the element of conduct that results in *gaining access* to such material. From the standpoint of the integrity of the criminalization, this prohibited conduct therefore filled an important gap in the net of criminalization, since there are technological ways of viewing material that do not necessarily also include possession, such as *on-demand live streaming*.

531. The case of viewing sexual acts via webcam (*webcam sex*) is similar, as the image is streamed in real time and the data is not stored on the local device. Although this is a relatively new phenomenon and criminal law does not (yet) know any special instances of criminalization that would apply precisely to child webcam sex, such conduct is, however, punishable in most countries under the criminalization that prohibits child pornography,[569] more precisely, as the prohibited conduct of accessing material, in the case of past recordings (paragraph 3 of Article 176 KZ-1), or as the prohibited conduct of attending a performance, in the case of live streams of child webcam sex (paragraph 2 of Article 176 KZ-1). Two positions are possible regarding the role of the perpetrator in sexual activities via webcam:

(1) if the perpetrator *him- or herself* incited, solicited, or encouraged a minor (a person under 15 years of age) to *participate* in an online pornographic or other sexual performance or for the *production* of pornographic or other sexual material him- or herself, he or she is liable under paragraph 2 of Article 176;
(2) but if such a meeting was organized by *another* person who provided users access to such a performance, the perpetrator, as a user or viewer, committed a criminal offence under paragraph 3 of Article 176 KZ-1, and the persons that organized the meeting (for example, typically parents of the children, for a fee) committed the criminal offence of distributing or providing material (also under paragraph 3 of Article 176). Both the production and consumption of such pornographic presentations are criminalized.

532. Paragraph 4 criminalizes *aggravated cases*, if the criminal offences under paragraphs 2 or 3 were committed within a criminal organization for committing such criminal offences. All of the provisions of the general part of the KZ-1 that apply to criminal organizations are therefore particularly relevant in relation to paragraph 4 of Article 176 KZ-1 (especially Article 41 KZ-1, as well as Article 77a KZ-1). A criminal organization is defined in paragraph 1 of Article 41 KZ-1 (somewhat logically twisted) as ‘an organization of at least three persons’.

533. The offence as stipulated in paragraphs 2, 3, and 4 of Article 176 KZ-1 must be committed with *intent*, be it direct or conditional, which follows the international acts. But the perpetrator is required to have direct intent for the prohibited conduct in paragraph 4, as it is impossible to participate in a criminal organization

569. B. W. Schermer, I. Georgieva, S. Van der Hof, and B.-J. Koops, pp. 18 and 19.

with conditional intent. Conditional intent also does not suffice for the criminalization covered by the form of conduct in paragraph 2, which contains the term *knowingly* (being knowingly present in a pornographic or other sexual performance depicting a minor); this case also requires direct intent.

534. *The attempt* to commit an intentional criminal offence under paragraphs 2, 3 (except in the criminalization of the status of possession under property law), and 4 is punishable under the general rules of the KZ-1, since it is a criminal offence for which a term of imprisonment of three years or more can be imposed.

535. Regarding attempted possession of child sexual abuse material, we must emphasize that merely downloading such material for the purpose of viewing it without the intent to permanently store it does not suffice. For theorists who wish to regard possession as conduct (which is certainly controversial, at least from the standpoint of the classical theory of the multi-part general concept of a criminal offence) and therefore also wish to see the possibility of attempted possession, it is generally enough for the beginning of an attempt to possess pornographic material if the perpetrator downloads a file onto his or her computer with the intent of deciding whether to permanently store it only after viewing the material.[570] The problem of determining possession could be avoided by regarding the transfer of the material onto one's own terminal device as a form of dissemination (and not possession). Such an interpretation seems particularly appropriate as regards downloading or possessing material by joining a P2P network (possession generally corresponds to dissemination). An attempt to attend or participate in a pornographic or sexual performance begins when a person expresses the wish to participate or be present. The question as to when an attempt is completed arises particularly in relation to the dissemination of child pornography. Dissemination is completed when a file containing pornographic content reaches a computer (or other electronic device that allows storage, for example a tablet computer or smartphone), regardless of whether the user opened the file or not.[571] In some forms of conduct entailing a criminal offence under paragraph 3 of Article 176 KZ-1, we can regard the attempt itself as a completed criminal offence (providing child pornography, encouraging a minor to produce pornographic material or to participate in a pornographic or sexual performance).

536. Conceptually, in the case of a criminal offence under paragraphs 2, 3, and 4 of Article 176 KZ-1, an *inappropriate attempt* is also possible, for example if the perpetrator of the criminal offence falsely believes that the person is under 18 years of age, but is actually older.[572] In such case, the perpetrator may be acquitted. In the opposite case, however, when the perpetrator of a criminal offence falsely believes

570. D. Korošec, p. 309.
571. *Ibid.*, p. 308.
572. *Ibid.*, p. 327.

that the person is over 18 years of age but is in reality still a minor (misconception as to the actual age of the person), this constitutes a *mistake of fact,* which excludes intent.[573]

537. An offence under Article 176 KZ-1 is *common* in terms of the possible perpetrator (*delictum commune*), as it can be committed by anyone without any special characteristics, rights, or position.[574] As opposed to the criminalization of child pornography in the German StGB, which explicitly excludes the possession of child pornography by researchers, defence counsels, police officers, experts, etc., from the essence of the criminalization, the KZ-1 does not have such an exclusion.

538. The forms of criminalization under Article 176 KZ-1 are included in the list of *indelible* criminal offences. On the basis of a legally justified request by institutions or associations to which children or minors are entrusted to be educated, schooled, protected, or cared for, information on expunged convictions for the criminal offence in question is also released from the criminal record (Article 84 KZ-1). This is in line with Article 10 of Directive 2011/93/EU on combating the sexual abuse and sexual exploitation of children and child pornography.

539. The prescribed penalty for a criminal offence under paragraph 1 of Article 176 KZ-1 is a fine or a prison sentence of up to two years, whereas a prison sentence of six months to eight years is prescribed for the offences under paragraphs 2 and 3. And if a criminal offence is committed within a criminal organization for committing such criminal offences, the minimum sentence prescribed is one year in prison. The penalties determined by Article 176 KZ-1 are lower than those set in Directive 2011/93/EU on combating the sexual abuse and sexual exploitation of children and child pornography.

540. The KZ-1 also stipulates that material depicting the sexual exploitation of a child (the KZ-1 speaks of pornographic or other sexual material) referred to in paragraphs 2, 3, and 4 of Article 176 shall be seized or its use appropriately disabled. The security measure of disabling use is subsidiary and applicable only in cases where the seizure of the object is not possible due to the nature of the object itself.

541. In accordance with Article 90 KZ-1, criminal prosecution for a criminal offence under paragraph 1 of Article 176 is barred after ten years and after twenty years for criminal offences under paragraphs 2, 3, and 4.

542. In accordance with Article 25 of the Liability of Legal Persons for Criminal Offences Act (ZOPOKD), a legal person can also be liable for a criminal offence.

573. Korošec, p. 327.
574. Bavcon *et al.* (2014), pp. 110 and 199.

Chapter 3. The Application of Criminal Procedure Law in the Area of ICT

§1. Jurisdiction

543. The jurisdiction of Slovenian law enforcement bodies (jurisdiction to enforce) follows the rules on the territorial application of substantive criminal law (jurisdiction to prescribe). These are determined in Articles 12 and 13 KZ-1. In addition to the territorial principle, the following also apply:

- the passive nationality principle, providing for jurisdiction to prosecute perpetrators of offences committed abroad against Slovenian nationals;
- the active nationality principle, providing for jurisdiction to prosecute Slovenian nationals for offences committed abroad; and
- the principle of universal jurisdiction, providing for jurisdiction to prosecute foreign nationals for offences committed abroad.

The latter, in particular, follows the principle *aut dedere aut iudicare* and the principle of the identity of criminal norms. As stipulated by paragraph 2 of Article 13 KZ-1:

> A criminal law Act of the Republic of Slovenia shall also apply to any foreign citizen who, in a foreign country, commits a criminal offence against a third country or any of its citizens if he or she has been apprehended in the territory of the Republic of Slovenia but has not been extradited to the foreign country. In such cases, the court shall not impose a sentence on the perpetrator that is more severe than the sentence prescribed by the relevant Act of the country in which the offence was committed.

544. The principle of universal jurisdiction also applies to the prosecution of a perpetrator of criminal offences abroad 'who, under the relevant international agreements or general legal principles recognized by the international community, is subject to prosecution, regardless of the location where it was committed' (paragraph 3 of Article 13 KZ-1).

§2. Electronic Evidence

545. Under Slovenian law, electronic evidence is today recognized as a separate type of evidence that may be presented to a court of law.[575] The notion of electronic evidence applies to any piece of evidence that originates independently of the activities of law enforcement bodies and contains computer data in the sense of Article 1(a) of the Budapest Convention (i.e., data represented in a manner suitable for processing in a computer system).

575. Šugman & Gorkič (2011).

546. The taking of electronic evidence requires three steps, which are governed separately by the ZKP:

(1) the seizure of the data carrier, i.e., of electronic devices (the term used by the ZKP);
(2) the preservation of data held by the electronic device; and
(3) the search of electronic data and its presentation to the court.

547. The seizure of electronic devices is governed by general rules, allowing law enforcement authorities to seize objects 'that must be seized under criminal law or may serve as evidence in criminal proceedings' (paragraph 1 of Article 220 ZKP). The seizure of an electronic device may be executed by the police (under statutory authorization, Article 164 ZKP) or in the execution of a court order authorizing a search of premises, vehicles, or persons (Articles 214–218 ZKP), if the execution of the seizure entails an interference with the right to one's private life. The authorization of seizure does not include the authorization to inspect the computer data held by the seized device.[576] The seized device is to be handled in accordance with the rules on the chain of evidence.

548. The next step required by law is the preservation of computer data. As a general principle, 'data in electronic form shall be secured by storing them on another appropriate data storage device in such a manner so as to preserve the identity and integrity of the data and the possibility of using them in further proceedings' (paragraph 1 of Article 223a ZKP). Typically, an identical copy of the entire data storage device will be made. Alternatively, the electronic device or a part thereof (if possible) will be sealed (and, at a later stage, inspected). If the preservation of computer data takes place prior to a court order authorizing the search of data and no such authorization is issued within the next twelve hours, any copies made for the purposes of data preservation must be destroyed (paragraph 2 of Article 223a ZKP).

549. Finally, the search (inspection) of the computer data may only take place with a prior court authorization (Article 219a ZKP). As most computer systems today function as means of communication, the rules on searching (inspecting) computer data must comply with the safeguards provided under Article 37 of the Constitution, requiring, *inter alia*, the aforementioned *ex ante* court authorization. Court authorization is not needed if 'prior written consent of the owner and the users of the electronic device known by and accessible to the police who have reasonable expectations of privacy' concerning the device is provided (paragraph 2 of Article 219a ZKP). The search will typically be conducted by police experts. The ZKP, however, does allow other experts (e.g., defence experts) to be appointed and to inspect the computer data.

576. Decision of the Constitutional Court of the Republic of Slovenia No. Up-106/05, 2 Oct. 2008.

550. In all three stages, care must be taken to respect the confidentiality of computer data. This issue may arise if data are either classified[577] or subject to a confidentiality privilege (e.g., the client-lawyer privilege). If at any stage there is reason to believe that the inspected data contains classified or privileged information, steps must be taken to preserve the data confidentiality by submitting the data to the court for a 'sifting' procedure (Article 222a ZKP). In the case of data falling under the client-lawyer privilege, this entails a prohibition on the police and prosecutor inspecting (and even preserving, if inspection is inevitable) the data without a prior sifting procedure (Article 222a and paragraph 7 of Article 223a ZKP).

551. Access to computer data is a matter of the forensic procedures available to the police. In the case of protected or encrypted data, the police may request that the user or the administrator of the computer system provide access by submitting a password or encryption key (Article 219a ZKP). Refusal to do so results in a fine or imprisonment (up to ten days). Sanctions, however, do not apply to persons privileged to refuse testimony (suspects/defendants and witnesses exempt from the duty to testify – Articles 235 and 236 ZKP).

552. The final stage in presenting electronic evidence consists of two parts: reading out reports and interrogating (as needed) the officials and experts that took part in any of the three steps necessary to produce electronic evidence.

§3. Communications Traffic Data Preservation, Retention, and Access

553. Following the aforementioned decision of the Constitutional Court (relying strongly on the CJEU Digital Rights judgment), ZEKom-1 no longer contains any rules on mandatory data retention. Traffic data may only be accessed if stored by IT operators (i) on a contractual basis in their commercial data collection, or (ii) when authorized by a court order.

554. To this end, the ZKP provides the following tools:

(i) a data freeze order (Article 149e ZKP), issued by the police, prosecutor or a judge, requiring that the data administrator, user, or IT operator secure the identified data for a maximum of sixty days, in anticipation of a court order that would allow access to such data;
(ii) a data production order (Article 149b ZKP), issued by an investigating judge, requiring the IT operator or information-service provider to submit identified traffic data (already stored and available to the IT operator or service provider);

577. Under the Classified Information Act, Official Gazette of the Republic of Slovenia, No. 87/01 with subsequent amendments.

(iii) a data preservation order (Article 149c ZKP), issued by an investigating judge, requiring the IT operator or the information-service provider to preserve and produce the identified traffic data (applicable, therefore, to any future communications that may take place); and
(iv) a subscriber data production order (Article 149č ZKP), issued by either the police, prosecutor, or an investigative judge, requiring the IT operator or information-service provider to submit personal data unrelated to a specific communication event.

555. These tools are designed as covert investigative measures, which are carried out in the stages of a preliminary criminal investigation. Orders under Articles 149b and 149c ZKP are subject to time restrictions and can only be applied when investigating the offences specified by the ZKP.

§4. The Interception of Electronic Communications Data

556. The covert interception of electronic communications data is governed by Article 150 ZKP. It provides a statutory basis for the 'surveillance of electronic communications, including interception and recording, and the control and safeguarding of evidence of all forms of communication transmitted over the electronic communications network' (paragraph 1 of Article 150 ZKP).

557. Surveillance authorization can be issued by an investigating judge, upon a motion of the public prosecutor. The execution thereof is entrusted to the police, with IT operators under the obligation to provide assistance. Both the motion and the authorization are typically issued in writing; in exceptional cases of particular urgency, they can be issued orally (Article 152 ZKP).

558. As to the substantive scope of a surveillance authorization, it can only be made in reference to the list of offences determined by paragraph 2 of Article 150 ZKP. These include the following:

(i) criminal offences against the security of the Republic of Slovenia and its constitutional order, and crimes against humanity and international law, if punishable by a sentence of imprisonment of five or more years;
(ii) any criminal offence punishable by a sentence of imprisonment of eight or more years; and
(iii) a list of criminal offences, among which the following may be of particular importance due to cyber-related *modi operandi*: the solicitation of persons under 15 years of age for sexual purposes; the presentation, manufacture, possession, and distribution of pornographic material; the illicit manufacture of and trade in narcotic drugs, illicit substances in sport, and illicit drug precursors; extortion and blackmail; the illegal manufacture of and trafficking in weapons or explosives; and the unlawful management of nuclear and other hazardous radioactive substances.

559. Due to the invasiveness of such surveillance, it is deemed to be only a subsidiary measure, where other investigative measures are not expected to yield any results or where alternative means of investigation would result in the endangerment of human life.

560. At this point, ZKP does not offer any statutory basis for measures counteracting any measures aimed at concealing the content of communication – encryption. If encryption is imposed by IT operators, they are under the obligation to provide unencrypted content (paragraph 4 of Article 5 of the Rules on the Equipment and Interfaces for the Lawful Interception of Communications[578]). There is, however, no statutory basis for making use of the tools available for overcoming end-to-end encryption methods. An attempt at introducing a statutory basis for the use of software enabling surveillance 'at the source' failed in 2013.

§5. Remote Access to Computer Systems

561. Currently, there are three provisions in ZKP that (to some extent) allow remote access to computer systems of interest.

562. The first provision allows for the 'control of the computer systems of banks or other legal entities engaged in financial or other commercial activities' (paragraph 1 of Article 150 ZKP). The same rules apply regarding its authorization and execution as with the surveillance of electronic communications. However, not only is the measure limited to computer systems operated by commercial legal entities, but it also appears to be under-regulated and at odds with the principle of legality. For this reason, the measure has not been used in practice.

563. The second provision allows for the 'use of special technical means for monitoring mobile telephony signals' in order to determine the (i) information required for the identification of the communication medium number and electronic communication numbers, or (ii) the location of the communication medium (Article 150a ZKP). This provision authorizes the use of so-called IMSI catchers, either in preparation for the further surveillance of electronic communications or as a mode of conducting the surveillance of a person's movements and activities (otherwise regulated by Article 149a ZKP). As the law stands, the application of the provision has been temporarily restricted pending the decision of the Constitutional Court on its constitutionality.[579]

564. The third provision offering a statutory basis for remote access to computer systems is embedded in the definition of an 'electronic device' that may be subject to inspection under Article 219a ZKP (*see* above). Originally, the rules on the search of electronic devices presupposed that the possession of such a device has been

578. Official Gazette of the Republic of Slovenia, Nos. 89/13 and 189/21.
579. Order of the Constitutional Court of the Republic of Slovenia No. U-I-144/19-16, 4 Jul. 2019.

secured (by means of seizure). However, recent developments have led to a widening of the concept of an electronic device that now includes 'network-connected and accessible information systems where data is stored' (paragraph 1 of Article 219a ZKP). The amendment in 2019 was introduced to allow the inspection of data stored in computing clouds, where its location is essentially unknown and the device cannot be seized. The potential scope of its application, at this time, remains unknown. The wording of the statute is broad, allowing the inspection of devices that share the same network and their connection is yet to be established (thus making the device 'accessible'). As the term 'electronic communications network' is understood broadly,[580] the potential for the application of remote searching of electronic devices under this provision appears significant.

§6. The Admissibility of Evidence (Obtained Abroad)

565. The Slovenian rules on the admissibility of illegally obtained evidence were introduced in 1995 and persist unchanged to this day. They are fairly strict, stipulating a non-balancing approach to the exclusion of illegally obtained evidence, extending the rule by including the so-called fruit of the poisonous tree doctrine. As paragraph 2 of Article 18 ZKP puts it, 'The court may not base its decision on evidence obtained in violation of human rights and basic freedoms guaranteed by the Constitution, nor on evidence obtained in violation of the provisions of the criminal procedure and which under this Act may not serve as the basis for a court decision, or which has been obtained on the basis of such inadmissible evidence.'

566. In terms of cross-border cybercrime, the aforementioned constitutional rule on the prior judicial authorization of an interference with the right to communication privacy is being closely examined. The requirement of *ex ante* judicial authorization (with no statutory exceptions), coupled with a non-balancing approach, make the issue of admissibility particularly challenging. This rigidity of the exclusionary rule makes any prosecution resting on evidence from abroad particularly uncertain. At this point, the courts are still engaged in determining a settled approach to dealing with the admissibility of evidence obtained abroad. The trends show that the exclusionary rules are being revisited as regards both (i) the issue of determining whether a violation of the evidentiary rules has taken place and (ii) the issue of whether such a violation should be met with the exclusion of the tainted evidence.

567. In general, the position of the Constitutional Court requires that evidence obtained abroad be examined (in terms of its admissibility) from the perspective of

580. Article 3 ZEKom-1: '4. "Electronic communications network" means transmission systems and, where applicable, switching or routing equipment and other resources, including inactive network elements, which permit the conveyance of signals by wire, by radio, by optical or by other electromagnetic means, including satellite networks, fixed (circuit- and packet-switched, including Internet) and mobile terrestrial networks, electricity cable systems, if they are used for the purpose of transmitting signals, networks used for radio and television broadcasting, and cable television networks, irrespective of the type of information conveyed.'

human rights as safeguarded by the Constitution.[581] The issue remains, however, to what extent the Slovenian Constitution applies – in particular, the requirement of *ex ante* judicial authorization.

568. As the law stands, the court has made a distinction between (i) evidence obtained independently of Slovenian authorities and (ii) evidence obtained abroad pursuant to a request by or in cooperation with Slovenian authorities.[582] The application of constitutional requirements may be more relaxed in the case of evidence obtained independently. The Constitution does not require full compliance with its provisions. It does, however, command compliance with the principle of a fair trial, which requires that the courts examine the evidence in question and its adherence to the principle of legality ('in accordance with the law') and the principle of proportionality.

581. Decision of the Constitutional Court of the Republic of Slovenia No. Up-519/12-19, 18 Sep. 2014.
582. Decision of the Constitutional Court of the Republic of Slovenia No. Up-127/16, 20 Jan. 2022.

Selected Bibliography

Ambrož Matjaž, Council Framework Decision on Combating the Sexual Exploitation of Children and Child Pornography and the Slovenian Criminal Law. *European Law and National Criminal Legislation* 33 (2007): 140–151.

Ana Vlahek & Matija Damjan (eds), *Varstvo potrošnikov pri spletnem poslovanju* (GV Založba 2017).

Bavcon Ljubo, Šelih Alenka, Korošec Damjan, Ambrož Matjaž, Filipčič Katja, *Kazensko pravo. Splošni del*, XIV edition (Uradni list Republike Slovenije 2014).

Damjan Možina & Ana Vlahek, *Contract Law in Slovenia*. 1st edn (Kluwer 2019).

Eugen Ulmer & Gerhard Schricker (eds), *International Encyclopedia of Comparative Law*, Copyright, Vol. XIV (Mohr Siebeck 2007).

Informacijski Pooblaščenec, Kdaj lahko uporabimo piškotke? Smernice Informacijskega pooblaščenca: Kako prilagoditi uporabo piškotkov na spletnih straneh novim zahtevam zakonodaje? (Information Commisioner 2013).

Irini Stamatoudi & Torremans Paul, *EU Copyright law* (Edward Elgar Publishing Limited 2014).

Korošec, Damjan, *Spolnost in kazensko pravo: od prazgodovine do t. i. modernega spolnega kazenskega prava* (Uradni list Republike Slovenije, Ljubljana 2008).

Maja Bogataj Jančič et al., *Pravni vodnik po internetu* (GV Založba 2007).

Marko Pavliha et al., *Zakon o elektronskem poslovanju in elektronskem podpisu s komentarjem* (GV Založba 2002).

Matija Damjan, *Odprta vsebina, Pravice in dolžnosti uporabnikov* (GV Založba 2011).

Matija Damjan, *Pravo v informacijski družbi* (GV Založba 2014).

Mežnar, Špelca, Civilna odgovornost za anonimne komentarje na internetu, In Damjan, M. (ed.). *Pravo v informacijski družbi* (Ius Software 2014).

Miha Trampuž et al. (eds), *Zakon o avtorski in sorodnih pravicah s komentarjem* (GV Založba 1997).

Mozetič Polona, Bavcon Ljubo, K vprašanju o stopnjah uresničevanja kaznivega dejanja – pripravljalna dejanja, In: A. Šelih, *Sodobne usmeritve kazenskega materialnega prava*. Inštitut za kriminologijo pri Pravni fakulteti, Ljubljana 2007, pp. 181–197.

Nika Skvarča, Kaznivo dejanje zvijačnega zapeljevanja – primerno orodje za preprečevanje spolnih zlorab otrok?, *Pravna praksa*, 2015, 10: 20.

Schermer, B.W., Georgieva, I., Van der Hof, S. & Koops, B-J., *Legal Aspects of Sweetie 2.0.* (TILT, Leiden/Tilburg 2016)

Selected Bibliography

Selinšek, L. Computer Forensics in Criminal Procedure, Needed New Approaches in Slovenia. *Zbornik Pravne fakultete Univerze v Mariboru* 4(1) (2008): 237–248.

Šepec, M., *Kazniva dejanja kibernetskega kriminala – značilnosti in posebnosti sodobnega kazenskega prava*, PhD thesis, Univerza v Mariboru Pravna fakulteta, Maribor 2015.

Šugman Katja & Gorkič Primož, *Dokazovanje v kazenskem postopku* (GV Založba 2011).

Legal sources

Council Framework Decision 2005/222/JHA of 24 February 2005 on attacks against information systems

Council Framework Decision 2008/841/JHA of 24 October 2008 on the fight against organised crime

Council of Europe, Convention on the rights of a child, 1989

Council of Europe, Recommendation No. R (89) 9 On Computer-Related Crime, 1989

Council of Europe, Explanatory report to the Council of Europe Convention on Cybercrime, 2001

Council of Europe, Explanatory Report to the Council of Europe Convention on the protection of children against sexual exploitation and sexual abuse (Lanzarote Convention), 25.X.2007

Council of Europe, Cybercrime Convention Committee (T-CY), T-CY Guidance Note No. 11, from 15 November 2016

Directive 2008/114/ES from 8 December 2008 on the identification and designation of European critical infrastructures and the assessment of the need to improve their protection

Directive 2011/92/EU of 13 December 2011 on combating the sexual abuse and sexual exploitation of children and child pornography, and replacing Council Framework Decision 2004/68/JHA

Directive 2013/40/EU of 12 August 2013 on attacks against information systems and replacing Council Framework Decision 2005/222/JHA

EU Code of Conduct on countering illegal hate speech online from 2018, available at: https://ec.europa.eu/info/policies/justice-and-fundamental-rights/combatting-discrimination/racism-and-xenophobia/eu-code-conduct-countering-illegal-hate-speech-online_en, accessed 21 June 2022

Optional Protocol to the Convention on the Rights of the Child on the sale of children, child prostitution, and child pornography, 2000

The Council of Europe Convention on Protection of Children against Sexual Exploitation and Sexual Abuse, 2007

United Nations Office on Drugs and Crime (UNODC), Expert Group to Conduct a Comprehensive Study on Cybercrime, Comprehensive study of the problem of cybercrime and responses to it by Member States, the international community and the private sector, 2013

Index

The numbers given here refers to paragraph numbers.

Index

Index

www.ingramcontent.com/pod-product-compliance
Ingram Content Group UK Ltd.
Pitfield, Milton Keynes, MK11 3LW, UK
UKHW020142290926
15471UKWH00004B/657

9 789403 52266